Dushan G. Monchilovich

Lina Surianto

Discovering Your Career in Business

D1110802

Discovering Your Career in Business

Timothy Butler, Ph.D.
James Waldroop, Ph.D.

▲▼ *Addison-Wesley Publishing Company, Inc.*

Reading, Massachusetts   Menlo Park, California   New York
Don Mills, Ontario   Harlow, England   Amsterdam   Bonn
Sydney   Singapore   Tokyo   Madrid   San Juan
Paris   Seoul   Milan   Mexico City   Taipei

Many of the designations used by manufacturers and sellers to distinguish their products are claimed as trademarks. Where those designations appear in this book and Addison-Wesley was aware of a trademark claim, the designations have been printed in initial capital letters.

Library of Congress Cataloging-in-Publication Data
Butler, Timothy.
    Discovering your career in business / Timothy Butler, James Waldroop.
        p.   cm.
    Includes bibliographical references and index.
    ISBN 0-201-46135-8
    1. Vocational guidance.   2. Vocational interests.   I. Waldroop, James. II. Title.
    HF5381.B798   1996
    331.7′02—dc20   96–22356
                                                     CIP

Copyright © 1997 by Timothy Butler and James Waldroop

All rights reserved. No part of this publication may be reproduced, stored in a retrieval system, or transmitted, in any form or by any means, electronic, mechanical, photocopying, recording, or otherwise, without the prior written permission of the publisher. Printed in the United States of America. Published simultaneously in Canada.

Cover design by Suzanne Heiser
Text design by Diane Levy
Set in 12-point Adobe Garamond by Shepard Poorman Communications Corporation

4 5 6 7 8 9-MA-0201009998
Fourth printing, December 1997

Addison-Wesley books are available at special discounts for bulk purchases by corporations, institutions, and other organizations. For more information, please contact the Corporate, Government, and Special Sales Department, Addison-Wesley Publishing Company, Reading, MA 01867, 1-800-238-9682.

For Linda and Kiera, and for my parents.
T.B.

For Valerie, Max, and Daniel, and for my parents.
J.W.

There is a flood-tide within us on which we are borne . . . my vocation is my response to the voice of my most intimate and secret being, when this response remains totally unaffected either by my will, or by the impressions made upon me by things without.

—Louis LaVelle, *The Dilemma of Narcissus.*

— CONTENTS

Introduction   1

ONE • Finding Our Way   8

TWO • Losing Our Way: Sirens' Songs and Other Distractions   17

THREE • The Imagination of Work   44

FOUR • Using the *Business Career Interest Inventory*   59

FIVE • The Basic Dimensions of Business Work   76

SIX • Scoring and Analyzing Your Active Imagination Exercises   92

SEVEN • Analyzing Your Business Career Profile   105

EIGHT • The Alchemical Heat: Conflict, Doubt, and Choice   163

NINE • The Business Career Profile: Case Examples   180

TEN • Evaluating Work Opportunities   208

Epilogue   223
Appendix   225
Chapter Notes   243
Index   245

── ACKNOWLEDGMENTS

WE WANT TO take this opportunity to express our gratitude to the many people who have contributed to this effort. David LeLacheur and Steven Robbins were instrumental in creating the computer disk version of the *Business Career Interest Inventory.* Marlys Rogers and her crew put in long hours creating and analyzing our database. Carol Trager gave us invaluable advice and assistance. Our agent, Kris Dahl of ICM, provided us with encouragement and counsel. Ellie McCarthy and Bill Patrick of Addison-Wesley helped us at every stage of the editorial process. We are also grateful to our friends and colleagues who offered valuable criticism and helped in the development of the *BCII.* A very special thanks goes to our many clients, who have taught us so much about so many things over the years.

Many people at the Harvard Business School have provided encouragement and support for our research. In particular, we want to thank Dr. Patricia Light, who brought us together at Harvard; Bob Scalise and Professor Len Schlesinger, who have both been champions of the career development program; and Kirsten Moss, Director of MBA Recruiting Services, who has been a valued colleague and supporter of the project. We also want to acknowledge all of our colleagues, past and present, at MBA Career Services and MBA Counseling Services, for their insights and for their friendship.

Finally, we want to thank our families, and especially our wives, Linda and Valerie, for their help and understanding as we ran full speed toward the realization of this project. Without their love, helpful criticism, and support we would not be where we are. Our greatest thanks go to you.

— A NOTE TO THE READER

www.careerdiscovery.com

THE ADVENT OF the Internet has brought new possibilities to the worlds of research and publishing. Our World Wide Web site, www.careerdiscovery.com, allows us to provide you with the results of our latest research on career development. Already this site has new interactive interpretive tools that will enhance the information available in this book. The site also has information on how to get further assistance with career counseling and coaching. We will be updating the site on a regular basis.

— INTRODUCTION

Mark Young* had moved steadily up the management ladder in the marketing department of a large manufacturing company, and was now the youngest person in the company at his level. He had been promoted three times in just five years, but he'd been stalled in his last position for almost two years and could see no promise of progress in the near future. The senior executive team was young and turnover was low. When Mark came to us he was considering several alternatives: he could join a startup business in a related industry, take a position as vice president of marketing in a college friend's business, or make a lateral move to a marketing position with a company of similar size that competed with his current employer. Mark had worked for only one company throughout his career, so he had a narrow frame of reference to use in assessing his opportunities.

Caroline Greeley was a highly intelligent (as our testing showed), very creative woman in her early twenties who came to see us on the recommendation of a friend with whom we had worked. Despite her intelligence and creativity, Caroline lacked self-confidence, and this was her primary limitation. She was working in what appeared to be a good position for her in the marketing area of a film production company in Hollywood. As we talked, her main question emerged: "I like the work I'm doing, so why do I feel so uncomfortable with this job?"

Elaine Littleton left a successful career with a management consulting firm because she had misgivings about the lifestyle her work dictated (the norm was eighty- to one-hundred-hour workweeks,

---

*All names and sufficient identifying information to protect the confidentiality of our clients have been changed.

with extensive travel). An exceptionally intelligent individual in her mid-thirties, Elaine loved problem solving and learning about new businesses. Her career dilemma was how to fill her nearly insatiable desire for new problems to solve without spending three or four days on the road and working such long hours.

For the past fifteen years, business professionals have been coming to us for help with their careers. We have had the chance to work with these individuals as they struggle with one of the most important questions any of us faces: "Where can I go, what can I do, to find work that is right for me and truly satisfying?" Our clients have included many hundreds of men and women of all ages and in all stages of their careers, from recent college graduates to seasoned executives in their late fifties and early sixties. We have worked with presidents and CEOs, as well as individuals in entry-level positions and at all levels in between.

Our clients have held management positions in both the for-profit and not-for-profit sectors, including manufacturing and service firms, high technology, medical services, management consulting, commercial and investment banking, investment management, entertainment, venture capital, diversified financial services, consumer goods manufacturing, telecommunications, computer hardware and software, insurance, and retailing, among many other areas. We have worked with consultants, bankers, marketers, controllers, vice presidents of operations and of finance, people in sales and sales management, human resource professionals, accountants, strategic planners, and individuals in many other business functions. Our clients come from all over the United States, as well as from Asia, Europe, and Latin America. In addition, we have consulted to thousands of students in the MBA program at the Harvard Business School, where we have worked as career psychologists for a collective twenty-five years. The majority of these students enter Harvard with the intention of changing careers, and we work with them to choose the best paths to attain their individual career objectives.

Our clients have taught us a great deal about how they have made their life choices and how they've decided what to do at different points in their careers. From each client we learn a little more about people, human nature, the forces at work when people make career decisions, and what makes a good "marriage" between a person and a career. We help our clients and they teach us; they have provided us with the insights about work and the process of career decision making that we will share with you in this book. Our book will help you do for yourself something of what we do for our clients.

Through the years, we have been struck by the fact that job status, level of compensation, and history of accomplishment are not necessarily good predictors of satisfaction with work. They may be indicators of past work satisfaction, but we now understand that the human instinct for fulfillment seeks expression and renewal throughout a lifetime. We may find ourselves, like Dante, lost in a dark wood at any point in life's journey, whether we are new managers or CEOs. Then, if we are to find our way forward, we must look deeply into the question of what will truly bring us satisfaction and a sense of being completely engaged in our work and our lives. This book is not about résumé writing, networking, or where the best jobs for the next decade will be. It is about what "looking deeply" means—about the unique unfolding of the individual self that seeks, above all, meaning and a sense of fulfillment in the realm of business work.

Maintaining a focus on business allows us to look at business careers in much greater depth than if we attempted to include all careers. In fact, a major reason we developed the *Business Career Interest Inventory*, the psychological inventory that accompanies this book on disk, was that other interest inventories do a good job of looking at careers across the widest possible spectrum but sacrifice detail and nuance. We wanted to turn up the power on the microscope and look through the lens at careers in business (including law, engineering, administration of nonprofit organizations such as universities and hospitals, and other business-related areas), giving you the benefit of that depth of view. What we have learned about the career decision-making process, however, applies to individuals facing career choices in any area.

Reading this book and exploring your core interests through use of the *Business Career Interest Inventory,* will help you address the same issues that we would work on together if you were to come to see us in person. We want to help you to discover your "right work" in the field of business, whether you are just beginning your career or are making a mid-career shift.

The Changing Landscape of Business

To say that the world of business is undergoing a revolution is, if anything, an understatement. We are in the midst of a confluence of a number of radical changes, including the globalization of the economy; the changeover from the industrial age to the information age; the reengineering of the processes performed by many corporations, resulting in flatter structures and fewer middle managers; and the rending of the implicit social contract between employees and corporations, which once held that if you worked hard you would have employment for a lifetime.

As little as a generation ago the most suitable analog for white-collar work in business was that of a tree. You were planted at the beginning of your career, put down roots, grew, and stayed in the same place (that is, with the same company) for the rest of your (working) life. The old security of the tree is so much a thing of the past that someone recently told us he didn't want another salaried position, because working for someone else is too risky! It is almost unimaginable that we would have heard those words uttered in the 1960s, or even through the middle of the 1980s.

Today the most appropriate analog seems to be that of a surfer riding the waves. You are on your own platform, constantly moving, supported by an ever-changing base, always on the alert, responsible for your own ride, expecting to be dunked a number of times, needing to be able to get back up on the board and keep going, and constantly on the alert for new dangers, opportunities, and needed additions to your skill set. Moreover, you are probably going to have to decide which wave to catch several times in your career. This book provides you with a means of sizing up the opportunities that come along and deciding which ones are worth the ride.

This time of revolutionary change is, understandably, frightening for many people. As a result, individuals increasingly tend to make impulsive, ultimately poor career choices out of fear, just when they can least afford to do so. It requires courage to find your own direction and stick to it, resisting the impulse to do what seems conventionally safe. It is more difficult to define that direction when the landscape is changing constantly. This book and the *Business Career Interest Inventory* will serve as a compass to help you find your path through this changing landscape of business, now and in the future.

If the scenario of riding a series of waves on your surfboard sounds like much more work than being a tree, it is. A radically different mind-set is necessary to succeed in today's business world, which is far more competitive and much less forgiving of career mistakes than it once was. Success in today's business world requires that each of us plan and manage our careers with care and with attention both to what is happening around us and to what career direction will be fulfilling and satisfying for us.

Our experience is that people who find their own "right work" not only are happier but are much more likely to be successful by other measures. Our aim in writing this book, then, is *not* to help people find the best career path for themselves in an idealized world. Using our model to assess your interests and specific work opportunities in terms of the actual daily activities they comprise will increase your chances for success and will help you decide whether a job will take you in the right direction. Discovering what career in business is best for you, whatever your age and stage of career, can make the difference not just between success and mediocrity but between success and failure.

Using This Book

At the heart of this book is the *Business Career Interest Inventory* (*BCII*), a psychological interest inventory that we developed to assess the way in which people's unique patterns of interests are related to what our research has shown to be the basic dimensions of business work. If we were working with you in person, we would not give you this instrument immediately. Before doing any formal psychological assessment, we would have you talk about your life, what you imagine your future to be, how that picture may have changed over the years, and about the myriad, less obvious aspects of your current relationships and commitments that will shape your decisions about work. In addition to gathering valuable information, we would be helping you enter into the process of creative imagination that is the essence of any self-assessment endeavor. If you wish to most closely approximate our counseling process, we recommend that you engage your imagination by reading the first three chapters before taking the *BCII*, which is introduced in Chapter 4.

In Chapter 1, "Finding Our Way," you will learn something about the research behind the *BCII*, what makes it different from other interest inventories you may have taken in the past, and why we believe that assessing your interest in the basic activities of business work is the best way to ensure success and satisfaction in your career. In Chapter 2, "Losing Our Way: Sirens' Songs and Other Distractions," you will learn about the various ways in which people can be pulled off course as they pursue their careers. Chapter 3, "The Imagination of Work," provides you with a series of exercises that will help you prepare for taking the *BCII* by gaining access to parts of yourself that may lie out of your conscious awareness. The last step before sitting down to take the *BCII* is to read Chapter 4, "Using the *Business Career Interest Inventory*," which will instruct you in using the disk that accompanies this book. (Or you may choose to begin by reading Chapter 4 and taking the *BCII*, returning to the earlier chapters at your leisure.)

After completing the *BCII*, which will take about thirty minutes, you should read Chapter 5, "The Basic Dimensions of Business Work," which will discuss our research findings on the underlying dimensions of business work as they relate to core interest patterns. Chapter 6, "Scoring and Analyzing Your Active Imagination Exercises," will allow you to analyze the exercises you completed in Chapter 3 and combine these analyses with your *BCII* results to arrive at a richer, more accurate, and more subtle self-assessment. Chapter 7, "Analyzing Your Business Career Profile," will allow you to apply the model that has emerged from our research to help you understand how your *business career profile* is related to specific business work roles and environments. Chapter 8, "The Alchemical Heat: Conflict, Doubt, and Choice," shares what we have learned about the difficult psychological process of making career decisions. In Chapter 9, "The Business Career Profile: Case Examples," you will read case histories of business professionals with particular business career profile types. Finally, in Chapter 10, "Evaluating Work Opportunities," you will learn how to use the model of *business core functions* to analyze work opportunities in terms of their match with your pattern of interests.

ONE

Finding Our Way

THE FIRST THING *Tony Gutierrez said when he came to see us was that he wasn't sure why he had come. Tony had an MBA from a top-tier business school and a B.S. in electrical engineering from an Ivy League school, and he was moving right along in his career at a top management consulting firm. As we talked it emerged that Tony had majored in engineering because he was exceptionally gifted in math and science, and had been encouraged by his teachers and parents to go with this strength. Further, as an only child and a first-generation American (his parents came to the United States from Guatemala), Tony felt pressure to "make good" and follow a path that would lead to financial success, even if he didn't enjoy the trip.*

Tony was quite good at just about anything he tried. In some ways this was a gift; at the same time, being good at everything meant that life experience didn't push him in one particular direction or another. For example, in college Tony had taken a smattering of courses in art and architecture and done very well. His professors had encouraged him to seriously consider a career in academia, teaching history at the college level.

After graduating, Tony applied to business school. A number of his friends from college had gone on for MBAs, so it was a world with which he was somewhat familiar. He enjoyed business school; was a good student, bright and articulate; and received offers from several of the most prestigious management consulting firms that visited the campus to recruit. Offers in the management consulting field were highly sought after by students in his program, and although he had some reservations about the work and the lifestyle, Tony couldn't bring himself to turn down what appeared to be a career move with no downside potential.

So why was Tony sitting in our office? He was doing well, on track for a promotion, and well liked by his peers, the partners in the firm, and the firm's clients. The only obvious reason for his dissatisfaction was that he had been assigned to one project with a team leader who had been very hard on him. Tony was used to being a star, a leader, someone other people liked and wanted to be liked by in return; he was unaccustomed to being criticized. That this team leader was also critical of everyone else on the team did little to make Tony feel any better about it.

Tony didn't feel that this one experience explained why he was unhappy in his work. If anything, he said, it was just a wake-up call, getting him to step back and reevaluate his career path. "If something like this can make me seriously question my career, maybe that says more about my match with the career than about the individual incident." We didn't take this at face value, because we have worked with many people who were so easily bruised by criticism that just one hurt really would make them want to move on. After further exploration, however, it seemed that Tony was right.

Tony just didn't find the work of being a consultant truly satisfying. Many of his colleagues in consulting loved their work, were truly passionate about it. Although Tony was good at it, in some vague way it was not enough for him. As we discussed his nonwork interests and analyzed a comprehensive battery of career assessment instruments, it became clear that what really excited Tony was more directly creative work, ideally where the product itself or the service that came out of the work had a creative aspect to it. We also saw that he wasn't really motivated by power and influence, as were many of his peers in consulting.

We noted that not only had he done well in art and architecture courses he had taken in college, but most of his friends had been in those areas, not from the school of engineering. In fact, Tony had never really felt at home with engineers, or with MBA students or consultants, for that matter. That told us that he was instinctively *drawn to people who were more creative than analytical. He may have gone into engineering and studied for an MBA because it seemed logical and other people told him he should, but he chose his friends with no concern for who they should be. The work he was doing was intellectually stimulating (and somewhat creative in that way), very challenging, and demanding, but it simply wasn't enough.*

Tony ultimately decided to leave consulting and pursue a career in new product development and marketing in the software field. This made use of his business education and, to a limited extent, his engineering training, while allowing him to infuse his daily work with a much greater element of creativity.

Learning by Doing

The type of work that will bring greater self-knowledge, satisfaction, and meaning is different for each of us, and each of us walks a different path of career discovery. As we grow into and through adulthood, two types of learning take place. The first type is learning about the world "out there"; in business career terms, this means learning about different industries and work roles. The second type is learning about the self. Different psychologists have different definitions for *self,* but for our purposes we may say simply that the self is our developing consciousness of the full being that we are. As we grow older, we must do the work of making meaning, the work of discovering what is most deeply satisfying and what activities consistently bring with them a sense of excitement, energy, and connection with the world. As career psychologists we have focused, in our research and in our consulting practice, on the way in which people come to know what they want in life, and in their business working lives in particular.

It is a paradox that only by *engaging* in work can we discover what type of work is most satisfying and meaningful. Career self-assessment requires us to become better and better observers of ourselves as we learn about our individual psychological realities through day-to-day experience. With experience comes a greater ability to recognize more directly which tasks, assignments, and work opportunities are more likely to be fulfilling. Finding the best work is not a task that is accomplished once and for all; it is a continual process of doing, and listening to what we have learned and how we have changed because of our doing. We find our way to meaningful work by pursuing specific activities and, through them, learning which are most fulfilling.

Through activity our inner energies and enthusiasms find their way to the surface in our lives. Different aspects of the self are realized through different types of activities. For some people, writing a poem can be a powerful activity that increases self-knowledge. For others, mediating a worker argument on the production line or working on a new computer model of a national economy may be an equally powerful vehicle for self-realization.

Because you are reading this book, you have probably already reached, at least tentatively, the conclusion that for you the types of activities that hold the most promise for excitement and meaning lie in the realm of business. In our business career consultation we place particular emphasis on two goals: first, helping our clients understand the unique pattern of deep interests and enthusiasms that seeks expression in their lives; and second, helping our clients understand what types of business activities will best allow this expression. From our research and consulting practice we have developed a model of eight basic underlying categories of business activities, which we refer to as *business core functions*.

One example of a business core function is *Quantitative Analysis*. Thinking about events in terms of mathematical relationships is one fundamental approach to understanding the world. The core function of mathematical reasoning may be expressed in a variety of specific business activities, such as analyzing corporate financial reports, conducting a market research study, or developing a model to predict optimal inventory levels. All of these activities are expressions of a common underlying function that for some people will be very interesting and rewarding. The Quantitative Analysis business core function is used here as an example. We do not want to risk biasing your responses to the assessment, so we will not describe the other business core functions until you have completed the *Business Career Interest*

Inventory and done some of the preliminary exercises described in Chapter 3.

Your Unique Pattern of Interests

Earlier approaches to career assessment focused largely on matching personality profiles with specific jobs, assuming that jobs in business would have a great deal of constancy in content over time. However, as the changes that are sweeping the world of business accelerate, business career decisions will be based more and more on choosing shorter-term work opportunities that will facilitate a person's next stage of personal and career development. More than ever, the business professional will be personally responsible for thinking at a deeper level not only about what work will make him or her attractive to future employers, but about what will allow for a sense of satisfying commitment in a world where traditional career structures are becoming increasingly unrecognizable. Yet many of our clients, even sophisticated senior executives, continue to think in terms of job titles and traditional business functions rather than in terms of the real work activities that make up a position. Thus, our approach to career self-assessment differs in a fundamental way from approaches that try to match personality traits with specific jobs. This book will help you develop your understanding of the kinds and combinations of business activities likely to hold the most meaning for you.

Let us take a closer look at our first assessment emphasis, the idea that each of us has a unique pattern of interests, a "potential self," that seeks expression. One of the most interesting findings in career psychology research is that underlying patterns of work interest are a relatively enduring feature of a person. Substantial research evidence demonstrates that these underlying individual patterns of work-related interests exist at least as early as adolescence. There is also evidence that people show progressively more consistency in their interests as they mature through adolescence, young adulthood, and full adulthood. Adults *know* their interest patterns better than teenagers do. Through the activities of their living and working, they have acquired greater knowledge of themselves. Further, there is evidence that, amid this stability, new experiences in work environments continue to influence the development of interests, *but within the contours of the deep interest pattern.*

We want to distinguish between the deep structure of an individual's interests and the specific manifestations of that deep structure. *Deep structure* interests are one of the most basic features of an individual's personality. They are deeply rooted and enduring, and they naturally push us to find an avenue for their expression, just as an underground pool of geothermally heated water pushes its way to the surface. Like the water that can make its way up through any number of routes and emerge as a hot spring or a geyser, any deep structure interest can be expressed through several different routes as an observable *specific interest.* For example, Andy Warhol's deep structure creative interest was realized through his work in advertising, his paintings, and his films; the physicist Richard Feynman's deep structure creative interest is seen in his scientific research, his writings, and his famously creative and entertaining lectures.

Specific interests develop when the necessary life experiences and opportunities for development of deep structure interests are present. Someone's deep structure interest in quantitative analysis may not develop into a specific interest such as technical equities analysis unless he or she is exposed to the field of investments. Given the opportunity, those interests develop into specific interests that may be either work-related or avocational pursuits. They may develop along one of several potentially fulfilling career paths, but work that is *not* grounded in an individual's unique pattern of deep structure interests will not sustain a career over a lifetime. Albert Einstein might have become a mathematician or chemist rather than a physicist, but he would never have lasted in a career as a military officer. Bill Gates, the founder of Microsoft, might have become a commodities trader or started a business providing cellular telephone communication service, but it is unlikely that he would have become a food service manager.

Every individual has a unique pattern of deep structure interests, and by early adulthood the basic features of this interest pattern have assumed a recognizable shape, even if the specific work interests and roles that will allow the pattern to become fully realized have not been identified. The search for the right kind of work is really a search for the way in which deep structure interest patterns will be most fully realized.

What About Aptitude?

Why do we focus our discussion on *interest* patterns? There are many approaches to describing the energies and capacities of the emerging self. We could focus on patterns of skills and aptitudes. To be sure, we do assess skills in our career consulting, but often we find people to be overfocused on abilities and aptitudes. People ask, "What am I good at?" or "Where does my competitive advantage lie?" They may have given considerable sums of money to career counselors who focus on assessing aptitudes, and found the results disappointing. Certainly an assessment of skills is important, but, just as the question "What should I do?" should be subordinate to "What do I want to do?" the question "Do I have what it takes to be good at . . . ?" should be subordinate to "Am I interested in . . . ?" Our competitive advantage always resides with those endeavors to which we bring our greatest enthusiasm and passion.

In our view, aptitude or skill level should be a "go/no go" factor for pursuing a career. On one hand, if you are truly interested in music but have poor fine motor coordination and a poor singing voice, that lack of aptitude may result in a "no go" for a career as a performing musician. On the other hand, you might channel your interest in music into a career as a music producer, a songwriter, or radio disc jockey. Lack of aptitude should never preclude exploring and deepening an interest.

Drifting to the Wrong Place

We see many people who have made their career decisions based on what they were *good* at with little or no concern for their *interest* in it. In fact, we have worked with many people who were very successful at what they were doing, who were at the top of their fields, but who had little authentic interest in the work they were doing. They had often drifted into whatever they were doing and, because they happened to be good at it, stayed even though they didn't really find it interesting. The result is the "golden handcuffs" scenario, in which people are making so much money doing what they don't like that they find it exceedingly difficult to change to something that they would find more satisfying.

Realistically, of course, unless you are independently wealthy you have to pursue a career in which you can earn a living. You may want to be a poet or professional basketball player or television talk show host, but following your heart down these paths may involve more risk than you can afford. John Lam provides an example of how, in real life, people can take what they learn about their core interests and put that knowledge to work in the context of the demands and constraints of other aspects of their lives.

John was a senior-level marketing manager at a thriving software firm, earning a very good salary. He was in his mid-forties and married, with two children. He had been with the company for sixteen years, during which time he was promoted steadily and was seen as a high performer. Unfortunately, he was unhappy in his work. He felt no particular love for the product; disliked the politics of management; was uncomfortable working in a rather cutthroat, unsupportive culture; and felt constantly stressed. He frequently arrived home from work feeling irritable and moody.

By his own description, John had fallen into the high-tech field. When he graduated from college it was a booming area in which work was easy to find. He had initially enjoyed the challenge, the glamour, and his early successes. Within a few years, however, the challenge had become relentless pressure, the glamour had worn thin, and the success he experienced became an expectation to continue always to do well.

From an early age John had been interested in a career in optometry. It was technically challenging, provided for a great deal of independence and autonomy, and was a respected profession. He had been dissuaded from pursuing this interest by his father, who was an extremely successful businessman himself. By choosing to go with an easy strength rather than with his interest, John had put himself in a bind: On one hand, could he afford to forgo his income to go to school for four years, pay the tuition to become an optometrist, and then start a new career at substantially less than his current salary?

On the other hand, could he afford to remain in a job in which he was unhappy?

In the course of our consultation, John determined that, rather than take the radical step of leaving his work (and placing his family under considerable financial stress) to go back to school, he would first try a move to a career position that might be better, if not ideal. He actively began to look for a work opportunity that would allow him more of the independence and autonomy that attracted him to optometry. He looked for a smaller company whose culture was more supportive, where his contribution would be more recognized and he would be personally respected. Even the act of looking helped him to feel better about where he was, and when he did make a move his overall mood improved dramatically.

To arrive at an understanding of the pattern of our deep structure interests so that it can become real in our work, we must learn to think and to listen in the native language of the self, the language of disciplined imagination. In Chapter 3 we will explore the relationship between imagination and the process of career discovery. In Chapter 5 we will describe in detail the second emphasis in our research: the relationship between patterns of deep structure interests and the specific business core functions that will allow for their realization. But first, in the next chapter, "Losing Our Way: Sirens' Songs and Other Distractions," we will look at obstacles that lie in the way of the life-long task of finding satisfying and fulfilling work.

TWO

Losing Our Way: Sirens' Songs and Other Distractions

THE PREDOMINANT USE of the word *career* to describe people's work is relatively recent. Today we have "career counselors" and "career interest inventories," whereas just a few years ago people had "vocations" and were "vocational counselors" using "vocational interest tests." According to the *American Heritage Dictionary,* the word *career* derives from the Latin *carrus,* which was a type of wagon, and from the Old French *carrière,* meaning "racecourse." Career used as a verb means "to move or run at full speed; rush." *Vocation,* by contrast, derives from the Latin *vocare,* "to call," and *vocatio,* which means "calling." This calling could be from God or from the deeper layers of the self. A hundred years ago someone might have said that it was his calling to be physician, a farmer, or a cobbler. People have moved away from thinking about work as something that called out to them, beckoning them to it, and now use a word that connotes movement and speed. In our work as career psychologists, we prefer to think of work as a calling, something that strikes a chord within people, resonating and feeling right.

Numerous and powerful forces can pull you away from your true calling, however, and understanding what they are can help you stay true to that deeper voice. Over the years we have been consulted by any number of bright, successful people who have made bad judgments in choosing and managing their careers. In many cases these were people with advanced degrees, some of whom had taken career self-assessment courses in their MBA programs or had consulted other career counselors at previous decision points. Their errors caused us to wonder: If people have a calling signaling them to pursue a course, how do they get off course? How do "bad jobs" happen to "good people"? Obviously there are countless idiosyncratic circumstances that can lead people to lose their way in pursuing their careers, but we generally see them falling into four broad categories: Sirens' songs, fears and discomforts, a gap in a person's knowledge of opportunities, and a gap in knowledge about oneself.

In each of these cases we are looking at influences of one kind or another that pull people off course. There are general societal and cultural influences that affect us—the everyday background elements that we grow accustomed to and don't really notice but that affect us nonetheless. For example, fifty or a hundred years ago many people accepted without questioning, or even noticing, societal and cultural prescriptions about kinds of work that were and were not appropriate for women. (And probably fifty or a hundred years from now people will be able to see clearly the cultural influences of which we are unaware today.) Our families and smaller social circles influence us, too. Again, they affect us almost without our knowing it, because they are constant, almost like background noise. The *unspoken messages* about what we Smiths do or what sorts of careers are appropriate for us Johnsons become our underlying assumptions, the things that can guide us without our ever knowing we are being guided. They may close out certain whole fields of options, subtly but powerfully shaping our thinking.

Finally, discrete events can have a profound impact on your thinking about your career. If, for example, your father was laid off after thirty years' faithful service to the same company, that singular event might substantially affect your thinking about working for a big company. If your mother left her job and began an entrepreneurial venture that became wildly successful, that experience might substantially affect your thinking about working for yourself.

In the following sections, we will describe in more detail these forces that can cause us to lose our way. As you read, think about your career thus far, about what missteps you have made or have narrowly avoided making. Think about people you know: friends, siblings, parents, other family members. What Sirens' songs, fears, and knowledge deficits have affected your and their lives and careers? Looking forward, what do you see as your vulnerabilities, what is most likely to draw you off course? The more you know about your own tendencies to go astray, the more you can avoid falling prey to them. First, let us consider the lures of the Sirens' songs.

The Sirens' Songs

In Homer's *The Odyssey*, Odysseus and his men pass close to an island where the Sirens' beautifully seductive songs have for many years lured sailors to their death on the rocks. The Sirens' songs of today are the distracting attractions that can obscure the calling and take people away from their true course—lures such as money, power, prestige, and the approval of peers, family, or society.

Nothing is inherently wrong with desiring any of these things. But if the desire is being fostered by the Sirens, the attractions may take on an importance out of proportion to how much satisfaction they are likely to bring, and in this way pull you off course. If amassing a certain amount of wealth, for example, *is* your true calling, you need to follow that course; if it is someone else's notion of what *should be* your calling, you must recognize that and not let it distract you.

Money and Status

Today the Sirens' song of wealth is enormously powerful and very difficult to resist. Fifty years ago, if you were living in a small town in Iowa, you were fairly well insulated from that lure. You didn't turn on your television and see the glitter of the Academy Awards, and so you didn't receive those particular messages that great wealth was something you should aspire to. Similarly, you didn't go to work and see people driving seventy-thousand-dollar cars along the street, talking on cellular phones. Today things are different.

We see many people who have made career decisions based primarily on how much wealth they were likely to accrue, and how quickly. This is not to say that money or the desire for it is bad, but to point out that it often works to pull people away from other things they want, effectively drowning out those signals. We have worked with many people who were dissatisfied with the actual content of their work but were unwilling or unable to seriously consider making a change that would result in greater pleasure but less compensation.

> *Rob Turner was simply not cut out to be a banker. He was prone to feeling anxious, and avoided confrontation and arguments whenever possible. As a commercial lender he effectively had to sell money and then hope that the borrower would make good on the debt. After the lending crisis of the late 1980s, banks were increasingly risk averse. The result was that getting the credit committee's approval for a loan application grew increasingly difficult. Meetings were more confrontational, and it was made clear to lending officers that if a loan went bad their jobs were on the line. Rob frequently found his stomach tied in knots. He hated his work but could not, unfortunately, resist the lure of wealth. He thought hard about leaving banking, or at least leaving the high-pressure bank for which he worked, but the constant call of the money and prestige was too strong.*

We helped someone else narrowly avert a career crisis brought on by the sudden and dramatic financial success of a friend. In this case our client was on the verge of throwing away a successful career out of sheer envy.

> *David Chen was a successful manufacturers' sales representative. He had been in the field for almost ten years and had developed a customer base of sufficient size to provide him with a steady stream of business and sizable income. During a period when the local real estate market was very hot, a broker friend of his was making money hand over fist, as people rushed to sell their homes and buy new property. Watching his friend "printing money" was driving David crazy. He came to us for counsel regarding the idea of leaving his business and joining his friend. We advised him that the career risk would be very high; that he was in fact in a very good field that provided him with freedom, variety, and financial gain; and, most important, that at some point the market would cool off (which, of*

course, it did). The Sirens had come within a hairsbreadth of luring David onto the rocks.

Less dramatic examples of people being lured away from what they love by the attraction of money and status abound. Most common is that of the person who enjoys doing one thing and is good at it, but accepts a promotion for the money and higher status. These people often have thought about what they will be giving up in making such a change, but are attracted by the money and prestige and are encouraged by their friends. "You're not seriously thinking about turning down that promotion are you?" they hear. Or "I'd sell my grandmother for an offer to work at. . . ." It is very difficult indeed to resist the Sirens when everyone around you is encouraging you to tune in and turn up the volume.

Mary Woislaw was a successful producer/director of public television programs. She pursued her craft in this highly competitive arena for several years and won a number of awards for her work. She was offered a position in management with an organization that produced commercial programs at a considerably higher level of compensation, which she accepted primarily for that reason (with her friends and associates urging her on). After a couple of years, however, Mary found that she missed the directly creative aspect of her previous position. Unfortunately, the door had more or less closed and locked behind her, and she had a great deal of difficulty getting back into production work.

Expecting Too Much

Another form of Sirens' song comes from people looking to their work to do too much for them, to satisfy too many of their needs and make them happy. In fact, our culture encourages people to have unrealistically high expectations for marriage as well as for work. When these expectations are unmet, people are naturally disappointed. If the expectations themselves are not questioned and modified, people may then conclude that they simply are married to the wrong person or have the wrong job. We have been consulted by a number of people who have gone from job to job and from company to company, each time thinking that they heard a promise of something that would make them truly happy, only to be disappointed once again.

> *Work dominated the landscape of Lisa Castro's life. She had few friends outside work, had never married, and was not close to her family. Lisa looked to her work, and specifically to the group of people she managed, to provide her with happiness. Lisa could not be an effective manager because she was too dependent on the people who reported to her for filling up her life. She was also unwilling to consider moving into other areas within the organization where she could develop other administrative and managerial skills, preferring to hang on to a role within a group that was clearly outliving its usefulness to the company. Unfortunately, the Sirens' song lyrics suggesting that "all happiness comes through work" blinded Lisa to the handwriting on the wall until it was too late and her work group was reengineered out of existence.*

Looking to work to fulfill all of our needs is like investing every penny in one stock in the market. It is a high-risk strategy for investing either money or psychic capital. We have seen a number of people whose unrealistic expectations of their work could not be fulfilled, and who went into a mid-career crisis. They made poorly considered and radical career changes in the hope of meeting those expectations, only to find that it was the expectations—not the area of work—that needed to be changed.

Family Expectations

Much of what people become is a function of what is encouraged and discouraged in their families. We will talk later in more detail about the career consequences of people learning early that some part of *themselves* is unacceptable, but let us consider now those instances in which the family puts out a clear message about which *careers* are and are not acceptable.

> *Guy Burke's father was a "giant among men": a Rhodes scholar, a man who influenced many events of significance at both the national and international levels. He had attended an Ivy League*

college and law school, and then distinguished himself at every stop along the way in his career. His father was quite frank with Guy, telling him that if Guy's career success did not equal or surpass his own, both his respect and his love would be diminished. To Guy this meant that his future was predetermined: he would win a Rhodes scholarship (which he did), pursue a career on Wall Street as an investment banker, become a partner in a successful bank, make millions of dollars, and wield great influence. His own happiness was not a great consideration to him. His father's approval was of paramount importance. Guy had totally adopted his father's frame of reference: "I guess I'd love my own son less too if he weren't very successful," he told us.

Guy's circumstance is unusual for its starkness. We do occasionally see people whose parents told them "You *will* be a doctor" (or "take over the family business when I retire," and so on). More often the imperative from family members is felt rather than clearly stated. That feeling may even be caused wholly by the imagination of the individual in question, so that if the person were ever to ask the family whether they intended for the person to follow a certain path, he or she would be met with genuine amazement.

Arlene Lieberson's mother was a tenured professor in a small liberal arts college in the Midwest, with a doctorate in the humanities. Arlene herself was interested in the health sciences and had become an occupational therapist with specialty in pediatric OT. She enjoyed her work, but Arlene always felt compelled to take courses toward a Ph.D. Although she was interested neither in a teaching career nor in doing research, Arlene could not feel content in her work without earning a doctoral degree. She was being called by the Sirens' song that urged her toward a level of academic achievement she neither needed to practice her profession nor really wanted personally.

Competitive Strivings

Competition with one or another parent often plays the role of the Siren. Healthy competition can provide a positive spark of ambition.

Take, for example, someone whose parents immigrated to this country and made it up from ground zero to a modest level of success. That person then sets a goal of making it to the next level (going to college or getting a professional degree, for example), feeling as if each generation can receive a boost from the former and make the most of it. This can be a healthy wish to "do better than." Another example might be two siblings who have found careers they enjoy, possibly even in the same field, and who enjoy a good-natured competition over who has better sales, whose company's stock price has appreciated more, and so forth. But the results of unhealthy competitive strivings can be disastrous.

> *Jack Daumer's father had a master's degree in public health and taught epidemiology at a medical school in the Southwest. Jack grew up feeling that his father, who was rather poorly compensated relative to other faculty members who were medical doctors (and to the physicians they trained), had missed the boat by not becoming a physician. He was determined to go for the gold ring himself. After graduating from business school, he violated one of the cardinal principles of entrepreneurship and attempted to start a business in a field about which he knew very little and with partners whom he did not know well. The business failed. Jack was so determined to outdo his father that he had not used good business judgment. His Siren was calling him to surpass his father and to do it* now.

Of course, as noted above, competition is not always with a parent. People can be pulled off course by their competitive feelings toward brothers, sisters, cousins, and other kin. Louis Correa provides an example of sibling rivalry gone too far.

> *In the early stages of his career, Louis was so hyperaggressive that he alienated both his peers and his managers. Essentially, no matter where he was or what he was doing, he was fighting a battle with his brother, who was an enormously successful venture capitalist. Louis's managers, understandably, failed to appreciate his aggressive, combative style, and he was fired from several positions before he gained control over his competitive strivings. Once Louis's competitive feelings were under control his career improved, and he was able*

to find work that he enjoyed, that suited his personality and aptitudes, and that he could perform quite successfully.

Unexpected Family Influences

Family influences can have a variety of effects—and not always those
intended by the elders. It is not uncommon for people to react against
their parents' stated wishes and choose career paths diametrically
opposed to the "officially" sanctioned ones. The result is often a career that neither fulfills the wishes of the parent nor satisfies the
individual.

> *Julia Klopp grew up in an upper-middle-class home, with very con-*
> *servative parents. Their conservatism extended to what was consid-*
> *ered an appropriate role for a woman: to be a wife and mother, keep*
> *a lovely home, not have opinions that differed from her husband,*
> *and lunch with other ladies at the country club. As Julia put it, she*
> *was scripted "to be a Stepford Wife" (referring to the film in which*
> *the men in the suburban community of Stepford replaced their wives*
> *with compliant automatons). Julia responded by choosing a career*
> *that demanded every ounce of her energy and every moment of her*
> *time and that paid her a great deal of money (all of which she spent,*
> *thus keeping her beholden to her employer). She was anything but a*
> *Stepford Wife, but she was also deeply unhappy with her work. In*
> *refusing to follow one set of Sirens' songs, she had created another*
> *and was steering toward a different set of rocks.*

Families can have a multitude of influences on people. Some people are drawn to compete with parents, others to compensate for their
real or perceived failings.

> *Eric Hauser's father had been a successful businessman, but under*
> *the influence of his business partner had pushed the limits of the*
> *law, been convicted of fraud, barred from practicing his profession*
> *in the investments field, and sentenced to prison. Eric, determined*
> *to make up for his father's failure at any cost, made success in busi-*
> *ness his sole aim in life. Succeed he did, but at a significant cost:*
> *He had no time to spend with his children when they were young.*

Looking back on his life, he deeply regretted having been driven to make amends for sins he had not even committed.

Other individuals are drawn into areas of work they hope will make their parents proud or make their parents pay attention to them. We have seen many examples of this dynamic, which in our experience is all too common with very bright, capable women who were not given the encouragement and recognition they deserved and might have received had they been boys.

Kyra Furlong's father had a family real estate business. She was highly intelligent, but, unlike her two brothers, she was never thought of in the context of joining her father in the family business. Kyra was determined to succeed and to gain her father's recognition. She pursued an MBA after college, graduating at the top of her class from a top school. Even at this point Kyra's brothers had the inside track, so she pursued a career in real estate development with a firm with a national presence, without even considering other options for which she might have been suited. In Kyra's case the Sirens' song, created by the approval and encouragement she never received from her father, was so prominent that she could hear no others.

Kyra replayed her experience in her family by going into the same business as her father and brothers. Her ambition was obvious to all, and she acknowledged it freely. Often, however, the nature of this type of reenactment is more subtle and difficult to identify, and the person is not aware of it. Consider the case of Jerry Fortunata.

Jerry came from a troubled home in which he never felt wanted. His mother had died when Jerry was a young boy and his father had remarried. His stepmother seemed to view Jerry as competition for her new husband's attention. She accepted Jerry's younger sister, but Jerry himself always felt rejected. In looking at his work history, we could see that he had held a number of jobs in which he had placed himself in the position of having to win over a constituency that was initially hostile to him. Jerry was bright, charming, articulate, and hardworking, and always succeeded eventually. The cost of working to overcome rejection was high, however. For Jerry the Sirens' song was not mere acceptance, but acceptance that was suffered for and won.

Jerry's story is a specific example of a much wider pattern, which has as its hallmark the assumption that if something is hard to get, it must be good. As Groucho Marx put it, "I wouldn't want to belong to any club that would have me as a member." Some people look to work to fill a void in themselves, to attempt to make up for some damage to the self. Perhaps not surprisingly, once they *get* the job that was impossible to get, they often dislike it and do not, in fact, feel more whole or fulfilled. In other instances the need for recognition can lead to errors in career management other than choice of career per se. Tamika Jones's situation exemplifies this sort of scenario.

Tamika was an exceptionally intelligent, vibrant, attractive woman in her early fifties. Like Kyra, her giftedness had not been recognized by her family (especially her father), and she craved attention. She was drawn to career positions in which a powerful, preferably charismatic and attractive man paid a lot of attention to her. This had presented no major problems in her career prior to the position she occupied before coming to consult with us. During her tenure in this position a management shakeup had resulted in the installation of a new president, to whom she reported directly. This individual ran very hot and cold toward Tamika, and when he failed to shine his light on her she felt hurt and angry. Unable to rely on him as a steady source of recognition and approval, she ill-advisedly left her position precipitously.

Other Scenarios

Of course, there are many other Sirens' songs that may have nothing at all to with our families. Having seen many hundreds of people in career transition over the years, we could have written a book on this topic alone. Instead, we will present several representatives of common songs. One has to do with fatal attractions to people with huge intellects (and huge egos).

Betsy Gifford had an unerring instinct that led her to seek out brilliant, narcissistic men for whom to work. She would bask in their approval when they gave it, feel miserable when they withheld it, and do anything possible to ensure that she got as much of their attention as possible. Her bosses, for their part, loved having an attractive woman who was very intelligent and accomplished in her own right as an adoring acolyte. The bad news in these relationships was that her geniuses were typically very mercurial, narcissistic, and self-absorbed, leaving Betsy unhappy much of the time.

Other people we have worked with have chosen careers to compensate for some inadequacy they felt themselves to have. The inadequacy can be real or imagined; it is real to that person, whether or not the rest of the world perceives it. It can have to do with any aspect of the self, such as appearance, intelligence, or social attractiveness.

Barbara Gold grew up in a small town in Idaho. She knew she was bright but questioned whether she was really bright enough to make it in the larger world. She attended a good college, earned superior grades, was recruited by a prestigious investment management firm as an analyst, received an MBA from a top school, and went to work for an investment bank with an excellent reputation, where she did very well. When she called us, however, Barbara was miserable. Her life was out of balance in the extreme. She did nothing but work and had no time for friends or a love life. She still saw the world in terms of goals to be achieved, which would prove once and for all that she was intelligent, and not just for "a small town in the middle of nowhere," as she put it. Clearly, no level of objective achievement was going to quiet Barbara's Sirens.

Another element of Barbara's story was that she was unusually attractive, which often leads people to feel they must prove that they are not "just a pretty (or handsome) face" achieving success on the basis of looks alone. This is akin to someone with a great deal of money who is concerned that people like him or her only because of the money (or family name, or connections). Susan Murray struggled with this issue.

Susan had always been a head-turner, as an infant, as a toddler, as a young girl, and as a woman. She had also always done quite well academically, to the pleasure of her parents and especially of her father. Like Barbara, Susan sought out the most difficult and challenging work she could find after graduating from college, to prove her worth in the world of work. She went into the sales and marketing area of a growing computer software company, where she was quite successful despite not having any technical training. Soon she found herself wearing "golden handcuffs," earning a high salary but not being truly interested in the products her company sold, or even in the software industry as a whole. She had proven to herself that she could succeed, but found herself stuck in an industry in which she had little interest.

In some instances the genesis of the Sirens' song is not as clear as in the examples we have described thus far. Nevertheless, the individual's behavior and decisions make it clear that there is, for some reason, an alluring voice leading the person off course. Ron Cody and Andy O'Hara provide two examples.

Unlike some of the other people we have discussed, Ron was laboring under no apparent familial or societal "shoulds." He appeared to have nothing for which he felt a need to compensate, no need to prove himself. Yet he was fatally drawn to the "big time," to the "big deal." Ron, by his own choosing, had left a successful career as a consulting engineer to set off on his own as a deal maker in his arena of work. Unfortunately, on his own he was unable to serve his former clients, who needed more "brain hours" than he could provide as an individual. In addition, developing new business was, to say the least, a struggle for Ron, who was quite introverted and sensitive to rejection. As the months passed he was unable to grow his consulting practice. It was clear that Ron had made an error in his decision to leave a situation where he was not solely responsible for bringing in clients. His desire to make it big on his own, however, kept him from reconsidering and going back to work for his old firm or going to another organization.

Andy was also clearly being pulled by the song of the Sirens, but the source of the song was not clear. He was a bright young investment banker, but after getting his MBA he had been rejected for positions with the most prestigious "bulge bracket firms." Andy became almost obsessed with the idea of getting into one of those banks and made a series of high-risk career moves with the sole goal of putting himself there. The desire to be in the "big pond" outweighed all other considerations for him.

The question of how one distinguishes a Sirens' song from a true calling is difficult to answer. (If it were easy, the Sirens would not have had such success luring sailors to their death.) The case of Andy may provide one clue, however, in its obsessiveness. If you find yourself unable to consider *any* other options, if you feel utterly compelled to pursue a certain path, you might consider that a warning that you are hearing the voice of a Siren. Words like "If I can only . . .," "I know I can never be happy unless I . . .," and "I'm miserable now, but later . . ." are signs that you should look carefully inside yourself for the source of those assertions. Obviously, if you are following a trail that has been clearly marked for you by others (family members or peers), you should examine whether this path is really the right one *for you.* If you are making career decisions that are very high risk or that don't seem to make any sense, even to you, think twice. The louder the song the more you should question it.

Keep in mind also that we are most easily seduced by the things we most crave. If you were never praised as a child, you may be especially attracted to an otherwise poorly matching work opportunity if you are highly praised in the process of interviewing. If you were always compared with a brother or sister, you may be especially prone to seduction by a work situation in which there is a "sibling" rivalry in place that you have an opportunity to win.

Of course, one person's foolish path toward the rocks is another's inspired vision, and only history allows us to distinguish the Wright brothers, Thomas Edison, and Alexander Graham Bell from thousands of others. Furthermore, as we discuss in Chapter 8, even when people determine that they have gone down a wrong path for them, that journey has not been for nought. Deciding to change directions does not mean that, by definition, you have made an error in judgment or that your previous travel is of no value. We often find that people have *needed* to go down those blind alleys, to find themselves washed up on the shore of the island of the Sirens, in order to learn where they do want to go.

Fears and Discomforts

Just as Sirens' songs pull people toward something wrong, fears push people away from what is right for them. Social psychologists talk about approach-approach conflicts and approach-avoidance conflicts. In an approach-approach conflict, people are pulled between two attractive alternatives ("Do I want that delicious cake or that ice cream?"), whereas in an approach-avoidance conflict they are both attracted to and repelled by the same thing ("Do I want that honey badly enough to risk being stung by the bees in the hive?"). The Sirens' songs create approach-approach conflicts, whereas our fears create approach-avoidance conflicts.

Clients often ask us whether they "have what it takes" to be entrepreneurs. What most people mean by that is "Can I tolerate the risk inherent in starting my own business? Will I be able to live with the anxiety?" Everyone experiences fear, of course, and entrepreneurs are no different from anyone else. (In fact, successful entrepreneurs do everything they can to minimize risk; that is why they are *successful* entrepreneurs.) Fear is no more a reason *not* to pursue a course of action than excitement is a reason *to* pursue it. It is a bit of emotional data, but nothing more.

The *American Heritage Dictionary* defines *courage* as "the state . . . of mind or spirit that enables one to face danger, *fear* [emphasis ours] or vicissitudes with self-possession, confidence and resolution." It is not that some people are fearless but rather that they do not allow their fears to divert them from taking the actions necessary to achieve their goals. This is true in every area of life, including career and personal relationships.

Lacking the courage to face fears of many sorts leads people to steer away from their true career paths. Although it may not lead to the goal that is the truest expression of who they are, they seek safer routes that do not (seemingly) carry the risk inherent in really "going for the gold." We say "seemingly" because we have seen many people who played it safe only to find that their careers are in greater danger than if they had gone all out for their true goal. Let us consider some kinds and causes of these inhibiting fears.

Fear of Failing

That the most common fear is fear of failing in our attempts to reach our career goals is not surprising. Many people hold back from trying their hardest so that they have an excuse: They didn't really give it their best shot and thus did not really fail. There are many varieties of this fear, one being fear of the humiliation that would accompany failure for some people.

Remy Ball's father had founded an office furniture manufacturing business and, with the help of his brothers, had turned it into a very successful company. Remy's father and uncles seemed to have an unerring instinct for making the right business decisions, were good judges of talent, and, if they were not technical geniuses, were certainly highly competent in the engineering side of the business. Remy's career decisions had been guided by the fear that no matter what he did, he could not measure up. He chose a field of work that had absolutely nothing in common with the business his father had begun, making any comparison impossible.

Remy was self-employed as an advertising consultant, which had the added advantage that he never had to be reviewed for bonuses and promotions (and risk being humiliated by getting a negative review). Unfortunately, being self-employed meant that he had to generate all his own business, and the fear of humiliating rejection when making sales calls was just as strong as the fear of a humiliating poor review. Thus, Remy was paralyzed in his efforts even in this arena, for fear of trying and failing. He might have been better off working for someone else, where by successfully working through his initial fear of failure he would have gained some sense of security. On the path he had taken, he had to prove himself every time he made a call.

Feeling as if they have to live up to the great achievements of others has been the equivalent of career curare for many people. The father of one of our clients advised her not to try to surpass him, because luck had played such a great part in his success (an unusually candid and gracious acknowledgment of the role that random chance plays in all our careers). After an initial sense of shock, she found this counsel quite freeing. Rick Katz was not fortunate enough to have a father who could attribute part of his success to luck.

Rick's father was not enormously successful financially or in terms of prestige. He was, however, a true genius in the area of science and engineering. Literally everything he studied and did in his general area of expertise was easy for him. He could learn new material with a quick scan of the research, could pull together an important technical talk in a few hours, all with seemingly no effort. Rick concluded that if he were working on something and it was difficult, there was something wrong. His standard for what was normal was so skewed that when he encountered even a little difficulty he would immediately feel discouraged and give up. By the time he came to see us, he had gone through several colleges and majors, and a number of jobs, quitting each when he hit his first rough spot in the road.

A fear of the unknown was what stood in the way of Marty Daniels. Specifically, Marty was afraid of not knowing enough even to figure out what he didn't (but should) know. Thus, he feared not only failing but failing in a most humiliating manner—by not knowing something that *everyone* else knows.

Marty had been offered a position in a firm that was at that time exclusively populated by people with master's degrees in one or another field of engineering, or master's or doctorates in the hard sciences. Marty had certain expertise that others in the firm lacked, but, as he put it, it was like being the only person able to speak a foreign language that others needed to know, but not being fluent in the mother tongue. By not having training in either engineering or science, he felt he would be at a tremendous disadvantage, and even in interviews had been fearful of asking questions that might reveal an ignorance he "should not" have had. We discussed the crucial importance of being able to ask questions, especially in the early years in a new career, and persuaded Marty to lay his cards on the table. He sat down with the managing partner and made certain that the firm was absolutely clear about what it was—and was not—getting in him (sort of a "truth in advertising" approach), so that he would feel more comfortable asking questions even if every other person in the firm knew the answer. Happily, the match was made, and Marty succeeded with the company.

Fear of Losing Success

Experiencing the "flow of success," a concept written about by Sharon Parks, can work against people's efforts to find the right career. Consider two people as contrasting examples.

Jill Reyes had grown up in real poverty, deserted by her father, her mother an alcoholic, living with her sisters in a condemned building in the Bronx. Unlike many of her friends, Jill not only was a survivor but was determined to work her way out of that impoverished existence. She graduated from high school (that alone being a substantial achievement among her peer group) and went on to college, where she studied business. She then started her own temporary office work agency and was successful in that business, but wanted still more. She applied to business schools and was accepted by a top program. Although intimidated initially, she was successful in her academics by dint of hard work, good business savvy, and a willingness to risk being wrong in class discussions. As Jill put it, "I know I can survive anything, so what's the big deal if I take a position and it's wrong? On the street, or in my business, if I was wrong I could have lost everything, and even then I knew I could survive. This is a piece of cake by comparison."

To say the least, Jill had not grown up in the "flow of success." By contrast, for Tom Frier things had always come easily. This had consequences both positive and negative for him.

Tom had led an enviable life. He was bright, very attractive, an excellent athlete, and a natural leader, someone to whom others al-

most reflexively looked to be the captain or team leader. Tom's family was quite wealthy, which afforded him opportunities for excellent schooling, travel abroad, and lessons in whatever he might have an inclination toward. Also, because of his family's social position and the exclusive private schools he attended, Tom's personal network included the sons and daughters of other wealthy, influential people. Essentially, from the moment of his conception Tom had been directly in the flow of success. This is not to say that he did not work hard in school or on the playing fields, but no matter what he did, he was successful. There were two problems with Tom's seemingly ideal life. Because he had always been "in the flow," he had absolutely no confidence that he could swim in the colder, rougher waters outside the warm stream of success. And, related to this lack of experience and confidence, Tom had become extremely conservative and risk averse. It was far more important to him to reduce or eliminate the risk of being somehow pushed out of the flow of success than to take a chance at doing something new. The result was that Tom lived more in fear of loss than in the excitement of being able to take chances, knowing that he had a safety net under him. He had become entangled in that net instead.

This is analogous to a basketball team getting a ten-point lead early in the first quarter and deciding to try to "sit on it," to preserve that lead for the next three quarters (not a strategy that many coaches would advocate). We see this fear of loss of success in other situations as well. A classic trap that many entrepreneurs fall into is that of becoming too conservative once they have achieved a certain level of success. They become more concerned with not losing than with continuing to win, and so they turn away from opportunities that involve what should objectively be seen as an acceptable level of risk. They also forget that you have to spend money to make money, and refuse to continue to invest appropriately in their businesses.

Fear of Being Aggressive

A client who tells us that he refuses to play politics, and wants to work for a meritocratic company where he doesn't have to do so, may be afraid of his own aggressive instincts. There is nothing wrong with being aggressive and fighting for your own cause, and there is no group or organization that doesn't involve political maneuvering. John Schwartz's story shows some of the problems that can arise as a consequence of not being aggressive enough.

> *John was an exceptionally intelligent man who was exceedingly uncomfortable with any sort of conflict, no matter how strongly he felt about the position or how right he knew he was. He could push (a little) on behalf of his employees, but not for himself. As a result he was frequently taken advantage of by his superiors, his peers, and even his subordinates, all of whom knew he couldn't say "no." John could have made far more money if he had been willing to put himself on the market, but he did not feel comfortable "pushing" himself on other people. He also could have commanded more power and respect in his own firm had he been willing to be aggressive on his own account, but that also felt too self-promotional.*

Fear of Being Disliked

Fear of your own aggressiveness can express itself as an overwhelming need to be liked or, conversely, a fear of being disliked. If you are a lion and kill and eat a zebra for lunch, you are doing what a lion is supposed to do: surviving. But it is unlikely that the zebra is going to like you for it. There is nothing wrong with fighting hard to be the one who gets the promotion or the best assignment, who makes the sale, who is recognized by the manager for an accomplishment. None of these actions, by their nature, involves stabbing someone else in the back or taking unfair advantage. Of course, if only one person is going to make partner and it is you, others may be unhappy, but this does not mean that you did something wrong. A surprising number of people, however, are unwilling to risk the possibility of being disliked even if that results in their not succeeding in their careers.

> *Art Griffin was an accountant who, in his own words, "gave it away for free." Friends, relatives, friends of friends, friends of relatives, relatives of friends, would ask him for his advice, "just a minute of his time." Needless to say, a minute would become fifteen*

minutes, and twenty on a subsequent phone call, and then more and more. Furthermore, once the series of "just one minute" calls had been established as a "freebie," Art felt awkward about changing the arrangement. Worse, these people would give Art's name to their friends, not so they could become paying clients but so they could get free counsel as well. Of course, it takes two people to make this dynamic work. Art's part was that he allowed it, regardless of the personal cost to him. Why? Because he was afraid that if people asked him for his advice and he suggested that they call his office for an appointment, they would think him greedy, not acting as a true friend, making this no more than a business relationship.

Fear of Success

If fear of failure is a common impediment to success, fear of success itself is also surprisingly common. Many people imagine success to be accompanied by loss. The loss might be that of other people's love and affection or of the friendship of people who have not succeeded to a similar degree. Or it might be a loss of an old, familiar sense of oneself as someone who is not very successful. Fears can be instilled in any number of ways and for any number of reasons. Often they come with the best of intentions, like teaching your children to be careful when crossing the street, for fear of their being run over. Mack Hayes presents an interesting example.

Mack's parents warned him not to think too highly of himself (pride being one of the seven deadly sins, of course). Mack had grown up in Great Britain and his parents were acutely class conscious. They sought to protect their son, wanting him to "know his place" and not try to "rise above his station" in life, efforts that they believed would engender retribution from people born into a higher social class. Fortunately, Mack did not allow this fear to keep him from becoming successful in his career.

In Mack's case the fear of success was engendered by a somewhat abstract and general admonition. Such messages, even when delivered rather generally, can be powerful. We may learn not to aspire to certain levels of success because of our race, or class, or gender.

The above examples show how allowing fears too much power can drastically affect both people's career choices and their ability to succeed in moving along whatever path they have chosen. It would be as if Odysseus, having successfully escaped the Sirens, then turned away from his goal of returning to Ithaca for fear that he would not be given a hero's welcome. Whether the cause was the Sirens' songs or his own fears, the result would have been the same: the failure to follow his calling, his intended course.

Lack of Knowledge About the World

The most common manifestation of this means of losing one's way is relatively straightforward: If you don't know what something is, only by sheer chance will you get there. Of course, if you *do* know it, you may still not arrive at the destination but at least you will have known to chart your course for it. The creatively gifted child who is never exposed to a museum, art class, symphony, or play is unlikely to become an artist, composer, musician, playwright, or actor. Exposure to the world is essential for our most fundamental interests to be realized. David Fritz provides a good example.

David grew up on the South Side of Chicago. His father and uncles were "city workers," and as his older siblings and cousins grew up, they too took jobs working for the city. David was a bright student and won a full scholarship to an excellent university in the city, where he majored in public policy and management. After graduating, he too went to work for the city, albeit in a much higher level position than anyone else in his family had held. It wasn't until several years later that David began to question whether he would have been happier working in the private sector, where attention to the bottom line would have made for a better fit for his ambitious, results-oriented personality. Had he really known about life inside an investment bank or fast-growing high-tech company, David might have made a very different initial career choice. Of course he knew that those businesses existed, but his knowledge was so sketchy, especially as compared with his knowledge about how the city worked, that the former was really terra incognita for him.

Another, less obvious form of lack of knowledge has caused many people we have seen to regret their career decisions. In this instance it is the confusion between learning and practicing the career. The law is a prime example of a career in which a number of people enjoy the schooling but not the work itself.

> *Janet Levine had attended a liberal arts college where she studied political science. As a senior, Janet had no real idea about what sort of career she wanted to pursue, but several of her friends from school had already graduated and gone on to law school. She arranged to sit in on some classes and was delighted by what she saw. She took the LSATs, scored very well, and was accepted by a top-tier law school. Janet loved law school, thriving on debating the concepts of law (What really constitutes a contract? What did the authors of the Constitution intend when they wrote about the right to bear arms? Under what circumstances should judges recuse themselves from cases?). She made the* Law Review *and was recruited by top law firms for summer internships and a career position. To her dismay, she found that she loathed actually practicing law. Gone were the interesting debates about "big picture" elements of the law. In their place were long hours of tedious, detailed brief-writing and proof-reading. If she could have stayed in law school forever, Janet would have been delighted. She found law practice, however, to be boring much of the time.*

Law is certainly not the only area of work in which people make career missteps through not doing sufficient "due diligence" in investigating what the actual work entails. We see management consultants who have not thought through what it will really be like to work in an exclusively advisory capacity, or to travel extensively; people who go to work for large companies without really considering how they will like being but one part of a complex machine; people who, conversely, go to small firms without considering what it will be like on a day-to-day basis to work in such a lean organization.

> *Terry Washington had been offered the job of his (and his class-mates') dreams after business school: working for a small venture capital firm. The financial upside was enormous; the variety would*

be great; the work would call on his financial, analytical, and technical skills; and, best of all, as the only analyst he would be mentored, not lost in a huge bureaucracy. Terry lasted less than six months. On his first day the only one of the four partners not on the road spent about two hours with him, gave him a stack of business proposals to peruse and analyze, and left for the airport. Over the next several months Terry spent most of his time alone, received very little in the way of guidance, and, as he put it, "was going stir crazy." What had seemed like the ideal position turned out to be anything but.

Information is easy to come by these days. How is it, then, that lack of knowledge about the world can lead people to go down career paths that are poorly suited for them? Part of the answer lies in the previous two sections of this chapter. If we feel a powerful Sirens' call toward a particular area of work, we may close our eyes to information that would force us to question that call. That information would create conflict, or what is sometimes called "cognitive dissonance," which is uncomfortable, so we shut it out. In Chapter 8 we will discuss the importance of allowing those conflicts and feelings of discomfort to come to the fore in order to become more fully aware of how our psychic growth is either served or not served in a particular work role. Similarly, if we are overwhelmed by fear of success or of failure, or by any other fear, we will simply not gather information about a particular area of work. Doing so makes us feel anxious, so we prefer to keep ourselves in the dark.

In Chapter 10 we will describe a means of assessing different jobs and career paths in order to avoid the kinds of errors just described. At this point let us consider another type of lack of knowledge that can lead to careers going off course. This area is knowledge about the self: who we are, what we want, and what we're good at.

Lack of Knowledge About Ourselves

One or more of a whole range of life circumstances can keep people in the dark about some aspect of their selves. If you were raised in a family of ministers and social workers, in which personal ambition and aggressiveness were frowned on, you might not be in touch with the aggressive element of yourself. If, however, you were raised in a super-aggressive, very competitive family, you might not be well acquainted with the side of yourself that is more altruistic.

Another gap in self-knowledge can come from people's appraisal of their own areas of strength and weakness. For some perverse reason it seems to be human nature to think the worst of ourselves, to underestimate our abilities and attractive qualities. We have worked with many people who have made poor career choices because they grossly underestimated their capabilities. It is as if they look in the mirror and see someone different from the person the rest of us see. On the basis of this misperception they then go down career paths less challenging and less satisfying than they would have if they had seen themselves accurately.

Louise Alvarez grew up in a very small town in New Jersey. After graduating from high school she took a job as a secretary working for a pharmaceutical company. No one in her family had ever gone to college, and Louise never believed that she "had what it took" to pursue a college degree. She was quite successful in her work, however, and a manager encouraged her to try taking some college courses on a part-time basis. She did so and was encouraged to find that she did very well academically. Over the next several years she earned not only an undergraduate degree but a master's as well. Still, Louise's sense of her own competence and value lagged behind reality. Several more years passed until she gradually began to recognize, almost against her will, just how bright she really was. At that point she was able to take her place on the executive team of the company where she worked.

Lack of self-knowledge is by no means limited to people's sense of their intelligence or competence. Most people would rather not acknowledge certain aspects of who they are. Carl Jung, the Swiss psychoanalyst, labeled as "shadows" those parts of ourselves that make us so uncomfortable that we try to deny their existence. The shadow self-aspect is one that people identify as bad, even evil, a part of us that could easily get out of control and has to be kept locked up tight.

Some people, for example, turn their sexual feelings and aggressive impulses into their shadows.

> *Anne McDonald prided herself on her essential goodness: kindness and loyalty toward friends, concern for the environment, sense of empathy for the underprivileged and defenseless. Her career choice (human resource development) had been guided by this sense of herself that was true, but incomplete. What Anne failed to "own" was the aspect of herself that was self-interested, that wanted to win and to be associated with others who were winners as well. Not only was her career direction determined by this partial picture, her level of success was affected as well, for two reasons. First, to have enjoyed success would have been wrong, part of the shadow. Second, Anne's denial of the aggressive and self-interested aspects of her personality also resulted in her being quite judgmental and having difficulty getting along with coworkers who were not so purely altruistic as she thought they should be.*

Keith Jackson presents almost the mirror image of Anne. His shadow was his goodness, kindness, and generosity.

> *Keith prided himself on being tough, not "babying" people. He was brutally honest, could be scathingly critical, and had a caustic wit. Of course, all this covered a soft underbelly, but that could be inferred only indirectly. People either loved Keith or hated him. Those in the former camp enjoyed his intelligence and dry humor, and were sufficiently thick skinned not to be pricked by his thorns. The people who disliked him had been stung by his criticisms and felt mistrustful, felt that he was not someone they could turn their backs on. They saw him as selfish and aggressive to the point of ruthlessness, someone "who liked his steaks not just rare, but still alive." Just as Anne saw only part of herself, so did Keith, albeit a very different part. His partial self-perception also drove his career decision (equities trading on Wall Street), and his work style, which was even more aggressive than that of most of his peers.*

In summary, we find that people err in their career decision making for several reasons. The first is basing their choices on what they "should" do (or worshipping some other sort of false idol), rather than listening to their inner sense of what work they will find satisfying. The second is making decisions strongly influenced by fears, when they should confront the fears and hold the course steady. The third is lack of knowledge, either about the world of work or about themselves. It is important to understand your shoulds and fears as you move into the exercises in the next chapter and as you take the *Business Career Interest Inventory.*

THREE

The Imagination of Work

IN THIS CHAPTER we will introduce the first of two methods for identifying the business core functions that are most important for you. This method is called *active imagination,* a means for becoming aware of images associated with the most exciting types of work. The second method, the *Business Career Interest Inventory,* will be introduced in the next chapter. Just as a sailor uses two independent systems of measurement (electronic navigational readings and readings from the stars) to ensure that the boat's location is accurate, the best approach to self-assessment uses more than one method of data collection to develop the richest and most accurate picture of a person. It is best to combine information about yourself from three sources when conducting a career self-assessment. The first source is, simply put, you: your life history, your imagination of ideal work activities and settings, and your imagination of what you see your life becoming, including (but not limited to) your work. The second source is other people: how do they see you, what can they imagine you doing well and with deep satisfaction? The third is objective data from career-relevant psychological assessment instruments such as the *Business Career Interest Inventory.* In this chapter we will teach you how to collect active imagination information both from yourself and from people who know you well. By employing these active imagination exercises, you can verify the information you obtain from using a sophisticated psychological inventory such as the *Business Career Interest Inventory.* You may wish to do all of the exercises or only a few, but it is best to do at least one before proceeding to take the *BCII.*

Our clients come to us with varying degrees of knowledge about their work and their careers that they have gathered from carefully paying attention to their experience of what they find truly interesting. They have learned from those times when they have been deeply engaged in and excited about work. They have images of these experiences, which can then be used as gateways for new imaginative thinking about the roles and work environments that can bring a sustained experience of deeply engaging work. These images are rooted in the deep energies of the self, and come into our awareness through the act of creative imagination.

The Nature of Images

Images come to us in different ways. They arise from speech, from reading, from dreams and daydreams, from the experience of art, and from immediate encounter with our day-to-day world. Images are not simply sense impressions, but rather experiences that the mind has poetically re-created to represent the truth of a situation. Certain experiences attract our own psychological material, and we use such experiences from everyday life to bring psychological issues to our consciousness. We may not consciously notice the expression on our boss's face during a conversation at the time of the experience, but an image of that expression may return later with seemingly inexplicable persistence. The persistence of an image is an indication that it carries encoded information about the emerging self that is yet to be recognized and integrated.

Many times in career counseling we notice our clients pausing and briefly focusing inward. In such situations, we ask them to describe the image that has attracted their attention. This request is often met with resistance, such as "Oh it's nothing, my mind was just wandering" or "That seems irrelevant to what we were talking about." To the *ego,* the part of the self that tries to avoid change, imagery is often experienced as an interruption. The appearance of an image, however, is no interruption at all. It is the self's attempt to deepen the conversation and to bring more intuitive and feeling modes of consciousness to the ego's more discursive and abstract understanding of a situation.

It is important to differentiate image from fantasy. Fantasies are the playthings of the ego as it attempts to escape reality. They are flights from what is real, and they carry with them the consequence of leading us farther from the true energy of the self. Our clients often bring career fantasies with them to our sessions. The fantasies typically involve unrealistic degrees of convenience, authority, compensation, or leisure. They are pleasurable to entertain but cannot bring the individual into greater connection with the world and with work that is meaningful over time.

Images, however, are autonomous (free from manipulations of the ego), emotionally diverse, and grounded in a fuller reality of the situation from which they arise. An image is emotionally complex and compelling. It pulls us deeper, it disturbs and arouses us; we sense that the image has something to teach us. Most characteristically, an image requires *work;* we have to leave familiar territory to approach it. It brings news of a larger world, and we must strain to listen.

In our career consulting we teach our clients to work with images from their focus on work. The images often arise out of conversations in our sessions. We begin our initial session with the request that our clients tell us about their lives. We want to know about important people, relationships, events, and decisions. As the conversation turns to adulthood, we want to hear in particular about experiences in work settings. As we listen, it is as if two stories are being told. There is the narrative of the ego, giving us dates and sequences and already-thought-out summaries and analyses of life events. This story often has the aura of being "canned"; it is the ego's agreed-upon official biography.

As we listen to this narrative, we listen for the voice of the self. Unusual images or vignettes surface and are often shared in an off-hand fashion. An interesting detail added to an otherwise bland chronology, the beginnings of tears, a sudden shift in posture, a pause with an inward focus, a sudden memory that surprises the client—all of these are clues that the self wants this element of the life story to be told more deeply, and told from a different perspective. We return to these "openings of the self" and ask our clients to say more, to amplify them and take them further. We listen to the story of the same life, told both from the narrow perspective of the ego and, in a halting offering of images, from the depths of the self where the full story lies as if in some deep subterranean reservoir. Our job, before the consultation is complete, is to train our clients to be divers, able to explore that reservoir.

There are a number of ways to engage the work of the imagination of the self. Reading, be it Shakespeare or *The Wall Street Journal,* is perhaps the most powerful and accessible stimulus to the imaginative process. The image, however, resides not in what is read but in how the reading works on us. Two people reading the same article in *Fortune* will have different experiences. The first may read it quickly, move on to the next page, and never have another encounter with the writing or its ideas. The second may also read the piece quickly and move on to the next page, but wake early the following morning full of unexpected thoughts and ideas about the supposedly forgotten article. For this second reader the ideas in the writing were in some way sympathetic with energies of the self looking for the shape of image and language.

Paying attention to how we are being affected by images is a vital art for the work of self-understanding. The emotional content of an image is one of its most important ways of communicating. Unexpected enthusiasm, curiosity, excitement, anger, or anxiety provide essential clues to what may hold meaning for us. Experiencing an image without judgment or suppression, allowing it to speak fully, regardless of the message, is the essence of the discipline of imagination. We need to learn to *hold* an image without trying to analyze or categorize it. By holding the image we allow *it* to work on *us,* with our conscious participation.

Evoking an image, holding it, allowing it to develop and becoming aware of how it affects us, are the essential elements of the process known as active imagination, an approach to self-knowledge elaborated by Carl Jung and several of his followers. This process is quite different from what is commonly understood as "analyzing" dreams or other works of imagination for the purpose of discovering their "meaning" (which usually boils down to finding a previous category of our thinking in which to place them). To be sure, sound and sophisticated analysis is an important part of self-understanding, but its proper place is *after* we have allowed the thinking and feeling brought on by images to develop fully.

In the remainder of this chapter we will present an approach that uses active imagination as a tool for career self-assessment. This approach will include several exercises for accessing images that can help you identify meaningful work. We will present a method for analyzing these exercises in Chapter 6, after you have taken the *Business Career Interest Inventory.* In Chapter 7 you will learn how your business career profile is related to specific business work roles and work environments. We do not present a method for analyzing active imagination images here because we do not want to bias your responses to the *BCII* by explaining the model for analysis before you have taken the inventory.

Training the Mind's Eye

Active imagination is not passive fantasy. To engage in active imagination you must be wide awake and highly alert, but with an inward focus. Active imagination has much in common with the deliberate act of memory. To learn active imagination, let us start with a classical memory exercise. A popular memory technique used during the Renaissance was to mentally place objects representing topics for a speech in each room of a familiar house. Moving from room to room with the mind's eye, the speaker would recognize the object that he or she had "placed" there while preparing the speech. The imaginative movement through the house not only allowed for recall of the specific objects or speech topics but exercised the eye of imagination.

Pick a house that you know well, either the house or apartment where you now live or one from childhood. You are going to go on a journey through that house as a way of learning how to exercise the eye of the imagination.

First, find a quiet place where you will not be interrupted. Sit with a comfortable posture; your eyes should be neither fully closed nor wide open. Turn your attention inward. With your attention focused on your mind's eye, open the door to your house and step inside. Look around. What do you see? Don't think—look. Are you in a hallway or a room? What is the lighting like? Is it day or night? Take a few steps. Notice what is different now that you are standing in a slightly different place; look around again. Move into the nearest room. Take a few steps inside this room and pause. Slowly turn to your right and notice what you see. Look at the furniture; notice what is on the wall. Take your time.

Release your focus and become more aware of the full room, continuing to turn to your right. Again, what time of day or night is it? Are the lights on? Look up to the ceiling. Notice the distance between you and the ceiling. Look at the texture of the ceiling surface. Bring your head back to a position where you are looking straight ahead. Are you aware of the weather outside, perhaps through a window? Look at the floor immediately in front of you. Notice what shoes you are wearing. Don't *think* these things; don't worry whether or not you are "making them up." Simply look and allow your imagination to supply the image.

Look for the nearest door that leads to another room. Begin to move toward that door; become aware of what it feels like to be moving in this space of the imaginative world. Pause at the doorway. Look into the next room. What catches your eye? Take your time. Notice whether the lighting in this new room is different. Is it darker or lighter? Where is most of the light coming from? Slowly, turn and look back into the first room. Notice any change in light as you do so. Turn back again slowly and stop, looking into the new room. Step into the new room.

Now let go of this interior space altogether and come back to the room where you are actually sitting. Notice the shift from the act of interior looking to the act of looking into the immediate space around you. Become aware of this shift in attention from inner light to outer light.

You may want to take a break before moving on to our career imagination exercises, or to "visit" another house, or perhaps your office, strengthening your ability to use your imagination. When you are ready, read on and go through the exercises below.

For the following exercise, and for the other exercises in this chapter, record your experiences in a journal. Becoming an accurate and descriptive writer is a powerful tool for self-understanding. It is not important that your vocabulary be large or your syntax perfect. It *is* important that you push yourself to capture an image or feeling. What you are really doing with the journal writing is pushing back the frontier of ego, that narrow definition of who you are and what is important that is based on old thinking and old experience. Authentic writing is a discovery of new energy reserves within your self. You may want to work toward accomplishing the same goal by using a tape recorder as an intermediate step, speaking your images, thoughts, and feelings before reviewing them and making a written note. What is most important is that you do not in any way censor what comes into your mind. Don't worry about what it means or what it says about you; just gather the information.

Remembering the Experience of Flow

The psychologist Mihaly Csikszentmihalyi conducted a lengthy study of work satisfaction, asking large numbers of people to describe, as closely as possible, their experience when they were deeply enjoying their work. In reviewing the many accounts provided by his subjects, Csikszentmihalyi arrived at a description of the state of enjoyment one experiences when fully engaged in one's work. He called this experience of being deeply absorbed in work "flow," an experience with several characteristics:

> . . . a sense that one's skills are adequate to cope with the challenges at hand, in a goal-directed, rule-bound action system that provides clear clues as to how well one is performing. Concentration is so intense that there is no attention left over to think about anything irrelevant, or to worry about problems. Self-consciousness disappears, and the sense of time becomes distorted. An activity that produces such experiences is so gratifying that people are willing to do it for its own sake, with little concern for what they will get out of it, even when it is difficult, or dangerous.

Professional basketball players and other athletes have described this experience of flow as being "in the zone." They say that time seems to slow down, the basket seems to grow larger, they lose their sense of the crowd, they feel at one with the game. As psychologists we have on occasion had the experience of being so in tune with clients that it almost seemed as if we could read their minds. This, too, is flow.

Our first approach to career active imagination will borrow from

Csikszentmihalyi's idea of flow. Again sitting in a comfortable position, with an inner focus, read the above description of flow and pay attention to the images that begin to arise. As you reflect on Csikszentmihalyi's words, some sensations, feelings, and visual impressions may come to mind. Watch what is happening as you consider his words. Look at the images; let them develop. Where are you in the images? What place, what time? One image may be replaced by another. Go with the images; allow them to develop. At some point, they will begin to slow and there will develop a more persistent image of being at a particular place and engaging in some particular work or play that has the feeling indicated by Csikzentmihalyi's description of flow.

Focus your attention on this place where, in your mind's eye, you have returned to a particular experience of flow. Do not edit what you are experiencing. The place and the activity may surprise you. It may not be at all what you would normally think of as ideal work or your best job to date. It may not even be work at all. The activity, or that time in your life, may in fact have been difficult; but images are tied to specific experiences, specific activities. It is these specific moments of flow that we want to capture in this exercise. We are building a collage of these moments, from different activities and different times in life that we will later assemble and analyze.

Right now your task is simply to pay attention and to record just what you remember and feel. Allow the image to develop. Watch; be attentive. Notice where you are: what room of what building? What time of day or night is it? What is your posture—are you standing or sitting? What are you wearing? Are you alone or with others? Who else is there? Are you talking? Are they? Watch what you are doing. Allow this interior theater to continue. Perhaps you move into another room, make a telephone call, or change tasks. Pay attention as long as the performance lasts, as long as your imagination provides images of this remembered time of being deeply absorbed in work. Try to become aware of the *feeling* of flow; the feeling itself can generate more images.

When the experience has run its course, return to the present, to the space where you actually sit. Take some time for this transition. In your journal, capture as fully as possible the images that you experienced during the active imagination memory of an experience of flow. Focus on describing the specific tasks that comprised the activity. Spending fifteen or twenty minutes writing for every five minutes of active imagination can be used as a general guideline. If the session inspired further thinking and feeling about work, write more. Pay attention; become an increasingly skilled observer of your self.

Write just what you have seen and felt. Don't analyze or attempt to draw conclusions. The psychologist James Hillman talks about the importance of becoming a "naturalist" of the self. This is what we want you to do in our active imagination exercises—collect specimens and samples for later analysis that will employ the tools that you will be given in Chapters 6 and 7. Do this exercise thoroughly for one remembered experience, record your findings in your journal, and then set it aside. At a later time you may return to this exercise and explore another episode. If your flow experience this time was not one involving work, make a point of revisiting this exercise another time and see if you have had that experience in your work life.

The Work History Interview

The next exercise in career active imagination will require two aids: a tape recorder and a friend. Again, find a quiet place where you will not be interrupted. Allow at least an hour for the exercise—more time, if possible. For the purposes of this exercise work is defined very broadly, and will include experiences from school, volunteer activities, and other avocational pursuits. Your friend will play the role of interviewer and help you focus on each of your work experiences from your life to date, with an emphasis on what you found most engaging and what you found particularly frustrating, boring, and uninteresting. Try to select a friend who is a good listener, someone you know well and trust, someone you find to be insightful about people. The advantage of working with a friend is that he or she can encourage you to give more detail than you might do on your own, and point out inconsistencies. For these reasons we strongly recommend doing this exercise with a friend's help, but if for some reason that is impossible, you can do it on your own, and either tape record your answers or record them on paper or in your personal computer.

A good way to organize the interview is to use chronology as a guide. Have your friend ask you about each of the past several years. For each year your interviewer should begin by asking you to recall where you were during that year, and to recall as vividly as possible each work setting. You can give your friend the following list of questions for helping you recapture your true feelings about each work experience:

+ Where were you working? Describe the place.

+ With whom did you work? With whom did you enjoy working, and with whom did you not?

+ What did you like most about the entire work experience? What did you like least?

+ Describe in detail the individual tasks that your work comprised. Which did you find exciting and engaging? Which did you find tedious and uninspiring?

+ If you could have changed the work to make it more enjoyable, what would you have done?

You may find that you have greater emotional clarity with the work experiences that are most distant in time. Time itself is a crucible for self-understanding. Some kinds of knowledge about ourselves, about what we genuinely value, and about the world generally, are gained only when experience has had time to be absorbed and integrated with the slower, deeper rhythms of the psyche. Impressions about current or very recent work experiences may be more reactive—not yet fully worked through and grasped with deeper emotional understanding.

This interview should be recorded. When we return to analyze these data in Chapter 6, we will pay particular attention to that inventory of tasks across work experiences that you remembered as being most intriguing and absorbing. Again, it is important at this stage of information gathering that you *not* try to analyze, categorize, or draw conclusions about these tasks; that part of the work will come later.

Job Envy

We all have had the experience of envying someone else's job—in some instances only in passing, in others more persistently, over a longer period. These latter experiences in particular provide an opportunity to learn about our own core interest patterns. Envy has much more to do with our own psychology than with the work reality of the person we envy. It is essentially a projection of our own interest patterns that may not have been fully acknowledged. Like all psychological projections, we first see some unowned part of ourselves in another person. What we must do first is understand what that part of us is and what it means to us, and then reintegrate it into our own lives.

Again, in a comfortable setting where you will not be interrupted, search back over the past year, or further if necessary, for an experience of job envy that seemed stronger or more persistent than usual. Often people find that there is someone whose job they have envied over a very long period of time. This may be someone you know personally, someone you have read about, or even a kind of work about which you know something and envy, without a particular person attached to it. Distinguish between the passing fantasies that are rooted more in a curiosity about fame or wealth and the envy experiences where you have found yourself thinking that this person must have a deeply engaging and interesting day-to-day work life. Take your time; allow several instances to come to mind so that you remember the one about which you felt most intensely.

Once you have called to mind the person whose work life you seem to have envied most, recall this person vividly and the impressions you have about his or her life circumstances. We are not interested in gathering more information about or discovering the truth of this person's work reality—we are interested in *your imagination* of his or her work. Our investigation is, after all, about your psychological reality. Next, look at your imagination of what a typical workday for this person might be like. Write in your journal and be specific. What particular tasks and activities do you see him or her doing on a regular basis? Where is this person working? Is the individual alone much of the time or with many other people? Does he or she spend time at a desk or move around? Are the workdays long? Is this person in charge of other people or working more autonomously? Is the pace of the workday hurried and urgent or quiet and calm? As before, complete this exercise thoroughly for one person, record your findings in your journal, and then set it aside. At another time you may return to explore and describe another job envy experience.

The Job from Hell

Perhaps as frequent as the experience of job envy is the experience of saying to ourselves, "I'm glad I don't have *her* job!" We are speaking not of jobs that are odious by their nature—such as working in a foul-smelling sewage treatment plant or in a poorly lit, unventilated sweatshop—but of jobs that many people might enjoy but that involve tasks or circumstances that you personally would find distasteful. Again, when we have such strong reactions we can learn more about ourselves than about the person we are observing.

In a quiet setting with your journal nearby, try to recall times when you had this reaction to a work situation that you observed or heard about. Bring to mind as vividly as possible images of the person and his or her workplace and work activities. Imagine what his or her workday is like; be specific in terms of describing particular tasks and activities. From this list separate out the tasks that seem to represent the essence of what repels you about his or her job. Record your impressions, set the task aside, and return later to explore another "job from hell."

Feelings of Accomplishment

We are all familiar with the experience of completing a task that feels worthwhile and well done, of having days that feel particularly well spent and that bring more than their share of satisfaction when they come to an end. This exercise consists of taking an inventory of those experiences. Think back over the past six months or so and recall experiences of particular satisfaction and accomplishment. The task or outcome may not be highly significant; the sense of accomplishment may come from small tasks unnoticed by others.

The experiences may involve the feeling of flow that we discussed earlier, or they may not. Flow is an experience you have *in the moment*. Accomplishment is a feeling you have at the end of the day or at the end of the project, no matter how long it took. As you go through the exercise try to focus on the *feeling*, not the supposed merit of the accomplishment. Record in your journal as specifically as possible the activities that led to the sense of accomplishment. Do not try to draw conclusions or make the listed episodes fit any pattern. Simply record and describe them with as much detail and nuance as you can. Repeat this exercise for the previous six months, and then for the previous year or more, until you have recalled at least five or six accomplishments.

Even more useful than a retrospective gathering of data about personal accomplishment is the ability to become an observer of these feeling states as they happen, or immediately thereafter. At the end of a day that leaves you with a sense of accomplishment, take the time to review the activities that made up that day. In your journal, list those activities with as much detail as possible. This requires discipline, but if collected faithfully over a period of time, the analysis of the data can be extraordinarily useful, and often surprising.

Reading Patterns

Highly persistent reading patterns are important indicators of interests. When you open the newspaper, where do you turn first? To the business section? To the international news? To the editorial pages? What part of *The Wall Street Journal* do you read first? Which column on the front page? Are you more likely to read a book on technical stock market analysis or a self-help book on interpersonal behavior? Think back over the past six months and recall the business press articles that you have found most captivating (a good measure of importance is having read the piece in its entirety, or even more than once). Record, as closely as possible, the titles of the articles, and a description of their contents. Include books, both work related and otherwise. Make a note of what appealed to you about the article or book, if that is readily apparent to you. Repeat this exercise for the previous year (and for the previous five-year period, if there are any major differences in your reading patterns—you used to read a great many books dealing with war strategy, for example). Again, the practice of recording the titles of interesting books and articles on an ongoing basis will reveal patterns over time that are not immediately apparent.

Grazing for Clues

This exercise is related to, but broader than, the exercise just described. It involves simply paying attention to all the things that catch your eye—being a watchful observer of yourself as you go about your day. Make note, for example, of the things you buy (necessities aside), of the things you would like to buy, of the advertisements that draw your attention. If you are riding the train to work and you find your eye drawn for some reason to a particular individual, make note of it, trying to apprehend what about him or her has caught your attention. If you find yourself daydreaming about something that feels as if it might be relevant to this process of self-discovery, note it.

Go through your life over the next few weeks or months catching the random bits of data that draw your attention (versus your having purposefully turned your attention to them). You should get in the habit of carrying a notebook or other means of recording the things that draw your attention. The more information you acquire, the better your next career move is likely to be. You may find the task of gathering these data without attempting to analyze or categorize difficult at first; most business professionals tend to be far more action oriented than given to reflection. Be patient, and know that the observations you are compiling will be put to good use.

Letters About You

We request that individuals who come to us for career consultations select five to seven people who know them well and ask those people to write a letter about them and send it directly to us. The correspondents are told clearly that this is not a job reference, but is for the benefit of the client, and that they should be completely frank and honest in what they write.

In this exercise, you will choose several people who know you well and ask them to write *to* you, *about* you. Choose people who have insight into you, regardless of how you know them or for how long you have known them. You might choose, for example, one or more members of your family of origin, current or former business associates, friends from college or business school, social friends, your spouse, even an adult child. How well they know you is more important than how they know you. Ask them to write about you *in the third person* (John has trouble with . . . He enjoys . . .). This will help them to be less conscious of the fact that you will be reading what they write about you. They may send the letter anonymously if they wish, but if they do so they should separately send a note telling you that they have sent the letter.

In this exercise you will employ *their* active imagination. Ask them to address the following questions:

- What would be the ideal career for you?
- What seems to make you most fulfilled and most excited?
- What careers should you stay away from, and why?
- What do they see as your blind spots?
- What do they see as the aspects of yourself that you need to change in order to be successful?
- What do they see as the influences on you that may pull you off your course (Sirens' songs and so on)?

The last exercise to complete before moving into an analysis of your career imagination is that of taking the *Business Career Interest Inventory*. The *BCII* is a means of surveying those patterns of deep structure interests that we have discovered through our research with business professionals. It is the next step in the process of gathering data about yourself. Read the next chapter, "Using the *Business Career Interest Inventory*" and then respond to the inventory, using your personal computer. You will then learn how to analyze both the data you gathered from the active imagination exercises and your *BCII* results, and use that analysis to understand how your pattern of deep structure interests relate to *business core functions*.

FOUR

Using the
Business Career Interest Inventory

THE *BUSINESS CAREER INTEREST INVENTORY* (*BCII*) is designed to measure the match between patterns of deep structure interests and the *core functions* of business work. (In the next chapter you will learn about core functions and in particular about the eight business core functions that we have identified in our research.) This chapter will provide the information you need in order to take the computer version of the *BCII* that is included with this book.

The *BCII* is not a clinical (psychological) assessment instrument, and the results it provides are not a measure of psychological health. Nor is the *BCII* a complete career assessment tool. It *is* a sophisticated tool for evaluating your interests in terms of the fundamental activities that underlie business work. It is intended for use along with the active imagination exercises described in Chapter 3. In Chapter 6 you will learn how to apply the same model employed by the *BCII* to analyze data from your active imagination exercises. You will also learn how to combine those data with your *BCII* results to arrive at an assessment of your business-related interests based on multiple data sources. Any career self-assessment is more rich, subtle, and accurate if it employs information gathered from a variety of assessment techniques. It is important to note that the *BCII* is a *business* career inventory; it is not appropriate for evaluating interests associated with nonbusiness careers. In addition, the *BCII* was not designed to be a job selection or promotion assessment instrument, and should never be used as such.

Taking the *Business Career Interest Inventory* on Disk

The *BCII* is composed of 280 items, each of which requires a response on a scale from 0 to 3. Full directions for taking the inventory are given in the computer application itself. The inventory should take you about thirty minutes to complete. There are no right or wrong answers; the inventory measures features of your personality, not knowledge or aptitude. Move through the inventory carefully but quickly. You will receive the most accurate results if, for each item, you give your first intuitive response. Do not try to analyze the items or speculate about their intention. The inventory results are *for you,* and you should take the *BCII* with the knowledge that the results are for your benefit only; there is no need to impress anybody. Work rapidly, use your first response, and enjoy the assessment.

The computer program supplied with this book, provided as a Microsoft Windows application (it runs using Windows 95, Windows 98, and 3.1), is simple to use. If you are a Macintosh computer user, your office, your local library, or a friend very likely has a computer capable of running the program. Neither a printer nor a hard disk is required to use the *BCII* computer program. The application runs entirely from the enclosed disk itself, making use of a public computer easy. The user-friendly program will guide you through each step of the inventory process.

At the end of the program, the final screen will provide you with your scores on eight *business core function* scales (including a statement concerning which functions are your "personal highs"), an overall *business career profile type,* a statement about your score on a *General Business Interest Index,* and statements about the validity of your results. No interpretive information is provided on the disk itself; this chapter and Chapters 6 and 7 will guide you through an indepth analysis of your scores. At the end of the assessment, simply copy your eight profile scores, your General Business Interest Index score and your three-letter business career profile type, and Validity Statements on the page provided for that purpose at the end of this chapter. You may then return to this point in the chapter to begin your assessment interpretation. *It is best if you take the* BCII *before reading about assessment profile analysis in Chapters 6 and 7.*

◆ To run the *BCII* program using Windows 3.1, open Windows, then insert the *BCII* disk into your PC. From the File menu click on "Run", type in a:\bcii.exe and click on OK. Follow the instructions that come up on your screen.

◆ To run the *BCII* program using Windows 95 or 98, open Windows, then insert the *BCII* disk into your PC. Double click on the "My Computer" icon, then on the "3½" Floppy (A:)" icon, then on the "BCII" icon. Follow the instructions that come up on your screen.

◆ Depending on the speed of your computer and its floppy disk drive, there may be a pause of a few seconds between some of the initial screens you see as you run the *BCII*. This is normal, and no cause for concern.

AFTER TAKING THE *BCII,* RECORD YOUR SCORES ON THE PAGE PROVIDED FOR THAT PURPOSE AT THE END OF THIS CHAPTER. RETURN TO THIS POINT TO BEGIN YOUR *BCII* INTERPRETATION.

Understanding Your *Business Career Interest Inventory* Scale Scores

At this point you should have completed the *BCII* and recorded your scores on the eight business core function scales (with a notation as to which of these are "personal highs"), the statement about your General Business Interest Index score, the Validity Statements, and the three-letter business career profile type. Chapter 5 will describe in detail the eight business core functions, and Chapters 6 and 7 will help you go more deeply into the interpretation of your scores using your business career profile type. For now, let us look at the scores themselves.

Your scores on the eight business core function scales are adjusted standard scores. A standard score is a way of making different scales, with different numbers of items, comparable by placing them in a "standard" format. All of these scales have an average of 50; that is, 50 is the average score obtained by the group of business professionals with whom you are being compared when you take the BCII. About 40 percent of these professionals have scores between 45 and 54, inclusive, and scores that fall in this range may be generally described as average *for this professional group.* We emphasize this last statement because, obviously, a term such as *average* has meaning only in terms of the group with which you are being compared. Many interest inventories compare a test-taker's score with a group of "people in general," usually from the country where the inventory was normed. As we will explain in more detail below, we have not taken this approach but rather have compared your scores to individuals who are already established in the business profession. Scores between 55 and 59, inclusive, are considered to be high-range scores on each scale. Scores of 60 or above are considered to be in a very high range, and scores lower than 45 are considered to be low-range scores.

We have studied the *Business Career Interest Inventory* results of over 1700 individuals in the field of business. Your individual profile will be compared to a select group of over 350 business professionals from a wide range of functions and industries (the sample also includes some professionals from closely related professions such as law and educational administration). The majority of the individuals in our sample are not new to business, but have been in their careers for many years. A significant proportion of the comparison group is senior business executives. In other words, when you take the *BCII* you are comparing yourself with people *who have already chosen business careers and have established or begun to establish themselves in the business world.* You are not being compared with the general population. Thus, an average-range score on a scale such as Managing People or Enterprise Control indicates a significant interest in this function. It is in the average range compared only with people who have established themselves in a career where this function is prominent. Scores between 50 and 54 are substantial scores (comparable to an "average" business professional), scores between 55 and 59 are high, and scores of 60 and above are very high.

Although the purpose of using standard scores is to be able to compare scores from different scales, you must be careful when doing so. No scale conforms exactly to the "normal" bell-shaped distribution curve, and scales can actually experience a fair amount of discrepancy in their departures from the normal pattern. For this reason a standard score of "44" on one scale is not necessarily exactly the same as a score of "44" on another scale. When comparing scales, it is best to make comparisons at the general level of score elevation (very low, low, average, high, very high). If you want to make more precise comparisons, please refer to the Appendix, which provides the percentile equivalent for your standard score on each of the business core function scales. Comparing your percentile score on a given scale with your percentile score on another scale will give you a more precise sense of the extent to which the interest measured by one scale is higher or lower than the interest measured by the other.

We have explained the meaning of a standard score. Now let us explain the meaning of an *adjusted* standard score. When someone takes an inventory such as the *BCII,* he or she has his or her own "response set" or way of approaching the inventory. The majority of people use a full range of high and low responses. Some people, however, mark items positively across the entire test; others have a tendency to give lower-range responses, regardless of what the items are. Scores on the *BCII* are mathematically adjusted to correct for an unusually positive or negative response set. If you tended to mark most items unusually positively, your standard scores will be adjusted downward (to a different degree on each scale); if you tended to mark most items unusually negatively, your standard scores will be adjusted upward. In this way your attitude toward the test and the items generally will not distort your scale scores.

Your *BCII* scale scores are the result of your being compared with business professionals of *your same gender only.* That there are significant differences between the scores of men and women on many, if not most, interest inventory scales is a well-established fact. The reasons for this are interesting, and a matter of debate, but are not our topic for now. What is important is avoiding gender bias in reporting scores, and for this reason the *BCII* employs the standard practice of using same-gender comparison groups (see Appendix).

Frequently Asked Questions About *BCII* Scores

What Are Personal High Scale Scores?

Comparing your scores with those of a group of business professionals is one way to make them meaningful and useful. Another important way to understand your scores is to understand them relative to your other scale scores. In other words, it is important to ask the question, "Regardless of how high or low my scores are compared with other people, what are my high scores within my *own* pattern of interests?" Your personal high scores are those that define your "peak" business core function interest areas. Work role opportunities that allow you to develop these functional interests are more likely to be satisfying. The score summary screen indicates which of your eight business core functions are significantly higher than your personal business core function scale score average. To perform this calculation, the *BCII* scoring program calculates the average of all eight of your business core function scales. Any business core function scales that are five or more standard score points higher than this personal standard score average are considered to be *personal high* scores and are marked as such immediately to the right of the businesss core function standard scores on the score summary screen.

The number of personal high scores will vary from individual to individual. Some people have as many as five personal high scores; some will have none. Most people have between one and three personal high scores. In the next chapter, each of the eight business core function scales will be discussed in detail. In reading that chapter, you should pay particular attention both to all scores that are *absolutely* high (that is, high compared with the business professional sample) *and* to those core functions that were your personal high scores.

What If I Don't Have Any Personal High Scores?

Some people (about 3 percent of those taking the *BCII*) have no scores that are marked as personal high scores. This happens when the scores on all eight business core function scales are very close to each other in numerical value. The lack of designated personal high scores does *not* mean that you have no highly developed interests. On the contrary, a lack of personal high scores is sometimes explained by a large number of unusually high business core function scale scores. If your *BCII* scores are quite close together numerically, going through the exercises in Chapter 3 should help you to get a better sense of which of the eight business core functions are most important for you.

What If I Have Many Personal High Scores?

As mentioned above, most people have between one and three personal high scores. A small percentage of individuals taking the *BCII* have five or more personal high scores, which occurs if you have a wide variation in range among business core function scale scores (having several very high scores and some very low scores). This does not affect the importance of the personal high scores; they still represent your most important areas of interest. If you have five or more personal high scores, the exercises in Chapter 3 will help you to further differentiate these high-range scores.

Will My Scores Change Over Time?

As we mentioned in the first chapter, research on interest patterns indicates that by young adulthood, individual patterns of interest have a good deal of consistency over long periods of time. Scale scores on interest inventories have been shown to have very high correlations over periods of ten years or more. Fundamental interests for most people have discernible patterns that persist over their lifetimes. At the same time, research indicates that work and life experiences allow interests to *develop* and thus become more noticeable (and measurable) at later points in life. So while scores on individual interest inventory scales may vary somewhat over time, the general *pattern* of scores will have consistency.

The *Business Career Interest Inventory* is relatively new, and although its validity and reliability have been rigorously tested, it has not existed long enough to allow us to test scale consistency over very long periods of time. The intent of the analyses presented in this book, however, is to allow you to determine your underlying *pattern* of interests, and that pattern is likely to have significant stability over long periods of time. Some individual scale scores will be more likely to change based on interest *development*. In our culture we are exposed to some business core function activities early in our development, and thus have a better means to test their match with our interests. This can be illustrated by comparing the Application of Technology and Managing People business core functions.

In the next chapter you will read in greater detail about how the

Application of Technology business core function is concerned with interests associated with the design and use of tangible products and with engineering-like approaches to business problems. Even if you are relatively young (say, in your early twenties), if you have an interest in technology you probably have had a number of opportunities to allow development of the interest patterns associated with this business core function, through your education and experience with technology. High schools often place emphasis on math and science, and chances are that you have either considered or actually pursued an engineering major in college. Entry-level jobs in manufacturing industries often provide the opportunity to be directly involved with the company's products. In other words, at a relatively young age you have had opportunities to "test" the interests associated with this core function and to observe whether or not you have had a positive response to those activities. If you are a technology/engineering enthusiast at age twenty-one, it is unlikely that your interest will significantly decline over the coming years, and your score on the Application of Technology scale is very likely to remain consistently high throughout your professional career.

In contrast, few individuals in their early twenties have had significant work experience relevant to the interest patterns associated with the Managing People business core function (one notable exception is the leadership experience available at a relatively early age to many military service officers). If you have been a leader of teams or work groups in high school or college, you may have already had enough experience to test out your underlying interest in dealing with the day-to-day activity of managing people. Many people, however, may have a genuine but *latent* interest in the Managing People business core function, but have not yet had the experience which would allow them to become fully aware of the meaningfulness of that type of work for them. As they have the experiences that evoke their awareness of this source of work satisfaction, their scores on the Managing People business core function scale are likely to rise.

Managing People and Enterprise Control are examples of two business core function scales that may change more over time as individuals are exposed to developmental opportunities that help them recognize the match between these types of work activities and their patterns of deep structure interest. With more life experience comes a greater ability to recognize what "feeds the self" in terms of the work activities that are most satisfying. Even in young adulthood, however, tools such as the *Business Career Interest Inventory* can be powerful in evoking awareness of underlying interest patterns and suggesting how they may be realized in specific types of work.

What If All or Most of My Scale Scores Are in the High Range?

A small number of individuals will obtain *BCII* profiles where all or most of the scores are in the high range. In these cases the question we need to answer is, "Is this the result of an unusually wide range of interest in the full spectrum of business activities, or is it because you used mostly higher range responses (2s and 3s), throughout the inventory?" As we mentioned earlier, the scale scores are adjusted for this latter case (an unusually positive response set), but in more extreme cases the adjustment may not fully compensate for a consistent use of higher range scores. If you feel that you have responded to the items authentically and that it is true that you have unusually wide ranging interests and a broad enthusiasm for business generally, you should pay particular attention to your "personal high" scores.

Remember that these "personal high" designations identify the most important business core functions for you, regardless of the overall elevation of your scores. There is an important difference between a score of 57 and a score of 65, though both are in the high range. If you are unsure that your results are accurate, perhaps suspecting that you have an overly enthusiastic response to assessment inventories generally, then you should retake the inventory using a more balanced range of responses. In either case, you should also be sure to use the exercises presented in Chapter 3 to generate data that will provide you with a different approach to assessing your interests in the different business core functions.

What If All of My Scale Scores Are in the Average Range and Close Together?

A small number of individuals will have *BCII* profiles in which all eight business core function standard scores are in a narrow range, within a few points of each other, around the average standard score (50). We refer to such a profile as being *undifferentiated.* If you have this type of profile it does not mean that you do not have significant interest in a business career. On the contrary, your interests are in a range that is average for a group of experienced business professionals. Rather, it means that the particular technique employed by the *BCII* was not effective in delineating subtle differences in your levels of interest in different business work activities. If you obtained this type of profile, you should pay particular attention to the assessment exercises described in Chapter 3. Those exercises, analyzed using the techniques outlined in Chapter 6, will help you better to differentiate your interests in the eight business core functions. You may also want to take the *BCII* again in a few weeks or months to see if your profile is more differentiated.

What If All of My Scale Scores Are Low?

When someone has notably low scores on all eight business core functions, an important question is posed: Is this assessment true and accurate, or is it a "false negative," meaning that the person is in fact more interested in one or more of the business core functions than the test has measured? If you have taken the *Business Career Interest Inventory* and were low on all eight business core function scales, look at your Validity Statements (described in greater detail later in this chapter) to see if there is reason to doubt whether the instrument's assessment of your interests was valid.

The two Validity Statements most likely to point to a reason for someone receiving low scores on all the business core function scales have to do with omitting items and being generally negative in your responses to the items. If you failed to respond to a great many items as you went through the instrument, this fact in itself can produce low business core function scale scores. If the Omitted Items Validity Statement indicates that you omitted an unusually high number of items, you should retake the *BCII* and try to respond to as many items as possible. The other reason for low scores on all eight business core function scales involves your "response set" in taking the *BCII.* Using low-range responses (0 or 1) much more frequently than the average inventory-taker can produce low scores on the eight business core function scales. The Response Range Validity Statement tells you if you used lower range responses unusually often. There are a number of possible reasons for using an unusual number of low-range responses, but two are most common. The first involves your mood when you took the test. If you were feeling negatively about the world, about life, and especially about work, nothing looked good to you and you were likely to respond accordingly. Think about what kind of mood you were in when you went through the instrument, and if you were feeling especially down at the time, take it again in a few days or weeks when your mood is back to normal. The second reason you might have a negative response set is that you are just not very interested in a career in business. In this case the assessment of your interest in the eight business core functions as being low is accurate (a "true negative"), and you should not limit your career exploration to the realm of business.

Before reaching this conclusion, however, consider other data from the assessment. First, check the General Business Interest Index (GBII) score statement that is reported on the score summary screen. This is composed of a large number of business-specific items (activities that occur in traditional business settings). Your adjusted standard score on the GBII is compared with the general business sample and is reported on a scale from "very low" to "very high." If your score is in the high or very high range, your interest in this broad range of business roles and activities is at a level comparable to that of the general business sample. If your score is in the average range, your interest in the full range of business pursuits is somewhat less than that of the general business sample, but not markedly so. If your GBII score is in the low range, your interest in the types of activities and roles that are typically found in business settings is significantly lower than that of people who actually work in business settings. If your score is in the very low range, your interest in the full spectrum of business activities is markedly lower than that of the general business sample. If you feel that your *BCII* item responses were authentic and your GBII standard score is low or very low, you should probably consider careers in nonbusiness *and* business arenas. This is particularly true if your GBII score is in the very low range. If you want to explore nonbusiness career options you should use career self-assessment methods designed for assessing a wider range of career options.

If you had your sights set on a business career and were surprised to find your scores low on all business core function dimensions, do not take the scores as the ultimate authority on your interests. *You* are the ultimate authority on yourself. If your scores are all in the low range, it will be particularly important for you to work with the active imagination exercises in Chapter 3 and with the analyses of them described in Chapter 6. If your low scores persist after retaking the *BCII,* doing the active imagination exercises, and reading Chapters 6 and 7, and you still feel that the scores are not accurate, consider consulting a career counselor to discuss the discrepancy. A career counselor will probably want you to use an interest inventory that covers a wider spectrum of occupations. Such inventories compare your interests with those of people in a wide range of careers, whereas the *Business Career Interest Inventory* focuses exclusively on careers in business.

What If I Have One or More High Scores but My GBII Score Is Low?

As stated above, the General Business Interest Index is composed of a large number of business-specific items (that is, activities that occur in traditional business settings). Your adjusted standard score on the GBII is compared to the general business sample and is reported on a scale from "very low" to "very high." If your score is in the high or very high range, your interest in this broad range of business roles and activities is at a level comparable to the general business sample. If your score is in the average range, your interest in the full range of business pursuits is less than that of the general business sample, but not markedly so. If your GBII score is in the low range, your interest in the types of activities and roles that are typically found in business settings is significantly lower than the interest of people who actually work in business settings. Finally, if your score is in the very low range, your interest in the full spectrum of business activities is markedly below that of the general business sample.

People may have low GBII scores for either of two reasons. The most obvious is that they are simply not interested in the activities that make up most business careers, and respond to the GBII items accordingly. The second is that their interest is *very* focused in only one area of business, so much so that they respond negatively to all GBII items that do not relate to this area, producing a low score on the overall scale. Remember the GBII assesses interest in a *broad range* of business roles and activities, so you may receive a low GBII score because you have a very strong interest in a narrow range of business roles and activities.

Understanding Your Validity Statements

There are three Validity Statements that appear on the final screen of your *BCII* program. They have to do with how fully you completed the instrument (the Omitted Items Validity Statement), how consistent you were in your responses (the Consistency Validity Statement), how positive or negative your "response set" was when you took the *BCII* (the Response Range Validity Statement).

The Omitted Items Validity Statement

If you failed to respond to a great many items as you completed the instrument, this can produce an invalid assessment. There are three Validity Statements that you can obtain. The first states that "The number of items you omitted is in the average range" and means that there is no reason to question the validity of your assessment results. The second states that "You did not respond to a relatively high number of items" and refers you to this chapter. The third states that "You did not respond to a high number of items" and also refers you to this chapter. If you received *either* of the last two Validity Statements on your screen and all or most of your scale scores were low, you should retake the *BCII* and try to respond to as many items as possible (see the section above, *"What If All of My Scale Scores Are Low?"*). If you received the last Validity Statement, you should re-take the instrument regardless of your business core function scale scores, again trying to respond to as many items as possible, and see if your scale scores change the second time.

The Consistency Validity Statement

Another Validity Statement pertains to responding inconsistently to pairs of items that are quite similar to each other. If, for example, you respond by stating that you would very much enjoy the work of a "Marketing brand manager" (Item 82) but later state that that you would not like to "create a marketing strategy for a new product" (Item 205), these two responses are internally inconsistent. If there are many instances of such internal inconsistency, the validity of the assessment can be compromised. Again, there are three Validity Statements that you can obtain. The first states that "Your consistency score is in the average range" and means that there is no reason to question the validity of your assessment results. The second states that "There is significant inconsistency in your responses to pairs of inventory items" and refers you to this chapter. The third states "NOTE: There is a high degree of inconsistency in your responses to pairs of inventory items" and refers you to this chapter. There may be several causes for a high level of inconsistency. One is simply not being clear about what your interests are, about what really appeals to you, and having this confusion reflected in your responses. Another is a conflict between what you are really interested in and what you feel you should be interested in. The result in this circumstance can be the "want side" responding to one item in the pair and the "should side" responding to the other. If you received the second Consistency Validity Statement, you should first think about what might account for your responding inconsistently while taking the *BCII,* and consider retaking it a few week later, especially if your business core function scale scores were not well-defined. If you received the last Consistency Validity Statement, you should think about what might account for your responding so inconsistently while taking the *BCII,* and then definitely retake it a few weeks later.

The Response Range Validity Statement

There is a third Validity Statement that has to do with your "response set" or way of approaching the inventory. As noted earlier, most people use a full range of high and low responses in responding to the questions on an inventory such as the *BCII.* Some people, however, tend to respond in a generally positive manner to the questions on an inventory, regardless of the item content (stating that they would enjoy most of the occupations, subjects for study, activities, and so on). Others tend to respond in a generally negative manner to the questions, regardless of the item content (stating that they would *not* enjoy most of the types of work, subjects for study, activities, etc.). There are six Response Range Validity Statements that you can obtain. One states that "Your total raw score is in the average range." This means that the number of times you responded to items with 0s, 1s, 2s, and 3s was in the average range, that it was not necessary to adjust your business core function scale standard scores in either direction in order to compensate for your response set, and that there is no reason to question the validity of your assessment results. Two other Response Range Validity Statements state that "You had a tendency to use lower (or higher) range responses in endorsing items. Your business core function scale standard scores have been adjusted upward (or downward) to compensate for this." This means that your response set has been corrected for (see the section "Understanding Your *Business Career Interest Inventory* Scale Scores," earlier in this chapter), but that there is no reason to question the validity of your assessment results.

Two other Response Range Validity Statements state that "You had a strong tendency to use lower (or higher) range responses in endorsing items" and refer you to this chapter. If you received either of these two statements and your overall *BCII* assessment profile was rather undifferentiated (either all your business core function scale scores were low or all were high), you may want to retake the instrument in a few weeks and try to respond a bit more (or less) positively to the items. Do *not*, however, force yourself to give responses that do not reflect how you truly feel about the different occupations, subjects for study, activities, and so on. This is especially important if your response set was negative (you used lower range responses) because you really are not very interested in the activities that a career in business involves. In this case your assessment results are not invalid, they accurately reflect your feelings about business work. Refer back to the section *"What If All of My Scale Scores Are Low?"* for a more complete discussion of how negative response sets can affect your assessment results.

The last Response Range Validity Statement states that "You had a very strong tendency to use lower range responses in endorsing items, rendering this test administration invalid" and refers you to this chapter. Any assessment instrument's design includes certain assumptions about what it will be measuring, and extreme violations of those assumptions will render the measurement invalid. For example, you may have a thermometer (a temperature assessment instrument) for everyday use whose designers assumed that the temperatures it will be measuring will fall between, say, minus 30 degrees and 120 degrees Fahrenheit (minus 34 degrees and 49 degrees Celsius). If you attempted to use that assessment instrument in mid-winter in Antarctica, it would read minus 30 degrees F even if the temperature were truly minus 80 degrees F, *because the assumptions of its design have been violated to such an extent that it cannot provide a valid assessment.* Similarly, the *BCII* assumes a certain typical distribution of response sets, and if that assumption is violated to too great an extent we must consider its assessment results invalid. If you received this Response Range Validity Statement, you should consider taking the *BCII* again or perhaps working with a career counselor who may be able to help you explore various career options.

Interpreting Your *BCII* Scores

Chapter 5 will explain in detail the meaning of the eight business core functions. Chapter 6 will allow you to use the business core function model to analyze the data from your active imagination exercises and combine this information with your *BCII* results. By the end of Chapter 6, you will have clarified the meaning of the core functions that are most important for you.

Understanding Your Business Career Profile Type

Your *BCII* Score Summary screen provided you with a three-letter *business career profile type.* Chapter 7 will enable you to take your career assessment to a deeper level by showing how business career profile types are related to specific business work roles, organizational cultures, and industries.

Your Score Summary

Your Name: _____

Date of Testing: _____

	Scale Score	Personal High Scores
Application of Technology	51	40
Quantitative Analysis	52	49
Theory Development and Conceptual Thinking	64	37 ✓
Creative Production	56	✓ 51
Counseling and Mentoring	40	67
Managing People	29	63
Enterprise Control	36	43
Influence Through Language and Ideas	52	56
General Business Interest Index	Avg	High
Business Career Profile Type	HLM	MHH

Validity Statements
  Omitted Items: _Avg Rng____ Average

  Consistency: _Avg Rng____ High inconsistency

  Response Range: _Lower than avg_ Lower than average.

FIVE

The Basic Dimensions of Business Work

IN THIS CHAPTER we will describe the model that you will use to interpret your *Business Career Interest Inventory* scores and to analyze your active imagination exercises. *Do not read this chapter until you have completed the* Business Career Interest Inventory, *or you may compromise the results of your assessment.* Analyses and interpretations of both the *BCII* and the active imagination exercises are based on the business core function model. We will describe the business core function model and provide a detailed description of each of the functions for which you have scores from the *BCII*.

If you have taken the *BCII* but have not completed one or more of the active imagination exercises, you may choose to read this chapter and then go to Chapter 7, which will help you interpret your overall business work profile. However, if you have not completed any of the active imagination exercises, we recommend that you return to Chapter 3 and do at least one at this time. Gathering information from both assessment methods (*BCII* and active imagination) will provide richer, more accurate information about your core interests and how they relate to business work than will any single method.

The Evolution of Core Functions

In Chapter 1 we described the in-depth psychological assessment that comprises the heart of our career consultations with business professionals. In our research we have looked beneath the surface features of the assessment data to identify the deep structure of activities that compose all business work. We have looked for the core functions of the work that goes on in business organizations. Let us take a moment to consider what we mean by the term *core function*.

Our clients often think about business work in rather abstract and stereotyped ways, using conventional functional categories such as "marketing," "finance," "sales," "accounting" or "project management." These terms *seem* to represent work that actually goes on in the world of business, but on closer inspection they actually describe very little. An assistant brand manager at a consumer products company may be doing work that is substantially different from that of a product manager with the medical products division of a high-tech manufacturing company, yet both would be considered to be working in the "marketing" function. A given person might be thrilled with one job and deeply unhappy with the other. Does this individual like "marketing"? What *is* "marketing"? Any marketing job is composed of an array of different activities. Different marketing positions may emphasize very different activities, and some activities present in one marketing role are totally absent in others.

Thinking about work in broad, stereotyped ways and using worn, conventional language get in the way of the real work of career development, which is the deepening of our understanding of the activities that hold the most satisfaction for us. That is why in our research we have looked for language to talk about business work that is closer to the work itself, relevant to *any* business environment and not dependent on the labeling by any particular company. These business activities that underlie all business work are what we refer to as *business core functions*.

For more than a decade we studied the psychological testing patterns of the business professionals who consulted us. We looked for clusters of scales from different tests that covary (are related as a group, describing a common underlying phenomenon). When we found such a cluster of scales, we discussed the personality features and work histories of those clients who had high scores on the scale cluster and those who had low scores. We looked at the items on the different scales that comprised each cluster and we examined the scores in the light of information from our interviews with our clients. We wanted to know what any given cluster was really about—what specific work activity interests it actually was measuring. We looked at the clusters themselves and how they were related to each other. Sometimes we found that two clusters were so highly correlated that it made no sense to speak about them as being separate. At other times we found meaningful subclusters that provided important information. We were looking for a model of the essential "core" business activities that were independent of arbitrary job classification.

As we pursued our research and the pattern of our clusters began to emerge, we realized that we were going to benefit from the research of a career interest researcher whom we had long admired, John Holland. In the late 1950s, Holland advanced a theory of the underlying structure of general human interests. His model of six fundamental career interest themes has withstood the test of time and is now widely recognized as the most comprehensive and useful approach to describing *general* interest patterns. His categories, however, were *too* general for our purposes. They were not specific to business and not sufficiently nuanced for our work with business professionals. In addition, they were not activity based. Eventually, through our research we developed a model of eight *activity-based business* core functions.

The Business Core Function Model

Our model of business work comprises eight core functions: Application of Technology, Quantitative Analysis, Theory Development and Conceptual Thinking, Creative Production, Counseling and Mentoring, Managing People, Enterprise Control, and Influence Through Language and Ideas. As we describe these eight business core functions, bear in mind that no single function should be considered in isolation from the others. A high or low degree of interest in any one core function provides less useful information than the unique *pattern* of interests. Taking into account the full profile of high and low interests across the model provides us with a more meaningful picture of an individual's core interest pattern, the activities that will allow for the realization of that pattern, and the work settings in which those activities are likely to be predominant.

Application of Technology

The Application of Technology business core function represents interests that are realized through the general use of technology to accomplish business objectives, activities often associated with engineering, production and systems planning, product design, production and operations process analysis, production planning, and systems analysis. Individuals who are strongly interested in this function are intrigued by the inner workings of things and curious about finding better ways to bring technology to the task of solving business problems. They are also typically comfortable with the "language" of technology: mathematical analysis, computer programming, and representations of the world founded on the models of the physical sciences.

Scores on this business core function scale are significantly correlated with scores on other interest inventories that measure similarity of interests with individuals in occupations such as engineer, research and development manager, systems analyst, and computer programmer. We have also found scores on this core function to be significantly correlated with self-reported confidence in *skills* in hands-on practical work activities such as mechanical crafts and in the skills associated with the occupations of systems analyst and computer programmer. It is important to remember, however, that the *BCII* is *not* a measure of skill in a core function area. Individuals may have a strong interest pattern associated with a business core function but not have had the opportunity to develop their skill in that area. Perceived lack of skill in a core function in which you have a strong interest should not deter you from developing the skills necessary to engage in the activities related to that function.

It should not be surprising that business professionals with engineering degrees are well represented among people who have high *BCII* scores on the Application of Technology business core function scale. However, this is not always the case. In our work at the Harvard Business School, for example, we have found that many students with engineering degrees do *not* have elevations in this region. In interviews we have found that many of these students were good in math in high school (and thus counseled into engineering or the sciences) or came from families where engineering was seen either as a high-status career or as a stable, "safe" profession for those who showed early mathematical promise. We have found over the years that engineering, like law, is an early career choice that is vulnerable to the "you are good at it so you should do it" fallacy; and to the fallacy that stable, higher-status professions will inevitably provide satisfaction to those capable of mastering them. The "nonengineer" engineers at Harvard had grown to realize that no matter how successful they might be in it, the engineering profession would not sustain their enthusiasm over the course of a lifetime.

For engineer MBAs who *do* have significant score elevations in the Application of Technology function, we typically have some very specific advice. With an interest pattern that is backed up by academic credentials and significant work experience, they can leverage their "career capital" and have a competitive advantage in pursuing management and leadership careers in those industries and companies that value engineering training. Many (but by no means all) manufacturing and technology-oriented companies view an engineering degree as a "membership card" for participation in positions at higher management levels. (If a company is public, this is a relatively easy issue to research, because the professional background of top management is a matter of public record.) For students who are interested in leadership careers in manufacturing or technology-intensive companies and who do *not* have engineering credentials, companies with a strong professional engineer bias should probably be avoided unless an exceptional opportunity for training or early advancement in a functional area is offered. We should note that this is a business core function in which interest is not normally distributed in the population. Thus, it is more meaningful if you have a high score on the Application of Technology business core function scale than if your score is low. There is not much meaning in the difference between a medium- and low-range score. You should not over-interpret a low score on this business core function scale. A low score indicates that this function is not particularly meaningful for you; it does not indicate that you have an unusually low interest in this area relative to other people.

Quantitative Analysis

The Quantitative Analysis business core function represents interests that are realized through problem solving that relies on mathematical analysis. Work activities such as analyzing market research, building a computer model to determine optimal production scheduling, performing a discounted cash-flow analysis, determining net present value, analyzing the future performance of an investment instrument, determining the optimal debt/equity structure for a business, and performing other accounting procedures are all examples of work tasks that draw heavily on the interests represented by this core function. The Quantitative Analysis core function represents interests that overlap to a certain extent with the interests represented by the Application of Technology function.

Scores on this business core function scale are significantly correlated with scores on other interest inventories that measure similarity of interests with individuals in occupations such as accountant, credit manager, systems analyst, computer programmer, and mathematics teacher. We have found scores on this function to be significantly correlated with self-rated confidence in *skills* in mathematics and statistics and in skills associated with the specific occupations of statistician, computer programmer, accountant, bookkeeper, and financial planner. (Remember, though, the *BCII* itself is not a measure of skills. Skills may be developed if a strong interest is present.) In our career consultations we find high scorers on this function to be well represented in work roles such as strategy consulting, information systems consulting and management, all areas of finance, public accounting, strategic planning, and production and operations management. It is common to find this function elevated in concert with the two other functions most directly concerned with intellectual curiosity and methodical problem solving: the Application of Technology and the Theory Development and Conceptual Thinking functions.

When the elevation on this business core function scale occurs with an elevated interest in the Application of Technology function, there is often a "working with things" flavor to the individual's interests. It is not uncommon to find these people enjoying work that is directly involved with product design or production, or with problems that emerge in operations-intensive environments. When the elevated interest in the Quantitative Analysis function occurs together with elevated interest in the Theory Development and Conceptual Thinking core function, a strong "working with ideas" theme is typically present. (In Chapter 7 we will present a method for performing a full profile analysis of your *BCII* scores, and describe our findings concerning characteristics and interests associated with many different combinations of business core function interest elevations.)

Theory Development and Conceptual Thinking

The Theory Development and Conceptual Thinking business core function represents interests that are realized through activities involving broadly conceptual approaches to business problems. Examples of these activities include developing economic theory, developing a model that explains competition within a given industry, analyzing the competitive position of a business within a particular market, designing a new product development or product distribution process, and teaching business theory. Individuals with high scores on this function are comfortable and find challenge in the realms of ideas, imagination, and theory. They are at home with the intangible domains of plans, alternative business scenarios, and long-range forecasts. This function has a distinctly academic flavor and is, in fact, a frequent area of elevation among business academics.

Scores on this business core function scale are significantly correlated with scores on other interest inventories that measure similarity of interests with people in occupations such as college professor, sociologist, and science teacher. Theory Development and Conceptual Thinking function scale scores also correlate with scales measuring interests in science and writing. In our career consultation we find people with strong interest in this function to be well represented in areas such as management consulting (particularly strategic consulting), strategic planning, research and development management, product design, strategic finance, economic analysis, and business teaching. When interest in this function is elevated in combination with interest in the Quantitative Analysis function, there is an emphasis on the analytical nature of problem solving. When it is elevated together with interest in the Creative Production function, the emphasis is more on imaginative, visionary, and theoretical thinking.

Creative Production

The Creative Production business core function represents interests that are realized through highly creative activities such as new product design, development of marketing concepts, development of visual and verbal advertising concepts, generation of new business ideas, development of innovative approaches to business service delivery, planning of events, and public relations. Individuals with high scores on this function often see themselves, and are seen by others, as being particularly creative.

Scores on this business core function scale are significantly correlated with scales on other interest inventories that measure similarity of interests with individuals in occupations such as medical illustrator, commercial artist, photographer, and musician. Scores on the Creative Production function scale are also correlated with scales measuring interests in art, design, music, and writing. We have found scores on this core function scale to be significantly correlated with self-rated confidence in *skills* in the areas of art and design and with self-ratings on confidence in skills associated with the occupation of commercial artist. It is important to note, however, that someone may have a high score on the Creative Production business core function scale and average or low scores in specific artistic skill areas such as writing or design. The expression of creativity takes many forms and is realized through many media; the skill patterns of those with creative interests vary widely. Remember, as mentioned above, that the *BCII* is *not* a measure of skills.

The Creative Production business core function is correlated to a certain extent with the Influence Through Language and Ideas function. The Creative Production function is related to creative pursuits in general, whereas the Influence Through Language and Ideas function represents more specifically the creative use of *language* to influence and persuade.

In our career consultations we find an interest pattern profile that is not exceedingly common (occurring in less than 10 percent of our business professional clients) but that occurs frequently enough for us to have studied it—a pattern where interest in the Creative Production business core function is notably higher than interest in *all* other functions. For individuals with this profile type, the opportunity for creativity is at the very center of work satisfaction. We sometimes characterize the ideal job description for these individuals as being a "blank page," representing something that doesn't exist yet, whether it is a new product, a marketing plan, or an entirely new way of delivering a particular service.

We find that individuals with this pattern often have been somewhat ambivalent about entering the domain of business careers. In our consulting interviews, many of these "high need for creativity" people talk about having considered careers in journalism, publishing, creative writing, art, fashion, or architecture. During business graduate school they often have a more difficult time finding a focus for both internships and postgraduation employment. These people are not inherently indecisive; rather, they are grappling with the nature of business work itself. The work associated with many profile patterns is predictably found in certain industries and functions (for example, interests in the Quantitative Analysis and the Theory Development and Conceptual Thinking business core functions finding expression in management consulting). Highly creative work roles, however, may be found in a wide range of industries and functions, so there is no obvious choice of industry or function for these people.

Furthermore, work opportunities that allow for expression of a singularly high interest in the Creative Production business core function are often ephemeral. The work beginning a new project may be very creative but becomes more routine over time. Thus, the job that *was* a good match becomes less and less satisfying. In fact, our experience suggests that people with very high and singular Creative Production interest change jobs more frequently than average during the course of their careers. Their search for creative opportunity leads (or pushes) them on. It is important to realize that this employment pattern may well be a consequence of these individuals' innate interest structure and not necessarily a problem with commitment or perseverance.

Counseling and Mentoring

The Counseling and Mentoring business core function may not sound as if it belongs in a model of business activities, but it emerged as a distinct cluster in our research. This core function represents interests that are realized through developing relationships as an integral part of business work. Coaching, training, and mentoring are activities in business settings that represent the manifestation of interest in this function. Not every skilled manager will have a high or even average score on this function. There are many motivations for, and satisfactions to be derived from, management other than the enjoyment of helping subordinates, clients, and peers.

Three business core functions focus explicitly on the interpersonal aspects of business work: Counseling and Mentoring, Managing People, and Influence Through Language and Ideas. These functions are significantly correlated but have important differences from each other. Of the three, the Counseling and Mentoring function has the most specific focus on the importance of individual relationships for work satisfaction. People who have strong interest in this function prefer work environments where they feel they are making a significant contribution and adding value to the business endeavor through their teaching, counseling, and generally service-oriented relationships with fellow workers and business clients.

Scores on this business core function scale are significantly correlated with scales from other interest inventories measuring similarity of interest with individuals in occupations such as personnel director, school administrator, social worker, guidance counselor, and nursing home administrator. Scores on the Counseling and Mentoring function are also correlated with scales measuring interests in social services, adult development, and counseling. Scores on this function are significantly correlated with self-rated confidence in counseling *skill* and with skills associated with the occupations of social worker, psychologist, guidance counselor, and human resources director. (Again, the *BCII* in itself is not a measure of skill level.) In our career consulting we frequently find that individuals who score high on this function have high altruistic motivation and often look for avocational opportunities to realize interests related to this function. They are more likely to express interest in working for a nonprofit organization at some point in their careers.

Organizational culture is often an important determinant of work satisfaction for these individuals. Organizations that value the development of workers and that reward managers who invest energy and resources in personnel development are likely to be attractive to individuals who have high interest in the Counseling and Mentoring business core function.

Managing People

The Managing People business core function represents interests that are realized through working directly with people in the role of manager, director, or supervisor. Individuals who are interested in this function enjoy the people management aspect of leadership positions. They enjoy dealing with people and with interpersonal issues on a day-to-day basis, and they derive major work satisfaction from workplace relationships.

Scores on this business core function scale are significantly correlated with scales from other interest inventories measuring similarity of interest with individuals in occupations such as nursing home administrator, credit manager, food service manager, and business education teacher. Scores on the Managing People function scale are also correlated with scales measuring interests in business management, merchandising, office management, and supervision. Scores on this scale are correlated with scales measuring self-reported confidence in *skills* related to supervision, to the organizational tasks required for day-to-day management, and with skills associated with the occupations of bank manager, retail manager, hospital administrator, hotel manager, and school superintendent. As we have said in each of the sections above, it is important to remember that the *BCII* is not in itself a measure of skills.

A person's score on the Managing People function scale is *not* a measure of his or her ability as a manager. There are many skilled and successful managers whose interests are in business core functions other than Managing People, a function that emphasizes the *interpersonal* aspects of work. We have been consulted by a number of very senior managers who do not have high scores on this core function scale. Such individuals may enjoy the strategy and vision aspects of leadership or have high needs for control and dominance. As you will learn in Chapter 7, it is possible to have a high score on the Managing People business core function scale without a high score on the Enterprise Control function scale, and vice versa. If you have a high score on the Managing People scale, you probably enjoy and look forward to working with people, and will be more satisfied in a job that includes that activity.

It is also important to realize that your standard score on this function of the *Business Career Interest Inventory* is based on a comparison with people who have notably high interests in this area. Our general professional sample is composed mostly of business professionals who, as a group, have an interest in managing people that is higher than that of people in general. As a result, an average-range *BCII* score on this function is actually in the high range if you were to compare yourself with the general population. A high-range score indicates that even compared with business professionals your interest in directly managing people is significantly high.

Another important point to keep in mind is that if you are in an early stage of your career, you may not have been exposed to management roles. If this is the case, you may not yet have had the types of experiences that will allow you to truly develop your interest in managing people. Although the *BCII* can reveal underlying interest patterns that may not yet have been fully realized, your score on this function may be lower than it will be when you have had sufficient experience in the management area to inform your imagination about this type of work. Therefore, if you are younger and have not yet had significant management experience, you should consider even average-range scores on this function as meaning that the management role is worth considering.

A markedly elevated interest in the Managing People business core function, regardless of other profile features, is one of our indicators for what we sometimes refer to as a "pure management" career model. Individuals with very high Managing People function scale scores have interests associated with working as managers in operating environments. They may have other interests as well, but they are indicating an interest in the manager role as such, versus a professional individual contributor role such as would be found in investment banking, management consulting, venture capital, or investment management. We encourage individuals with high scores on the Managing People scale to weigh this information carefully. In MBA environments in particular, the lure of the high compensation and the glamour often associated with professional services roles can be very seductive. The money and the glamour can become a Sirens' song for many people who would find more satisfaction in an operating environment.

In our consultations with MBA students, we often encounter individuals who suspect they will be more satisfied in a management role in an operating environment but nevertheless feel that a few years in a management consulting or venture capital firm will accelerate their careers. They hope that after two or three years in consulting they will be able to go into an operating company at a higher level than they would otherwise, or that a position with a venture capital firm will lead to a top management role in a portfolio company. No doubt this strategy works for some people, but in our experience the road from a professional services role to a significant line management position is not as easy as many hope. It is more common for consultants, on joining an operating company, first to be assigned to staff jobs in functions such as strategic planning or business development before being offered management positions. Some venture capital firms place their people in management roles in their portfolio companies, but those that do usually want seasoned managers in such positions.

Management consulting, venture capital, investment banking, and most other professional services firms do not offer significant management training, although they may offer valuable experience and training in other areas of business. So if you are aware that managing people is going to be a central aspect of your work satisfaction, you should also consider career paths that take you directly to that role, especially if you have a strong interest in a particular industry. You might want to examine companies that offer management development programs in which high-potential new employees are rotated through several different areas of the business (sales, finance, marketing, operations, and so on) over the course of one to two years, being groomed for rapid advancement to general management responsibility.

Enterprise Control

The Enterprise Control business core function represents interests that are realized through having ultimate decision-making authority for an enterprise. Individuals who have a strong interest in this function enjoy the authority and control of resources that enable them to actualize a business vision. Whether or not they enjoy managing people, they find satisfaction in making the decisions that will determine the direction taken by a work team, a business unit, a company division, or an entire organization. They find satisfaction in roles such as team leader, group or division manager, president, CFO, CEO, partner or director of a professional services company, entrepreneur, and elected public official. Individuals who enjoy autonomous roles in sales may also have elevations on this scale.

Scores on this business core function scale are significantly correlated with scales from other interest inventories measuring similarity of interests with individuals in occupations such as elected public official, realtor, marketing director, military officer, Chamber of Commerce executive, chief executive officer, and president. They also correlate highly with scales measuring interest in leadership, law, and politics. Scores on this core function scale are correlated with scales measuring self-rated *skills* associated with areas such as leadership, law, and politics and with the specific occupations of chief executive officer or president, realtor, media executive, marketing director, hospital administrator, and military officer. Because the *BCII* is not in itself a measure of skills, you should not be deterred if you are not sure of your skill level in activities associated with this core function. Skill in this function, perhaps more than any other, requires time and experience to develop. The Enterprise Control function has a moderate correlation with the Influence Through Language and Ideas function.

The latter function has more of an emphasis on *influence*, such as lawyers, consultants, or negotiators might exert in the course of their respective professional activities. The Enterprise Control core function has a greater emphasis on the *power* of direct authority.

Influence Through Language and Ideas

The Influence Through Language and Ideas business core function represents interests that are realized by exercising influence through the skillful use of written and spoken language. Negotiations, deal making, public relations, sales, and the design of advertising campaigns are examples of business activities that provide for the realization of interest in this core function. Individuals who have a strong interest in this function enjoy work with frequent interpersonal transactions. They enjoy language and ideas and typically see themselves as having strong communications skills.

Scores on this business core function scale are significantly correlated with scales from other interest inventories measuring similarity of interests with individuals in occupations such as elected public official, lawyer, public administrator, realtor, public relations director, school administrator, insurance agent, and Chamber of Commerce executive. Scores on this scale are also significantly correlated with other interest inventory scales measuring interests in areas such as public speaking, law and politics, writing, advertising, and marketing. Scores on the Influence Through Language and Ideas function scale are also correlated with self-rated confidence in *skills* associated with leadership, law and politics, public speaking, and sales, and with self-reported confidence in skills associated with the occupations of attorney, manufacturers' representative, realtor, marketing director, advertising account executive, media executive, public relations director, corporate trainer, writer, and editor. (Again, remember that the *BCII* is not in itself a measure of skills.) The Influence Through Language and Ideas function has a moderate correlation with the Enterprise Control function, and together these two functions compose the *Control and Influence* dimension element of the *business career profile type*. (You will learn in Chapter 7 about the three dimensions that comprise the eight business core functions.)

Understanding Your Business Core Function Profile

Understanding the meaning of your own interest pattern structure requires more than a grasp of the scale definitions for each of the *BCII* business score function scales in which your scores are in the high range: As you will learn in Chapter 7, the meaning of one core function scale score will change depending on the scores obtained on other core function scales. If you have completed one or more of the active imagination exercises, you will learn how to score and analyze the exercises and reconcile them with your scores from the *BCII* in Chapter 6. If you have not completed any of the active imagination exercises in Chapter 3, and do not wish to do so at this time, you should proceed directly to Chapter 7, where you will learn how to perform a complete profile analysis that will enable you to understand how your particular combination of scores is related to specific types of business work.

SIX

Scoring and Analyzing Your Active Imagination Exercises

ALTHOUGH THE *Business Career Interest Inventory* provides a sophisticated analysis of your pattern of deep structure interests in the eight business core functions, like all psychological inventories it is best used in conjunction with other assessment information. Self-assessment is most accurate, subtle, and reliable when it uses information obtained from different assessment methods. This chapter will teach you how to use the business core function model to analyze the results of your active imagination exercises from Chapter 3 and then to integrate these analyses with your *BCII* scores and best assess your interests in relation to the eight core functions.

The active imagination analysis requires a review of your journal entries for each completed exercise. The goal of the analysis is to arrive at a rating of each of the eight business core functions for each exercise. There are three ratings: no presence of the function (0), some presence of the function (+), and a dominant presence of the function (++). In the analysis we look for specific activities that can be categorized under each of the eight functions. If there are no activities for a particular function, the score is 0. If there is one activity for a function, the score is +. If there are two or more activities for a particular function and/or it is the dominant function of the active imagination event, the score is ++. It is possible that a particular imagination event has two dominant activities, but much less likely that it has three. If you are scoring several exercises with two or more

++ function scores, you are probably being too liberal with the use of that rating.

For the flow exercise you will rate each separate example of an experience of being in flow. For the work history interview exercise, you will rate the most satisfying work/educational experience from each year. For the job envy exercise, you will rate each separate incidence of job envy. For the job from hell exercise, any function represented in that job will receive a 0 rating. For your accomplishment exercise, you will rate each accomplishment event. For the reading exercise you will rate your reading interests for each period of time being considered (the past six months, one year, and five-year periods). For your grazing exercise, you will rate your notes from one week of grazing. For the letters exercise, you will score each of the letters separately.

Examples of Scorable Activities for the Eight Functions

Let us look at each of the eight business core functions and list some of the activities that might generate a + or ++ rating. It is important in these analyses to think *imaginatively.* Solving an engineering problem is an obvious example of an Application of Technology business core function activity, but enjoying a summer job in house construction is also a scorable activity. The lists below are intended to be representative examples but *not* a comprehensive list of scorable activities for each of the business core functions.

- *Application of Technology:* computer programming; systems analysis work; solving engineering problems; architecture; working on product design in any capacity; working or managing in a manufacturing environment; avocational pursuits in carpentry, electronics, auto or other mechanics, optics, astronomy, photography, or pottery and other crafts; reading in science and technology or in any of the fields mentioned above.

- *Quantitative Analysis:* accounting activities; financial analysis of all types; statistical analysis of all types; mathematical approaches to decision making; playing mathematical games or solving mathematical puzzles; economic forecasting.

♦ *Theory Development and Conceptual Thinking:* strategic planning; market analysis; marketing planning; strategy consulting; teaching or taking business theory courses; studying or developing economic theory; avocational interests in scientific, philosophical, mathematical, or literary theory.

♦ *Creative Production:* writing of any nature; art and design work of any nature; creation of new product ideas; avocational interests in art, crafts, fashion, interior design, writing, or music.

♦ *Counseling and Mentoring:* any form of counseling, mentoring, training, or teaching; avocational commitments that involve counseling, coaching, or teaching roles (such as Big Brother/Sister, Little League, Girl Scouts, crisis hotline).

♦ *Managing People:* any direct (day-to-day) management or supervisory roles; avocational commitments as a leader or organizer of civic, religious, or school groups or committees.

♦ *Enterprise Control:* operating or planning to operate your own business; being in or aspiring to top organizational leadership positions; holding or running for an elected office.

♦ *Influence Through Language and Ideas:* advertising account work; public relations activities; certain law-related activities; writing memos and reports; preparing and delivering work-related presentations; public speaking engagements; holding or running for an elected office; working with the media or in a media function; avocational interests in politics or debate.

Sample Active Imagination Ratings

The hypothetical journal entry scorings below will give you a better grasp of the rating process. Each entry is followed by a discussion of scoring issues raised by that example. Entries 1 and 5 are in the style of a flow active imagination exercise. Entry 2 is presented as a job envy exercise. Entry 3 is a hypothetical excerpt from a work history interview entry. Entry 4 is presented as an excerpt from a letter provided for the journal writer.

Journal Entry 1: A Flow Exercise

I am at my computer in my home office. I am writing from my notes and assembling quotations from several sources for a chapter of a book I am writing on decision-making theory. I stop for long periods to think and refer to books in my library to check sources that apply to the ideas that I am trying to articulate. Hours pass. I realize that I am putting into words things that I had been thinking for several months but had not previously articulated.

SCORING

- *Applied Technology:* 0 (The use of the computer is incidental)
- *Quantitative Analysis:* 0 (Absent)
- *Theory Development and Conceptual Thinking:* ++ (A major theme)
- *Creative Production:* ++ (Another major theme)
- *Counseling/Mentoring:* 0 (Absent)
- *Managing People:* 0 (Absent)
- *Enterprise Control:* 0 (Absent)
- *Influence Through Language and Ideas:* + (Borderline, see below)

This scoring is relatively straightforward. It is about creativity in the realm of concepts. Using a tool or piece of a technology such as a computer is not scorable if it is incidental to the actual work being accomplished. The one difficult aspect of the scoring is the + for Influencing Through Language and Ideas. The audience of the writing is not mentioned in the journal entry, and we do not get a feel for the persuasive intention of the writing. But in the end, writing a book chapter is in itself enough to earn a + score on this dimension.

Journal Entry 2: A Job Envy Exercise

It is past midnight. Robert and his staff have been working to finish the layout for the school newspaper since three o'clock that afternoon. Robert is production editor for this issue and most of the staff is present: Ray, Susan, Burt, and Roger, as well as a few "irregulars," friends who have agreed to help. It is the annual "lampoon" edition, and everyone is having a good time. The staff is tired, but they are able to concentrate and work well. Robert gives the overall directions, but last-minute ideas and changes flow from most of the people present. Robert and Susan are working with the graphics program and are pleased with the results. The actual setting of the text and graphics is fun, and at the end of the night everyone is proud of the finished product.

Scoring

- *Application of Technology:* + (Present, but not dominant)
- *Quantitative Analysis:* 0 (Absent)
- *Theory Development and Conceptual Thinking:* 0 (Absent)
- *Creative Production:* ++ (A major theme)
- *Counseling and Mentoring:* 0 (Absent)
- *Managing People:* ++ (Another major theme)
- *Enterprise Control:* 0 (Borderline, no explicit mention of being editor in chief or satisfaction from running the "whole show")
- *Influence Through Language and Ideas:* + (Barely scorable, but implied)

Scoring this active imagination journal entry presents a challenge. First getting a grasp of the major theme of the journal entry will help you score the excercises. In other words, what is really going on here? What is the main reason for this experience to be remembered as particularly meaningful? In this case, the entry is about an enjoyable, high-energy interpersonal situation. The entry writer envies being in charge in a Managing People function. Managing People is one major core function theme of the entry. Creative Production is also clearly important, so much so that it merits a ++ rating. Difficult to score are the Influence Through Language and Ideas and Enterprise Control functions. Both are implied rather than explicit, and both are on the borderline between 0 and + ratings.

The fact that the writer clearly is envying working on a newspaper merits a + for Influence Through Language and Ideas, even though the ideas of the paper are not mentioned directly. The scoring for Enterprise Control is more debatable. Clearly the Managing People function is more dominant than Enterprise Control. The writer is envying the manager, but we do not have enough information to know whether being in charge of the whole newspaper enterprise is important. If this were your own journal entry and you decided, on further reflection, that being in charge of the whole operation was also an important aspect of your enjoyment, then a rating of + would be indicated.

Journal Entry 3: A Work History Interview

The days prior to the mid-year sales meeting were personally high-energy, both scary and exciting. It was clear that my region was not going to meet the numbers for the year if we kept on the present course. I came to the conclusion that we would have to virtually drop our efforts in the low-end copier market and focus all our re-sources toward developing new accounts for the high-end 2000 Se-ries. As I anticipated, this plan met with resistance from the sales team. The 1000 Series had been out for three years and the reps had an established customer base. It was clear that not all 1000 Series customers would be good candidates for upgrades to the 2000 Series. Focusing on the higher margin new machines would mean prospecting and many cold calls.

The meeting was full of heated debate. I scheduled a number of one-on-one meetings to listen to each rep's reactions and concerns. I came out of the meeting feeling that I had strengthened my relation-ship with most of the team and, in the end, I got buy-in for the new strategy. The meeting, the days before, and the following four months during which the strategy was implemented were times in which I felt I was truly taking action and making something happen. It was a very creative period.

Scoring

- *Application of Technology:* 0 (Absent)
- *Quantitative Analysis:* 0 (Absent)
- *Theory Development and Conceptual Thinking:* + (Present, but not a major theme)
- *Creative Production:* 0 (Absent, see below)
- *Counseling and Mentoring:* 0 (Borderline, see below)
- *Managing People:* + (Present, but not a major theme)
- *Enterprise Control:* ++ (A major theme)
- *Influence Through Language and Ideas:* ++ (A major theme)

In this entry, Enterprise Control dominates. Making a decision that changes the direction of the organization is the major source of satisfaction. The mention of relationship-building at the sales meeting is enough to score a + for Managing People, but not explicit enough to be scorable for Counseling and Mentoring. Influence Through Language and Ideas merits a ++; presenting his ideas and being persuasive with members of the team were a meaningful part of the event for the writer. Theory Development and Conceptual Thinking is rated a + because the protagonist indicates that he made marketing strategy decisions. The use of the word *creative* in the last line is not enough in itself to make Creative Production scorable; this core function is concerned with an immediate creative product, almost always of a tangible or potentially tangible nature.

Journal Entry 4: A Letter

. . . Marcy is happiest when she is working in the midst of a busy operation. She likes being around people, particularly when she is the one organizing things. People trust Marcy and often come to her for advice; this is a role that she truly enjoys. . . .

SCORING

- *Application of Technology:* 0 (Absent)
- *Quantitative Analysis:* 0 (Absent)
- *Theory Development and Conceptual Thinking:* 0 (Absent)
- *Creative Production:* 0 (Absent)
- *Counseling and Mentoring:* ++ (A major theme)
- *Managing People:* ++ (Another major theme)
- *Enterprise Control:* 0 (Absent)
- *Influence Through Language and Ideas:* 0 (Absent)

In this excerpt from a letter sent by someone who knows Marcy well, satisfaction derived from relationships at work is the theme that dominates. This satisfaction does not need to be, as it is in this case, from a counseling relationship per se. Meaningful relationships with fellow workers and clients that are a major source of satisfaction and that continue over time are also scorable on the Counseling and Mentoring function. In this event the counseling and mentoring role took place, as it often (but not always) does, within the context of an explicitly important management activity; thus, Managing People also emerges as a dominant theme and is scored ++. This is a brief excerpt, focusing exclusively on the interpersonal realm of work. We do not know what type of "operations" Marcy would enjoy in particular. If the letter sample had been more expansive, other functions might have become scorable.

Journal Entry 5: A Flow Exercise

The consulting project for Southern Travel was particularly satisfying. They were misperceiving the needs of a major market, and when I made the final presentation, we all knew right away that I had really added value. Everything about the project felt good: designing and analyzing the surveys, doing the focus groups, talking with management, and making the presentations. It was a politically sensitive topic, in light of the investment of certain members of management in the company's established direction, so I felt particularly good about getting them to see the merits of the new strategy.

SCORING

- *Application of Technology:* 0 (Absent)
- *Quantitative Analysis:* + (Definitely present, but not as major as the Influence function)
- *Theory Development and Conceptual Thinking:* + (Borderline, more implied than explicitly stated)
- *Creative Production:* 0 (Absent)
- *Counseling and Mentoring:* 0 (Absent)
- *Managing People:* 0 (Absent)
- *Enterprise Control:* 0 (Absent)
- *Influence Through Language and Ideas:* ++ (A major theme)

The problem solving of consulting work is often strong on Quantitative Analysis, Influence Through Language and Ideas, and Theory Development and Conceptual Thinking. In this case, the Influence aspects of the client relationship emerge as the major theme.

Combining Ratings from the Active Imagination Exercises

Clearly, the more active imagination work you do and analyze, the richer, more subtle, and more accurate your information will be. In fact, there is some danger in viewing an analysis of just a few exercises as being definitive; it is unlikely that two or three exercises will fully sample recurring themes of major work satisfaction. You may want to begin your analysis with a few exercises, and return to it later as your journal entries grow. Over time, you will more easily recognize which business core functions emerge as dominant sources of satisfaction. The analysis of active imagination exercises provides information that you can use to corroborate or challenge data derived from the more mathematically sophisticated assessment offered in the *Business Career Interest Inventory.* The desired outcome of analyzing the combined ratings of your active imagination exercises is to arrive at a tentative description of the importance of each business core function as being high, middle, or low range.

You may take two approaches to an overall analysis that combines your ratings from all of the active imagination exercises: the first is a "big picture" intuitive summary, and the second is a more mathematically oriented approach. Each has its advantages and disadvantages. In the first approach, you review the ratings of each core function across all of the exercises rated. Look generally at the number of 0's, +'s, and ++'s scored. Based on the distribution of scores, classify each core function into a high, middle, or low range. Different combinations of scores may yield the same final classification. For example, in reviewing ten exercises you may find that a particular function received only one ++ score, but was present as a + in seven of the other exercises. Surely a function that occurs almost every time you imagine enjoyable work has a greater importance than the simple mathematical average of these scores would indicate. On the other hand, ++ ratings are very strong indicators of interest and should carry significant weight in your summary analysis. Thus a high classification might also result from a score pattern of two ++'s, three +'s, and five 0's.

The second approach is more mathematical (and may have particular appeal to readers with Quantitative Analysis interest). This approach works better as the number of analyzed exercises increases, and you should not use it unless you are analyzing five or more journal entries. For each function, assign a numerical weighting of 0 for 0 scores, 1 for every + score, and 2 for every ++ score. Find the average for each function by summing all ratings for that function and dividing by the total number of ratings. The cutoff points for the high, middle, and low classifications are arbitrary, but we suggest you start by considering scores of .2 or less to be low range, scores between .2 and .5 to be middle range, and scores of .5 or higher to be high range.

We can use the five sample journal entries above to illustrate this quantitative analysis. Let us look at each of the business core functions individually.

The Applied Technology business core function received scorings of one + and four 0's. The weighted average scoring is thus .2 (1 point for the + rating divided by the number of exercises being scored, which is 5). This would place the rating in the low range. The Quantitative Analysis function likewise received scorings of one + and four 0's. The weighted average is again .2, and the overall rating is again in the low range. The Theory Development and Conceptual Thinking function received ratings of one ++, two +'s, and two 0's. The weighted average is .8 (2 points for the ++ and 2 points for the +'s, divided by 5). This would place the overall rating of this function in the high range. The Creative Production function received ratings of two ++'s and three 0's. The weighted average is .8, and the overall rating is in the high range. The Counseling and Mentoring business core function received ratings of one ++ and four 0's. The weighted average is .4, placing the overall function rating in the middle range. The Managing People function received ratings of two ++'s, one +, and two 0's. The weighted average is 1, placing the overall function rating in the high range. The Enterprise Control function received ratings of one ++ and four 0's. The weighted average is .4, placing this function in the middle range. The Influence Through Language and Ideas function received ratings of two ++'s, two +'s, and one 0. The weighted average is 1.2, placing this function in the high range. Our combined ratings are summarized as follows:

Core Function	Weighted Average	Range
Application of Technology	0.2	Low
Quantitative Analysis	0.2	Low
Theory Development and Conceptual Thinking	0.8	High
Creative Production	0.8	High
Counseling and Mentoring	0.4	Middle
Managing People	1.0	High
Enterprise Control	0.4	Middle
Influence Through Language and Ideas	1.2	High

After reviewing this scoring, our hypothetical evaluator might decide that two of the ratings do not seem accurate. She might feel that the Enterprise Control business core function is more important than its middle range ranking. Perhaps it is a function with which she has had only recent and limited experience, and she feels strongly that it represents the expression of deep interests. She might change its final range rating to high. At the same time, she could decide that the Counseling and Mentoring rating was the result of one or two isolated events and belongs in the low range. In this way a review of the ratings becomes, in itself, a new active imagination exercise. Given the arbitrary nature of these weightings, do not be too literal or concrete about the final average ratings. You may even want to devise your own rating system. If you use this numerical approach, always use it in conjunction with the "big picture" analysis described earlier.

Integrating Active Imagination and *Business Career Interest Inventory* Scores

Once you have completed both the *BCII* and the analyses of a number of active imagination exercises, you will have been drawn deeply into an imaginative way of thinking about business work. The goal of both approaches to assessment is to provide *data for your creative imagination.* Even before you assign scores or relative values to the eight business core functions, you will be doing the work of assessment: becoming aware of new images, feelings, and thoughts about business work. Chapter 7 will return to a more formally analytical approach in helping you interpret the overall pattern of your interests; the chapter assumes that you have made, at least for the time being, a decision classifying each of the business core functions into the high, middle, or low range of interest. It is possible to do this using either your *BCII* or your active imagination scores alone, but we strongly recommend that you use a combination of the two methods in making your final classification. In doing so, keep the following points in mind.

One assessment method may be better at assessing a particular personality dimension for a particular individual. If you are at an early stage in your career, you may have had little actual experience with activities associated with business core functions such as Managing People or Enterprise Control. In that case, they may be less likely to show up in active imagination exercises (with the possible exception of exercises such as the one involving an ideal job) than in the *BCII.* The *BCII,* by suggesting possibilities within the items themselves, may elicit information about interests that have existed only in potential at the time of the assessment. For these two dimensions especially you may want to give more weight to the *BCII* results.

Also, whereas the *BCII* presents a finite number of images in its items, the possibilities for accessing images associated with business work through active imagination are virtually limitless. Any theoretical structure limits imagination at the same time that it clarifies understanding. You may decide, for example, that there are actually two categories of Counseling and Mentoring and that, although you do not particularly enjoy the counseling role, work environments where you act as a mentor are quite rewarding for you. You can discover distinctions such as these through active imagination and disciplined introspection, and you should use these insights to modify *BCII* scores when necessary. Perhaps the best way to think about self-assessment is as a never-ending alternation between the uncovering of new images of the self and an analysis of the images so that they become the basis for action. In Chapter 7 your current analysis and classification will be used as guides to understanding how your total pattern of interests is related to specific business work roles.

SEVEN

Analyzing Your Business Career Profile

IN THIS CHAPTER you will learn how to integrate your scores on the eight business core functions into an overall profile interpretation. You will then learn what our consulting experience and research have taught us concerning your particular business career profile type. We want to emphasize that this is *not* a "cookbook." If you simply look for the section that applies to you and expect to find *the answer* there, you will be disappointed (although we don't blame you for wishing you could). Our aim in this chapter is to take the model we presented in Chapter 5 and bring it to life, exploring some of the subtle nuances it holds. Please note, though, that it is still a *model*—a way we have developed to think about people's interests. We cannot explore all the other important aspects of who you are, such as your values, skills, and other dimensions of personality. Thus, you should use this chapter to help you do your thinking about your own life in all its complexity.

It is also important not to focus too much on the technology (the *Business Career Interest Inventory* and the exercises in Chapter 3). We discover people's interests in many ways, testing being only one. As an example, if we have only a few hours to meet with someone who is stopping over to consult with us on a trip from London to Chicago, we do not spend that time testing them. We talk with them about their lives and careers; but at the end of those few hours we would be able to think about them in terms of this model. In other words, the model exists and has value independent of any kind of testing.

Determining Your Business Career Profile Type

At this point you have completed the *BCII* and read in Chapter 4 about the various types of scores provided on the final Score Summary screen. You may also have done one or more of the active imagination exercises in Chapter 3 and scored them according to the directions in Chapter 6. To help you organize the interpretation of your scores on the eight business core function scales, we have classified them into three underlying dimensions. The three-letter *Business Career Profile Type* from the *BCII* Score Summary screen refers to these dimensions.

We call the first underlying dimension *Application of Expertise.* It includes the business core functions Application of Technology, Quantitative Analysis, Theory Development and Conceptual Thinking, and Creative Production. Each of these four business core functions involves using some sort of specialized expertise in a business setting. The second underlying dimension has to do with *Working with People,* and includes both the Counseling and Mentoring and the Managing People business core functions. The third dimension is *Control and Influence.* Its two business core functions are Enterprise Control and Influence Through Language and Ideas. The groupings of core functions are summarized below:

Application of Expertise	Working with People	Control and Influence
Application of Technology	Counseling and Mentoring	Enterprise Control
Quantitative Analysis	Managing People	Influence Through Language and Ideas
Theory Development and Conceptual Thinking		
Creative Production		

For each of the three fundamental dimensions you received a designation of high, medium, or low, depending on the elevation of the underlying business core function scales scores. Take Application of

Expertise, for example. If your score on *any one or more* of the four business core function scales comprising this group was high, your designation for the Application of Expertise dimension is "High." If *all four* of your scores were low, your designation for Application of Expertise is "Low." If none of your scores was high, but at least one of them was in the middle range, your designation on the Application of Expertise dimension is "Medium." Thus, you can be high (H), medium (M), or low (L) on each of the three fundamental dimensions and your *BCII* results provide you with that information. Your designations could form any of twenty-seven combinations: HHH, HHM, HHL, . . . all the way through LLL.

In theory, we could have divided the designations into high, moderately high, medium, moderately low, and low; or even into very high, high, moderately high, medium, and so on. At a certain point, however, what is gained in precision is lost in the ability to actually use the information (not to mention that the twenty-seven combinations would grow exponentially into the hundreds). In fact, we found that we could not truly make use of even the twenty-seven combinations of high, medium, and low designations on each of the three fundamental dimensions. However, we could not justify simply calling people Low if they were at the 49th percentile on a given business core function scale, or High if they were at the 51st percentile. You may, in fact, *be* low or high, but we do not feel that we are in a position to make that call.

But you are. So if you were assessed as medium on one of the three fundamental dimensions underlying the eight business core functions, we ask you to act as the tie-breaker and push yourself into either the high or low category. You will do this by looking at the business core functions that dimension comprises, and thinking about whether you are truly high or low on any of them. Going back to the active imagination exercises in Chapter 3 may help you to make these decisions. Bear in mind that we all have a tendency to want to score high on tests, so you may be more inclined to move a medium up to high than down to low. It is important to resist that tendency and to *accurately* make the changes. You can always, in your own mind, keep the subtle distinction that although you are calling yourself high or low, you are really at the low end of the highs or at the high end of the lows. Similarly, if your designation on one of the three dimensions was high, you may know you are in fact extremely high or only moderately high; or if you were designated low, you may know you are extremely low or only moderately low. Bringing all of your self-awareness to bear on this process will provide you with the most nuanced knowledge and the most useful outcome.

If you were assessed as medium on all three of the underlying dimensions, you might want to take the *BCII* again, this time using more 0's and 3's as you go through it, or simply wait two to three weeks and retake it without any conscious effort to change your distribution of responses. If taking the instrument again yields the same result, you may need to rely more heavily on the exercises from Chapter 3 and on your own general sense of yourself in pushing yourself into the high or low designation for those dimensions. After you have, if necessary, converted any medium designations into a high or low, you will find yourself in one of eight possible combinations of those two designations. Taking the dimensions Application of Expertise, Working with People, and Control and Influence in that order, you could be high on all three (HHH), high on two of the three (HHL, HLH, or LHH), high on only one of the three (HLL, LHL, or LLH), or low on all three (LLL). We use the term *business career profile types* for those eight combinations of high or low designations on the three fundamental dimensions underlying the different business core functions. Now we will use this model to help you return to the world of work and help you answer the key question: "What does this mean for *me,* for my career?" To this effort we bring to bear both our years of experience and our empirical research.

How to Use Your *BCII* Scores

First you want to compare your *BCII* results, assuming no question was raised concerning their validity, with what you learned from the active imagination exercises. If the results of the two sources of data are in agreement regarding your interest in the eight business core functions, that may give you increased confidence in the results.

(However, you should not construe agreement on any of the business core functions as additive, meaning that you are even higher, or lower, than either result alone would imply.)

If the results are not fully in agreement, you have some work to do. Reexamine the data you gathered from the active imagination exercises in Chapter 3, and ask yourself whether they really reflect who you are. Then reexamine your evaluation of those data and see whether you scored them according to the directions given in Chapter 6. Finally, consider your responses to the questions on the *BCII* and evaluate whether you answered them honestly. Look for contamination by feelings of what you *should* like both in the active imagination exercises and in the *BCII*. Reread the parts of Chapter 5 that describe those business core functions on which your data are not in agreement. Do you feel either an internal, spontaneous attraction to or repulsion from the particular business core function? Does reading the description clarify what it really means in such a way that you are able to fine-tune the results and resolve what may have appeared to be a conflict?

If you find that your responses and scoring were honest and accurate, but there were notably different conclusions drawn from the active imagination exercises and the *BCII* on one or more business core functions, there may be an internal tension within you related to those business core functions: Perhaps, for example, you are of two minds concerning your interest in running the show (Enterprise Control) or your interest in the softer side of business work (Counseling and Mentoring). If this seems to be the case, read Chapter 8, which addresses the issue of internal tensions that are part of making most meaningful changes.

When you feel confident that you know where you fall on the spectrum from great interest to no interest on each of the eight business core functions, read the following summary of what each function entails before proceeding. (Each function is discussed in detail in Chapter 5, but we repeat the descriptions here for those readers who have moved directly to profile interpretation after having taken the *BCII*. We recommend that every reader eventually read Chapter 5 in its entirety.)

♦ The Application of Technology business core function represents interests that are realized through the general use of technology to accomplish business objectives, activities often associated with engineering, production and systems planning, product design, production and operations process analysis, production planning, and systems analysis. Individuals who are strongly interested in this function are intrigued by the inner workings of things and curious about finding better ways to bring technology to the task of solving business problems. They are also typically comfortable with the "language" of technology: mathematical analysis, computer programming, and representations of the world founded on the models of the physical sciences.

♦ The Quantitative Analysis business core function represents interests that are realized through problem solving that relies on mathematical analysis. Work activities such as analyzing market research, building a computer model to determine optimal production scheduling, performing a discounted cashflow analysis, determining net present value, analyzing the future performance of an investment instrument, determining the optimal debt/equity structure for a business, and performing other accounting procedures are all examples of work tasks that draw heavily on the interests represented by this core function. The Quantitative Analysis core function represents interests that overlap to a certain extent with the interests represented by the Application of Technology function.

♦ The Theory Development and Conceptual Thinking business core function represents interests that are realized through activities involving broadly conceptual approaches to business problems. Examples of these activities include developing economic theory, developing a model that explains competition within a given industry, analyzing the competitive position of a business within a particular market, designing a new product development or product distribution process, and teaching business theory. Individuals with high scores on this function are comfortable and find challenge in the realms of ideas, imagination, and theory. They are at home with the intangible domains of plans, alternative business scenarios, and long-range forecasts. This function has a distinctly academic flavor and is, in fact, a frequent area of elevation among business academics.

+ The Creative Production business core function represents interests that are realized through highly creative activities such as new product design, development of marketing concepts, development of visual and verbal advertising concepts, generation of new business ideas, development of innovative approaches to business service delivery, planning of events, and public relations. Individuals with high scores on this function often see themselves, and are seen by others, as being particularly creative.

+ The Counseling and Mentoring business core function represents interests that are realized through activities involving development of one-on-one relationships as a rewarding aspect of business work. Coaching, training, and mentoring are activities in business settings that represent the manifestation of interest in this function. Not every skilled manager, however, will have a high, or even average, score on this function. There are many motivations for, and satisfactions to be derived from, management other than the enjoyment of helping subordinates, clients, and peers. This function has a specific focus on the importance of individual relationships for work satisfaction. People who have a strong interest in it prefer work environments where they feel they are making a significant contribution and adding value to the business endeavor through their teaching, counseling, and generally service-oriented relationships with fellow workers and business clients.

+ The Managing People business core function represents interests that are realized through working directly with people in the role of manager, director, or supervisor to accomplish business goals. Individuals who are interested in this function enjoy the *people management* aspect of leadership positions. They enjoy dealing with people and interpersonal issues on a day-to-day basis, and they derive major work satisfaction from workplace relationships.

♦ The Enterprise Control business core function represents interests that are realized through having ultimate decision-making authority for an enterprise. Individuals who have a stong interest in this function enjoy the authority and control of resources that enable them to actualize a business vision. Whether or not they enjoy managing people, they find satisfaction in making the decisions that will determine the direction taken by a work team, a business unit, a company division, or an entire organization. They find satisfaction in roles such as team leader, group or division manager, president, CFO, CEO, partner or director of a professional services company, entrepreneur, and elected public official. Individuals who enjoy autonomous roles in sales may also have elevations on this scale.

♦ The Influence Through Language and Ideas business core function represents interests that are realized by exercising influence through the skillful use of written and spoken language. Negotiations, deal making, public relations, sales, and the design of advertising campaigns are examples of business activities that provide for the realization of interest in this function. Individuals who have a strong interest in it enjoy work with frequent interpersonal transactions. They enjoy language and ideas and typically see themselves as having strong communications skills.

As you read the section that fits your individual business career profile type, treat it as food for thought. Read actively, "chewing" the information as you go, working to see how it applies to your unique set of experiences and personal attributes. The worst thing you can do is take the information at face value, "swallowing" it whole, which typically results in either of two reactions: the first is a too concrete and literal acceptance of the ideas, which can result in poor career decisions; the second, which is more common, is to reject the ideas and information completely, thus not benefiting from what they *can* give you.

People who consult us have often taken another, more general career interest inventory and been given an interpretation such as, "Well, Phil, you have a high score on the forester scale—have you ever considered a career in *forestry?*" Or they themselves have drawn the conclusion, telling us that "I took this test and it told me I should be a funeral director, so I blew it off." In explaining the various business career profile types, we use examples from our work as a means of making the concepts more "experience-near," bringing the abstract into the everyday world. The danger here is that you may be tempted to do with this precisely what people do when they see that they are similar to foresters or funeral directors, which is to take the examples too concretely. Remember, that they are *examples* and *illustrations* designed to help you understand and to inform your unique career development process, they are not prescriptions.

Also, some combinations of business core functions simply do not occur often enough for us to comment on them with any degree of confidence. This is another reason that this section of the book cannot be used as a career "cookbook." It is better than a cookbook; it supplies not recipes but real food for your imagination.

As you read, you may find one or another of the points we make, or an example we use, ringing especially true for you. Listen to those bells if they ring. Stop and think about how the point or example may apply to career decisions you have made or contemplated, or to changes you may be thinking about now. How does this information fit with your experiences of satisfaction or dissatisfaction with current and previous work activities, organizational mission, or organizational culture? Does it evoke any feelings of excitement, any fantasies, any regrets? The message here is to read slowly, to stop whenever something strikes you. Take some notes about your reactions and insights as you read. This chapter is your opportunity to take these data and put them to work for you, to customize and fine-tune what we are saying in print, and so to develop a deeply nuanced and textured understanding of what the information means for you.

The Eight Business Career Profile Types

We will now describe the eight different business career profile types and discuss the various combinations of business core functions that each of the three fundamental dimensions underlies. *Remember that the profile types are only a tool for organizing your thinking; the most important information is to be found in considering your scores on all of the eight business core functions, paying particular attention to your highest scores.* We will start with the profile type in which an individual is high on all three underlying dimensions, followed by the three profile types in which only one of the three dimensions is elevated, followed in turn by the three types in which there are designations of high on two of the underlying dimensions. Finally, we will consider the business career profile types on which all three fundamental dimensions are designated as low.

You will naturally be inclined to go directly to the business career profile type that the *Business Career Interest Inventory* and your active imagination exercises suggest is your own profile type. But we do recommend that at some point you read through the other seven business career profile types, for two reasons: They may stimulate your personal reflection in a way that you will find useful, perhaps adding some nuance to the business career profile type that best describes you; second, reading about other people's business career profile types will prove useful as you consider how best to manage and work with other people.

THE HHH BUSINESS CAREER PROFILE TYPE

- ◆ *Application of Expertise:* High
- ◆ *Working with People:* High
- ◆ *Control and Influence:* High

Among business executives, the HHH profile type is the most common of the eight business career profile types. Among MBA students this profile type has an extremely high frequency. If your profile type is HHH, you will need to base your interpretation of your profile on the specific pattern of the individual business core function scales. Because you have elevations on each of the three fundamental dimensions underlying the eight business core functions, you must look beneath the surface to consider what produced those elevations. (You should do this no matter what your business career profile type is, but it is *essential* for the HHH profile type.) One HHH profile type can be very different from another. For example, an individual whose HHH profile type derives from an elevation in the Creative Production area of Application of Expertise is likely to be very different from someone whose HHH profile results from an elevation in the Quantitative Analysis area.

In this section we will go into detail about various combinations of high business core function scale scores that can result in the HHH profile type, to make clear some of the distinctions contained in this grouping. More than a hundred different combinations of high scores on the eight business core function scales could result in an HHH profile type. We will not attempt to produce an exhaustive listing of the various combinations, for two reasons. Most obviously, such a compendium would be unwieldy in the extreme. Also, large numbers of the combinations are so rare as to make listing them simply for the sake of completeness a waste of time and paper. Instead we will concentrate on those that in our experience are more common and more likely to match your own profile, organizing the HHH types by their Application of Expertise interest elevation(s).

We will describe five varieties of HHH profile type separately, beginning with HHH profile types whose only Application of Expertise dimension elevation is on the Application of Technology business core function scale (calling them, for the purposes of this discussion, "AHH profile types"). We will then explore HHH profile types whose only Application of Expertise dimension elevation is on the Quantitative Analysis business core function scale (calling them "QHH profile types"). Next we will describe HHH profile types whose only Application of Expertise dimension elevation is on the Theory Development and Conceptual Thinking business core function scale ("THH profile types"). We will then discuss HHH profile types whose only Application of Expertise dimension elevation is on the Creative Production business core function scale ("CHH profile types"). Finally, we will also discuss several different *combinations* of the four business core functions that produce elevation in the Application of Expertise dimension.

If your business career profile type is HHH and you have more than one Application of Expertise business core function in the high range, you should read the descriptions given below for each of the relevant Application of Expertise business core functions that are elevated singly. Then read the appropriate paragraphs discussing the relevant Application of Expertise business core function combinations in this chapter and in Chapter 5.

Before we discuss specific areas of business expertise and their implications for the HHH profile type, it is important to understand the two Control and Influence business core functions, Enterprise Control and Influence Through Language and Ideas. We will describe the impact of differential interest in these two functions on each of the Application of Expertise functions, but first we want to describe them more fully as they apply to the HHH type independent of other functions.

In their pure forms these are the two ways in which people achieve their goals in business. As such they are almost supraordinate functions, influencing the ways in which all of the combinations of other business core functions are realized. Two people may have the exact same business objective, but will attempt to realize that objective through very different means if one of them is strongly weighted toward Enterprise Control and the other toward Influence Through Language and Ideas.

The Enterprise Control business core function describes activities that have to do with strategic thinking, the acquisition of the resources necessary to accomplish objectives, and engaging in the transactions that are a part of moving toward that objective. Enterprise Control is about being the captain of the aircraft carrier, or even of the fleet, strategically deploying ships in battle. Business professionals who are strongly interested in Enterprise Control activities (and not in Influence Through Language and Ideas) are more concerned with transactions, processes and products. They enjoy thinking about the big picture, leveraging resources, developing new markets, and business development through acquisition and the formation of business alliances. They enjoy doing deals and effecting change and growth through the most effective use of capital resources. There is a strong "strategic finance" element in the Enterprise Control core function because much of the strategic aspect of business is concerned with access to and efficient use of capital markets.

Because of their overwhelming interest in the big picture and strategy of the "game," high scorers on the Enterprise Control business core function scale who have moderate or low scores on the Influence Through Language and Ideas scale often have difficulty early in their careers, being impatient for the opportunity to play at the level they aspire to. They may need to learn the skills associated with the Influence function, even if they would prefer not to have to use them, being able to employ more command and control instead. These implications will hold true regardless of the mixture of elevated interests in other core functions which combine to produce the HHH business career profile type.

The Influence Through Language and Ideas business core function has to do with working with and through other people, making use of relationships and persuasive argument to gain people's support in accomplishing business objectives. Business professionals who are strongly interested in Influence Through Language and Ideas activities (and not in Enterprise Control) enjoy winning people over to their point of view, building consensus, "selling" their ideas. They enjoy working as part of a team, preferably in a leadership role, and their leadership style tends to be non-autocratic. They enjoy skillfully crafting formal presentations and planning how to informally introduce subjects for discussion, and tend to be skilled at putting themselves in other people's shoes to understand how best to appeal to them. If the business professional whose interests are in Enterprise Control enjoys dealing with transactions, processes and products, the individual whose interests are in Influence Through Language and Ideas will gravitate toward people, organizational dynamics and services. One could be thought of as the person who wants to be elected president, the other as the person who wants to be the powerful Speaker of the House or Senate leader, making things happen behind the scenes by skillful use of interpersonal persuasion and leadership qualities. People interested in Influence Through Language and Ideas will typically enjoy developing and maintaining client relationships, networking with other people in their organizations and in their industry more widely, and attempting to influence how decisions will be received by people both inside and outside the company.

If you are an HHH profile type you can be strongly interested in one function and not at all in the other, strongly interested in one and moderately interested in the other, or strongly interested in both. Typically when an individual's interests in both functions are strongly elevated, the Influence Through Language and Ideas function is what will be most visible to the casual observer, but Enterprise Control will be the person's core motivation. A substantial percentage of business professionals, and an even greater percentage of MBA students, have elevated interests in both functions. It is unusual for someone with an HHH profile type to have a very high level of interest in one of these two functions and very low interest in the other, but even if you have a differential of high and moderate interest this may be helpful to you in thinking about your dominant personal style and the work settings which will allow you to express your interest. As CEO, the HHH profile type is likely to want to act as Chief *Operating* Officer or president as well (unlike the HLH profile type). These are people who are likely to be quite hands-on in their management style, wanting to get involved in the details of the business.

> *Bob Gross was the president of a division of a retail apparel manufacturing company. He enjoyed the design aspect of the business as well as the marketing strategy and tactics, the overall business strategy, and the development of the people reporting to him. He was very involved in the day-to-day operations of the business and took great satisfaction in having good working relationships with people at all levels in the company, from his vice presidents to the workers in the factory. Thus, Bob's work and career clearly manifested all three of the fundamental dimensions that underlie the eight business core functions: Application of Expertise (Creative Production), Working with People (Counseling and Mentoring, Managing People), and Control and Influence (Enterprise Control and Influence Through Language and Ideas).*

Now let us talk more generally about the HHH business career profile type and about the business core functions that make up the Working with People dimension. A strong interest in the Managing People business core function, *regardless of other profile features*, is one of our indicators for what we sometimes refer to as a "pure management" career model. If your score on this function scale is high, refer back to the Managing People section of Chapter 5 for a discussion of the implications of this finding. As you do so, however, bear in mind that individuals with HHH profiles may have dominant Application of Expertise dimension scores that will make professional services firms such as management consulting attractive career alternatives—ones, however, that they will most fully enjoy at later career stages when they are partners or directors within those professional service organizations.

Regardless of the business core function that produces an elevation on the Application of Expertise dimension, the HHH profile type for whom the Counseling and Mentoring function is high but the Managing People and the Enterprise Control functions are *both low* is less likely to be interested in being a manager at all. This HHH profile type could be a teacher, an academically oriented consultant, or a human resource development trainer (for example) but is less likely to be a manager. Working for an organization that has an altruistic element to its mission may be important to a person with these core function interests.

Now let us take a closer look at the different Application of Expertise subspecies of the HHH profile type. If you are an HHH, you should certainly read the section that best applies to you, and we recommend that you read the others as well, for two reasons: It may help illuminate aspects of your interests of which you are currently not fully aware; and it may help you think about how best to work with colleagues or subordinates to whom the HHH profile type may apply (but due to elevation on a different business core function within the Application of Expertise dimension). Typically, HHH profile types are (or aspire to be) general managers and have a functional interest and/or industry focus tied to their area of expertise. The HHH profile type who becomes CEO of a company will typically have arrived at that position via a strong functional focus. The HHH with a strong interest in Application of Technology provides a clear example.

HHH with Application of Technology Elevated (AHH)

AHH profile types are interested in the way things work. Many people do not care at all about what's inside their personal computers. In fact, the PC revolution really took off only after graphic user interfaces like Windows made it possible for the average user to use the PC and know next to nothing about the disk operating system (DOS). AHH profile types, however, are *very* interested in what is going on inside the box. They may not be programmers, but they are nonetheless intrigued. Similarly, they may be interested in how their microwaves heat their leftovers, how magnetic resonance imaging (MRI) takes pictures of the brain at work, how genetic engineering is done, and so forth. (They may not, in fact, *know* any of these things, but they are likely to be interested in them.)

If they are working in business, AHH profile types are likely to be attracted to technologically more sophisticated products and services, and to the technical end of those businesses: to new product development, to information systems, to computer-assisted design and manufacture, to production planning and distribution systems. Commodity products, basic service management (such as restaurants), and professional services (such as law) are unlikely to appeal to AHH profile types.

With the Application of Technology business core function elevated, we might find someone who manages within or heads a company or division that produces a technologically sophisticated product or provides a service involving the use or understanding of sophisticated technology. Chuck Cohen is a good example of the AHH business career profile type.

> *Chuck Cohen had both a bachelor's and master's degree in electrical engineering, and had worked as an engineer and manager for a large aerospace company before getting a business degree. Within a few years of graduating he found himself president of a small, fast-growing high-tech company. He loved everything about the job: the product, the technology behind it, being in the position of president, and managing the people in the organization. Like many HHH business career profile types, he was actually too involved in the day-to-day management side of things and had to learn to delegate those responsibilities better.*

Another natural home for the AHH profile type would be at the partnership level of an engineering or information technology consulting firm.

Chris Kerrigan had worked as a strategic planner for several energy companies and utilities but found the role of internal planning too confining. He wanted to be in charge of his own destiny, and so he founded his own energy resource consulting firm. He was able to grow his client base to a point where he had about twenty full-time professionals working under him—but then he began to feel that a larger operation would take him too far away from the mixture of activities he enjoyed.

Managing the information systems group within a company would be another natural environment for the AHH profile type.

Mina Johann had worked as an engineer before getting her MBA. She subsequently worked in marketing for a high-tech firm but found that she wanted to be running the show, not just selling the product. She also enjoyed financial services, and found a position as head of the information systems group for one part of a diversified financial services firm. In this position Mina had internal profit and loss responsibility for her group, which had to compete with outside vendors for her internal customers' work.

Finally, let us consider how different levels of interest in the two Control and Influence dimension business core functions affect the AHH profile. We would look for the AHH whose only Control and Influence elevation is on the Enterprise Control function to be (or aspire to be) a general manager, CEO, or division head of a technically oriented company; and for the AHH whose only elevation is on the Influence Through Language and Ideas function to be drawn more to marketing, sales, product management, or perhaps to marketing communication. Dual elevation may have the AHH in the technically oriented company, aspiring to and moving toward the position of general manager or CEO, and doing so through the sales and marketing side of the business.

HHH WITH QUANTITATIVE ANALYSIS ELEVATED (QHH)

The QHH business career profile type is typically very interested in the quantitative side of life, especially in the financial analyses important to business decisions. The prototypical QHH profile type's career path could involve moving from financial analyst to manager of an internal audit group to assistant controller to controller to chief financial officer to CEO; or, depending on other factors (talent, ambition, good fortune), it could stop at any point along the way.

Terry Roper was able to move up this path with considerable speed. He had studied accounting as an undergraduate and gone to work for a "Big Six" firm on the audit side of their business. He did well, earned his CPA, and went to business school for an MBA. Terry then secured a position as the chief financial officer for a small company whose previous CFO was a friend from Terry's days in public accounting.

Another home for the QHH is as a manager of analysts. When we speak with analysts in investment management firms, they often want either to become portfolio managers (which involves managing only the investment of funds, not people) or to remain as analysts, with no aspiration for a management role. Some people, however, seek out management responsibility.

Lisa Nance had been an equities analyst with a large pension fund for several years when an opportunity arose for her to move into management. She did not hesitate to make the move, despite several of her colleagues expressing misgivings ("Are you sure you really want all the headaches of being a manager?" she was asked. "Why on earth would you want to do that?"). In fact, she did want all the headaches (and all the satisfaction) of managing a group.

Partnership or ownership of a firm that offers consulting of a quantitative nature could also be a good fit for a QHH. Such analysis would not be limited to financial analysis, as the case of Hugo Dickinson makes clear.

Hugo had worked for many years in the market research department of a large consumer packaged goods company before going out on his own as a consultant. Leveraging his industry contacts and credibility, he was able to build up his business to a comfortable size within a short time. His consulting practice relied heavily on sophisticated models of market analysis for advising clients on issues such as pricing and competitive strategies.

Finally, let us consider how different levels of interest in the two Control and Influence dimension business core functions affect the QHH profile. We might see the QHH whose only Control and Influence elevation is on the Enterprise Control function going up the finance ladder and becoming CFO on the way to the CEO position in a firm in any industry; working as a leader of investment portfolio managers or as head of a trading desk in an investment bank; or perhaps running a hedge fund. The QHH whose only elevation is on the Influence Through Language and Ideas function, on the other hand, might be drawn to sales of financial products and services or of investment advisory services; to providing financially oriented consulting (as a Certified Public Accountant, for example); or to work in investor relations. As interest in both functions becomes elevated we think about careers for the QHH in investment or merchant banking, either in mergers and acquisitions or in corporate finance; in commercial banking; in venture capital; or a leveraged buy-out firm.

HHH with Theory Development and Conceptual Thinking Elevated (THH)

Perhaps due to the highly academic flavor of the Theory Development and Conceptual Thinking business core function, the THH business career profile type is not one we often see. When we have seen it, the elevation on the Control and Influence dimension is most often due to the Influence Through Language and Ideas business core function rather than the Enterprise Control business core function.

> *Ben Ifill was a manager of quantitative analysts for a Wall Street investment bank. As a "quant" himself, he was well acquainted with the work and in fact served as a "player-coach," continuing to develop sophisticated models for the bank while developing and mentoring more junior analysts and managing the group.*

Finally, let us consider how different levels of interest in the two Control and Influence dimension business core functions affect the

THH profile. The THH whose only Control and Influence elevation is on the Enterprise Control function is relatively rare. The academic flavor of the Theory Development and Conceptual Thinking business core function, while not antithetical to the Enterprise Control function, makes for an unusual combination. If we were to see it, it would probably be in a partner of a rather academically oriented consulting firm. The THH whose only elevation is on the Influence Through Language and Ideas function, on the other hand, might be a business school professor, or someone who is weighing the option of going beyond the MBA for a Ph.D.; a strategic planning or business development specialist working in a corporate setting; or a "knowledge-base consultant." A THH business professional with elevated interest in both of the Control and Influence functions might become a partner or director in a strategic management consulting firm, where an interest (and skill) in Influence Through Language and Ideas is essential for developing business and working effectively with clients, and where interest in Enterprise Control is a necessary element of internal firm leadership.

HHH with Creative Production Elevated (CHH)

If the Creative Production business core function were the elevated area of expertise, we might see an editor of a publishing imprint or business magazine, or someone who trains business executives to be more effective presenters (especially if, in the latter case, the Working with People dimension elevation was due to interest in the Counseling and Mentoring business core function).

> *Lydia Almeida had worked in consumer packaged goods marketing before getting her MBA. Subsequently she moved into the media and communications industry and then became CEO of a company that retailed high-end women's apparel.*

The CHH may also be an entrepreneur. We frequently find high scores on the Creative Production business core function scale among individuals who are most interested in the newness of new ventures (versus the sheer potential for profit).

Brooks Lambert was a classic of this sort. Brooks had started several successful businesses. He enjoyed the creative challenge, recruiting the team, and running the operation—for a time. After the business was up and running successfully, Brooks was ready to move on.

Finally, let us consider how different levels of interest in the two Control and Influence dimension business core functions affect the CHH profile. We would look for the CHH whose only Control and Influence elevation is on the Enterprise Control function to be very interested in entrepreneurial ventures, regardless of the industry; or to be interested in having a high level position in an industry which has a strong creative aspect to its product or service, such as entertainment, media, advertising, fashion, travel and resorts, and trade shows. With elevated interest only in the Influence Through Language and Ideas function we might see the CHH as an advertising firm account executive or relationship manager; a consumer goods brand manager; someone involved in the sales and marketing of a creative product; or someone at the executive level in the media industry. The CHH business professional with elevated interest in both functions is going to look more like the Enterprise Control CHH than the Influence Through Language and Ideas CHH, due to the strong entrepreneurial influence of the Creative Production business core function.

HHH with Combinations of Application of Expertise Core Functions Elevated

These HHH business career profile types have a good deal in common with their HLL counterparts who also have two or more business core functions elevated in the Application of Expertise dimension. The difference between the HHH and the HLL profile types is in the interest in running the business (the HHH type) versus being an individual contributor (the HLL type). If your business career profile type is HHH and you have more than one Application of Expertise business core function elevated, you should read this section, and also read the HLL section for individuals with combinations of Application of Expertise business core functions elevated.

Like the HLL profile type with similar Application of Expertise elevations, the HHH profile type with both the Application of Technology and the Quantitative Analysis business core functions elevated is likely to be drawn to cutting-edge high-tech products and to the financial side of the business. Unlike the HLL profile type, though, the HHH is probably much more interested in becoming CEO of such a company. The HLL profile type is still interested more in working as an individual contributor; the HHH will either want to head the company or play another sort of dominant role, such as principal investor/venture capitalist or investment banker in a boutique firm specializing in high technology IPOs (initial public offerings).

The HHH profile type whose Application of Expertise elevations are in the Application of Technology and the Theory Development and Conceptual Thinking business core functions is characterized by the same "outside the box" thinking that we see in the HLL profile type with these elevations. This HHH type is typically interested in new technologies that push the envelope of what is currently possible or even envisioned. As an HHH profile type, however, this person is also interested in making those dreams a reality and in building and running the business that will accomplish this.

Ivor Kleinman had held a series of jobs in various technical fields, working for video productions houses, a television studio, and a desktop publishing software development firm. In this last position he found himself increasingly interested in the software industry in general, beyond desktop publishing. He had an idea for a new, qualititatively different approach to solving a problem that plagued software developers and end users. He formed a partnership with an associate who had complementary skills, experience, and credibility; raised funds from investors; and started a successful business.

The HHH profile type whose Application of Expertise elevations are in the Application of Technology and the Creative Production business core functions is, again, like the HLL type with similar expertise interests, interested in the marriage of creativity and technology.

Richard Vega enjoyed virtually everything about the advertising business: the psychology of understanding what appeals to people, the

creativity and technical aspects of producing the artwork, the craft-
ing of advertising copy for maximum persuasive power. He also
wanted the power to control his own destiny and to be a player in
the advertising business. He recognized that the only people in his
field who made larger sums of money and who seemed to have real
power were those who went beyond being good at the trade of craft-
ing compelling advertising—they ran advertising agencies. Richard
determined that he would prefer to move up through management
in the well-established agency for which he worked rather than go-
ing out on his own, and over a period of several years he accom-
plished this goal.

The individual whose business career profile type includes Application of Expertise elevations in the Quantitative Analysis and the Theory Development and Conceptual Thinking business core functions
might develop a computer program that makes use of innovative analytical techniques to draw inferences about bond yield curves. The
person whose business career profile type is HHH, however, will want
to take this intellectual property and make it into a business rather
than simply publishing it in a professional journal.

In our experience, the HHH profile type whose Application of Expertise elevations are either in the Quantitative Analysis and the Creative Production functions or in the Theory Development and
Conceptual Thinking and the Creative Production functions tends to
find expression for Creative Production interests avocationally, with
either the Quantitative Analysis or the Theory Development and
Conceptual Thinking business core function dominating the career.
Apparently the gap between Creative Production and either of the
other two functions is so great that combining them in a single career
is rather difficult.

A cautionary note: We live in a country where one of the cultural
norms is "More is better"—more money, more power, more intellect,
more athletic ability, higher test scores. We want to emphasize that,
unlike taking the SATs, scoring high on everything on the *Business
Career Interest Inventory* is in no way better than any combination of
highs and lows. We have encountered many very successful executives
who are not HHH profile types. The idea behind this book is to help

you to find the best fit for your unique self, one that will help you grow into the person you have the potential to become. The number of high scores on the eight business core functions is completely irrelevant to that goal.

The HLL Business Career Profile Type

- ◆ *Application of Expertise:* High
- ◆ *Working with People:* Low
- ◆ *Control and Influence:* Low

Sometimes as a very rough cut of careers we think about two groups: managers (who get things done through other people) and individual contributors (who do things themselves). A hospital administrator is an example of the first group; a neurosurgeon would be an example of the second. As a manager's career progresses, the kind of work the person does changes and the size of the part of the organization he or she manages grows. The person who begins a career at General Electric as a financial analyst and ends it as a CFO is ultimately doing very different things (and has a vastly larger number of subordinates). Career development for the management career is characterized by authority over a larger number of people and control over a greater amount of organizational resources.

The individual contributor, by contrast, does much the same thing at the beginning of his or her career as at the end. The neurosurgeon is still doing surgery; a currency trader on Wall Street is still trading currencies. Individual contributors may become much more skillful at what they do, and the means of making that contribution may change with advances in technology, but the basic activity remains much the same. Development for the individual contributor career is characterized by a growing body of expertise that is seen as increasing in value by organizations that seek expert services.

The HLL is, perhaps not surprisingly, the business career profile type we most commonly see among people in individual contributor roles *who are happy with that role and are much less likely to want to move into management.* These people derive the most satisfaction simply from doing what they do best, without yearning to have other people working for them. In fact, HLL types, if they do move up the ladder into management, frequently experience their work as less and less satisfying.

> *Ray Seaman had been hired out of business school as an assistant brand manager for a large consumer packaged goods company. After doing his time as an assistant he got his own brand to manage, which he enjoyed and did quite successfully. Eventually he was promoted to group brand manager, and after several years in that position he received yet another promotion to category manager. A year into this position he came to see us for consultation, saying "I loved being a brand manager. I felt ownership of the product, it was creative work, which I loved, and you could see the outcome of your efforts in market share and profitability. Now I manage people who manage people who are brand managers. I spend all my time in meetings, and I'm a million miles away from the front line, from doing what I really liked doing. I find myself envying the people two or three levels down from me."*

Another common outcome for individual contributors who make the mistake (sometimes being forced into making it) of moving into management is, simply, failure. As many high-tech companies discovered in the boom years when they were growing rapidly and desperately needed managers, a great engineer does not necessarily make a great, or even an acceptably good, manager. The engineer would often be pressed hard to become a manager, was always enticed with more money, sometimes forced at the point of a pink slip (or being marked as not willing to "do what it takes" for the company's benefit).

Forcing people into positions they are not suited for and do not want works no better in an American computer company than it did in the Soviet Union. The result was unhappy, ineffective managers who should have been retained as happy, productive individual contributor engineers. Fortunately, the industry eventually recognized this problem and many companies instituted "professional tracks" in which individual contributors could rise in both status and salary *without having to manage anyone.* This was an immense relief both to those engineers and to the people who would have been (badly) managed by them. If you are a clear HLL profile type, it is important that you not buy into the notion that managing is better or more prestigious. You may, in fact, want to *explore* the role of manager but do so on a provisional basis. The data one gathers from actual life experience, if properly analyzed, is valuable assessment information that cannot be duplicated by any assessment inventory. The point here is that HLL profile types should not burn their bridges to their areas of professional expertise. Our experience has shown us that often the expert role for this profile holds a great deal of their work satisfaction.

If you are an HLL profile type, read the descriptions below of the HLL profiles concerning the specific business core function(s) on which your interest score was elevated for information about the kind of expertise you might be interested in applying in your work and what the implications are for that specific variation of the HLL profile. You may also want to reread the section(s) of Chapter 5 that describe the Application of Expertise business core function(s) in which you are interested.

We recommend that you read the other varieties of the HLL profile type as well, for two reasons. First, reading about closely allied types may help illuminate aspects of your interests of which you are currently not fully aware. It may also help you think about how to best work with people to whom the HLL profile type may apply (but due to elevation on a different business core function within the Application of Expertise dimension).

HLL with Application of Technology Elevated (ALL)

People for whom Application of Technology is their sole elevated business core function are often found in careers in which engineering or engineering-like work is the predominant activity, such as process engineering and industrial engineering. Of course, technologically sophisticated manufacturing companies are where you will find the highest numbers of ALL business career profile types: automotive manufacturers, high tech, oil and chemicals, and public utilities, for example. Technologically sophisticated service businesses such as medical care and telecommunications also attract large numbers of ALL profile types.

But ALL profile types are also found in consumer goods companies (Procter & Gamble employs more Ph.D. scientists than are on the combined science faculties of the Massachusetts Institute of Technology, Harvard, and the University of California, Berkeley), in low tech manufacturers, transportation companies, and hotels. The *activity* is what counts, and Application of Technology HLL profile types are happy to roll up their sleeves and get their hands dirty (figuratively speaking) in any setting where it is needed.

We should distinguish here between ALL profile types, who enjoy engineering-related activities, and scientists. Many scientists, of course, make use of technology in their work, but they are engaged in basic research, with a much greater emphasis on theory development and creativity than the ALL profile type. In addition, some scientists are relatively unconcerned with the practical implications or applications of their work, which are of great concern to the ALL profile type.

ALL profile types may be attracted to research and development *management,* but the attraction will be due to their wanting to have more impact on the direction of development as the technical leader in charge of the product and to strongly influence decisions going into its development, rather than wanting to be in charge of other people on the team. By contrast, they would be unlikely to aspire to be vice president for research and development at a Hewlett-Packard; that individual would be more likely to be an HLH or HHH profile type, with the Application of Technology business core function elevated and the Enterprise Control business core function strong as well.

Like other HLL profile types, ALL profile types are most likely to be satisfied in an individual contributor role where their advancement is measured by their taking on more and more challenging projects, being compensated more highly, and perhaps being recognized with titles that signify their being more senior, all without the responsibilities of management.

ALL profile types are interested in the way things work. Many people do not care at all about what's inside their personal computers. In fact, the PC revolution really took off only after graphic user interfaces like Windows made it possible for the average user to use the PC and know next to nothing about the disk operating system (DOS). ALL profile types, however, are *very* interested in what is going on inside the box. They may not be programmers, but they are nonetheless intrigued. Similarly, they may be interested in how their microwaves heat their leftovers, how magnetic resonance imaging (MRI) takes pictures of the brain at work, how genetic engineering is done, and so forth. (They may not, in fact, *know* any of these things, but they are likely to be interested in them.)

If they are working in business, ALL profile types are likely to be attracted to technologically more sophisticated products and services, and to the technical end of those businesses: to new product development, to information systems, to robotics and computer-assisted design and manufacture, to production planning and distribution systems. Commodity products, basic service management (such as restaurants), and professional services (such as law) are unlikely to appeal to ALL profile types.

ALL profile types may be found in certain types of technically oriented consulting (information technology, for example), depending on how low their interest in Influence Through Language and Ideas business core function is (if it is very low, the individual would probably not be comfortable making presentations to client companies). Some of the larger management consulting firms employ ALL profile types either to meet their internal needs or for selected work on certain client engagements.

Amelia Scott had tried her hand at several careers before discovering computer programming. She pursued a bachelor's degree in computer science at night while working for a major computer hardware manufacturer. She spent several years writing code for the hardware's operating system; then, wanting a change of scene (and wanting to keep her technical skill set at the cutting edge), she went on for a master's degree in computer science and moved over to a software design firm. At the time of that decision she considered getting an

MBA, but determined that it was the technical side of things she most enjoyed and chose the technical master's degree instead.

HLL with Quantitative Analysis Elevated (QLL)

Individuals for whom the Quantitative Analysis business core function is the only elevation enjoy using mathematics to solve problems. In a sense, the Quantitative Analysis HLL business career profile type is at one level of abstraction higher than the ALL profile type. If the Quantitative Analysis business core function stands alone, the person will enjoy analyzing a business's financial statements, using computer models to analyze the financial markets, analyzing the performance of specific companies, and so forth. There is a definite financial analysis bent to the QLL profile type, as differentiated from the engineering flavor associated with the ALL profile type.

We find QLL profile types in actuarial sciences, equities analysis (especially on the "buy side," working for investment management firms; "sell side" analysts often have more elevation in the Influence Through Language and Ideas business core function). We also see Quantitative Analysis HLL profile types as portfolio managers in these firms. They are found in accounting firms or in the treasurer's office of any sort of company, working as financial analysts for those companies; and in the treasury area of commericial banks.

They are comfortable with analysis and want to use it to solve interesting problems, not simply to compile and track data. QLL profile types are also found in business doing marketing research (vis-à-vis in brand management "marketing"). They are also occasionally found in trading positions, especially when the commodity being traded is technically complex (financial derivatives, foreign currencies, and so on).

We have also found QLL profile types in strategy consulting firms, and in firms specializing in information system consulting or economic forecasting. One problem these people may have is that many such firms have an "up or out" policy—the consultant *must* become a project manager or leave the firm (and the manager must, in turn, make the leap to developing business as a partner).

Like other HLL profile types, QLL profile types do best in organizations that have a technical track. Some management consulting firms do provide such an option and hire technical specialists, thus providing the HLL profile type with the opportunity to make a career without moving into management of the firm.

> *Francine Cole was a classic QLL profile type. She had studied economics as an undergraduate, then gone on for an MBA, concentrating in finance. On graduating she had gone to Wall Street as an analyst (she had chosen not to interview for corporate finance or mergers and acquisitions positions). After two years in investment banking she made a move to the buy side, accepting a position as an analyst with a premier investment management firm. After a few more years as an industry analyst she went on to manage one of the firm's mutual funds.*

HLL with Theory Development and Conceptual Thinking Elevated (TLL)

If the Quantitative Analysis HLL business career profile type is one level more abstract than the Application of Technology HLL profile type, the Theory Development and Conceptual Thinking HLL profile type is still another level more abstract. TLL profile types enjoy activities involving working with theory and strategy at a highly conceptual level. They are interested in the development and application of new theoretical models to business situations and in bringing theory from other disciplines such as economics, sociology, psychology, population ecology, political science, and anthropology to bear on thinking about business.

TLL profile types may in fact be academics, found on the faculties of business schools, or in think tanks. In management consulting firms they are active in developing new frameworks for thinking about clients' business problems, and if their insights are consistently useful and the firms can support them, they may enjoy long and productive careers in consulting. TLL profile types are often attracted to more academically oriented consulting firms, where more Ph.D.s and M.D.s than people with MBAs may be walking the halls.

When we have found TLL profile types working in business, they often report feeling "different" from their colleagues. This feeling is well founded, because they *are* different. A challenge that TLL profile types often face is in translating their thinking into the language of their fellow workers, in working to fit into the dominant culture sufficiently well for their ideas to be given credence and to gain acceptance. Otherwise they run the risk of being seen as too theoretical and "ivory tower."

When we see TLL profile types they have often considered going back to graduate school for a master's degree or even a doctorate in economics or in some other academic discipline. If they are in business school or out in the business world, they feel a pull toward the theory of the work, toward academic pursuits. Like some of the students we have worked with who are pursuing joint law and business degrees, the TLL profile type often talks about feeling "neither fish nor fowl."

> *Michael Kennedy had graduated summa cum laude from college and near the top of his class in business school. He had his pick of offers from top management strategy consulting firms, investment banks, investment management firms, and strategic planning departments in top corporations, all of whom pursued him aggressively. They promised substantial financial compensation and the opportunity for him to "write his own ticket" in terms of the kinds of projects on which he might want to work. He struggled with the decision, but ultimately determined that he was, at heart, an academic. He turned down all of those offers, studied for his doctorate, and joined the faculty at a top business school.*

HLL with Creative Production Elevated (CLL)

HLL business career profile types for whom the Creative Production business core function is the only elevation are the people who bring the worlds of art and business together. They are commercial artists and designers of clothing, furniture, and packaging. Creative Production HLL profile types are found doing layouts for magazines or corporate annual reports, writing copy for advertisements, and working with engineers to design aesthetically attractive products of any sort. They are found in publishing, especially of trade books and magazines, in direct mail catalog production, and in the entertainment industry.

On the service side of business, CLL profile types may work in event planning, trade show display design, architecture, entertainment, and commercial interior design; as creatives in advertising agencies; and in other service industries in which creativity plays an important role. Whether in a service business or manufacturing, CLL profile types may be found engaged in the creation and design of new services and products.

In fact, CLL profile types may be found in companies in any industry, but they are attending to the aesthetics that are part of that company's success. They may design the logo for a manufacturer of industrial fasteners or supervise the layout of the catalog for a company that produces electrical equipment.

> *Ted Garsh was very successful in the field of consumer goods marketing. He had progressed to the position of group manager, found his work quite intellectually stimulating (which was very important to him), and enjoyed the lifestyle that his income and position provided. He had gone into marketing because he felt that it was the most creative of the various business functions he was qualified for after business school, and found that it did indeed satisfy much of his desire to "think outside the box." Missing for him, however, was the crucial element of pure creativity. He considered leaving business entirely to pursue a career as a writer, but ultimately determined to limit the energy and time he invested in his primary career objective in order to free up energy for writing as a serious avocational pursuit.*

Ted is a good example of someone whose work is almost good enough in meeting his need to express a core interest (that is, it contains some elements of that interest and is not antithetical to it in other ways) and who chooses to express that interest more fully avocationally.

A major challenge for HLL profile types with a dominant high score in Creative Production is to find enough creativity in their careers. Many business projects follow the pattern of requiring high creativity in early stages but later reach a steady state where innovation takes a backseat to assuring optimal day-to-day performance. In such situations, the CLL profile type often finds him- or herself restless and looking around for new creative challenges. High Creative Production individuals are more likely to find satisfaction in project-oriented (rather than steady-state) work with shorter time horizons.

The search for creative opportunities is likely to be a lifelong career quest. Although we have not yet conducted research to verify our observation, we see individuals with this profile type as likely to change jobs frequently in the course of a career. (This observation may be rendered moot in coming years, as more and more business professionals of all types will have careers characterized by frequent job changes.) In our consultations with MBA students, we have found that high Creative Production individuals often have considered careers altogether different from business before making the decision to enter an MBA program. Instead of saying that they struggled with choosing among the University of Chicago, Stanford, and Harvard, they are more likely to say that their choice was between Harvard and a graduate program in journalism, or between getting an MBA and going directly into the entertainment business.

HLL with Combinations of Application of Expertise Core Functions Elevated

There are many possible combinations of the four Application of Expertise functions, but we have found only a few with enough frequency to be able to comment knowledgeably.

One of the most frequent combinations, in our experience, is the HLL business career profile type with the Application of Technology and the Quantitative Analysis business core functions elevated together. This combination is, in a sense, "the financial analyst meets the engineer," the person who is knowledgeable about the technical aspects of a project but also concerned with the bottom-line implications. Still more of an individual contributor than manager, this combination may be found in certain technically oriented consulting firms that are also definitely business driven (such as firms that specialize in consulting about inventory and distribution planning, information technology, or energy resources).

This type is likely to be attracted to technically cutting-edge companies in which that technology is key to the companies' success, such as computer microprocessor manufacturers, software design firms, telecommunications companies, computers and computer peripherals, and high-tech medical equipment. These sorts of companies provide Application of Technology and Quantitative Analysis HLL profile types with interesting challenges, recognize the importance of their contributions, and reward them appropriately. Another possibility for this type would be working as an equities analyst covering, for example, part of the high-tech/telecommunications industry sector.

Steve Derkazarian had been an applied mathematics major as an undergraduate and had worked as an engineer for a high-tech manufacturing company for two years before pursuing a graduate business degree. After getting his MBA he considered obtaining a doctorate in business and making a career teaching in an MBA program. Unlike Michael Kennedy, Steve determined that he was not sufficiently academically inclined to make that career satisfying over the long term. Combining his undergraduate degree and previous work experience in engineering with his MBA, he was sought after by a number of high-tech firms, and took a high-profile fast-track position as a product manager with a very successful, fast-growing computer hardware firm.

Another combination we see fairly frequently is the HLL profile type with the Quantitative Analysis and the Theory Development and Conceptual Thinking business core functions elevated. The Quantitative Analysis function tends to predominate in this type in the sense that it is most visible to the outside world. Other people easily notice the facility with numbers and quantitative data analysis; the interest in theory and abstract concepts is less easily observable. So the HLL profile type with the Quantitative Analysis and the Theory Development and Conceptual Thinking functions elevated is analogous to a blended color such as blue-green, in which green is modified by blue (but, importantly, is not pure green). We might find someone of this type developing computer models (Quantitative Analysis) to perform meta-analyses of various economic forecasting measures (Theory Development and Conceptual Thinking). We might also find this type teaching in the economics department of a university and doing research in the application of game theory to capital markets.

Angelo Depina specialized in doing international risk analysis for a large investment management firm. He developed and used computer models to assess social and political factors that could impact foreign exchange rates and the economies of other countries. His work combined his interest and skill in quantitative analysis with his broader, more "big picture" interest in conceptual thinking and developing theories.

The HLL profile type with the Application of Technology and the Theory Development and Conceptual Thinking business core functions elevated is a relatively unusual combination. This person is interested in technology, and in new technologies, but is more "out there," almost in the realm of science fiction, thinking about what the next generation of computers will do, how the Internet may be used when . . . , or how cellular telephone communication would be altered if . . . , or how the perfection of controlled nuclear fusion will affect. . . . In writing about this profile we must omit parts of the scenarios because, by definition, they do not yet exist. If they did, they would not be what the HLL profile type with the Application of Technology and the Theory Development and Conceptual Thinking functions elevated is working on. Thomas Edison and Alexander Graham Bell are examples of people who come to mind who might have had this profile type.

Michael Allender was a phenomenally bright computer scientist who worked for an engineering consulting firm that did work for the Department of Defense that was truly beyond state of the art. Even at his firm, which was populated by uniformly extremely bright people, he was considered to be exceptionally gifted. Michael preferred to work on projects that were just in their inception, with so much to be defined that he was not restricted in his creative joining of theory and technology.

The HLL profile type with the Application of Technology and the Creative Production business core functions elevated wants to use technology in the service of his or her creativity. Much as the Quantitative Analysis function predominates in the HLL profile type in which the Quantitative Analysis and the Theory Development and Conceptual Thinking functions are elevated, the Creative Production function is usually the driver in this type. You could find the designer who became so enamored of computer-assisted design software that she learned programming and became a developer of software for this purpose. More likely, though, you would find the person who is expert at using that software in the creative enterprise. The enterprise itself could be desktop publishing, retouching or otherwise altering photographic images, doing animation or special effects for the entertainment industry, or any other creative enterprise.

> *Nate Fenster was an architect whose specialty was designing public buildings. Although the end product was always hard-copy blueprints for the builders to use, Nate used extremely sophisticated computer technology in both the design and marketing of his work. For example, he worked with software applications that would allow him to, on screen, allow his prospective clients to walk through the structure in three dimensions as it would appear after construction.*

The LHL Business Career Profile Type

- ◆ *Application of Expertise:* Low
- ◆ *Working with People:* High
- ◆ *Control and Influence:* Low

The LHL business career profile type finds working with people on a day-to-day basis to be critical to his or her enjoyment of a job. This is not someone for whom having and utilizing special expertise is of great interest, nor is it someone who wants to run the show. Rather, the LHL profile type enjoys managing and developing people.

If an elevation in the Counseling and Mentoring business core function is the reason the underlying Working with People dimension is designated as high, we would expect to find someone for whom the role of adviser is appealing, someone who takes a personal interest in employees and colleagues. This individual may be drawn to aspects of business work that allow that personal interest to be expressed as an important part of the job.

John Merotta had worked in several different business functions before settling into the outplacement industry. In his previous positions he had enjoyed helping people think through their career questions and personal problems. As an outplacement counselor he was able to make this the meat of his work. Perhaps because his motivation to help clients was so sincere, he was also highly successful in business development.

Doris Molina worked as a successful human resource development consultant, specializing in an industry undergoing great change (health care). She was adept at helping people cope with the feelings that accompany upheavals such as reorganizations and downsizings. Doris worked on her own and had no desire to build a consulting business with associates to manage. She had declined several offers from client organizations to go to work for them as an employee, preferring to concentrate on helping the people in the organization without having a reporting relationship with them.

Many LHL profile types with the Counseling and Mentoring business core function elevated find themselves, like Doris, drawn to industries where the mission is doing good, such as health care, assisted living for the elderly, and education. Others enjoy their work in manufacturing or in other service environments (such as banking or transportation) and in any function, whether operations management, finance, marketing, or human resource management. Whatever the industry or nominal "function," however, the aspect of the work they enjoy most is the counseling, mentoring, and relationship-building. Individuals with a high Counseling and Mentoring scale score, regardless of other features of their profile, often see relationships as one of the most important payoffs of their professional careers. When they look back on their careers over a period of time, the most important landmarks are likely to be meaningful relationships that have endured even after they left a particular organization.

It would, of course, be difficult for this type of person to find a comfortable home in an organization in which the culture itself was inimical to such good-hearted personal interest. We have seen several refugees from one such organization (which, for obvious reasons, shall go unnamed), famous for its cutthroat politics. These people left for many reasons, but a common denominator was their difficulty coping with the organizational culture.

Just as some HLL profile types who are elevated in the Creative Production business core function satisfy that creative impulse outside of their work, some LHL profile types who have the Counseling and Mentoring function elevated find expression for those altruistic aspects of themselves avocationally. These people are drawn to doing volunteer work in their nonworking hours, often activities of a counseling or mentoring nature such as being a Big Brother or Sister, being a "buddy" for someone with AIDS, tutoring illiterate adults, or working with someone who is physically or otherwise handicapped. Others may work less directly with the end client—behind the scenes in a soup kitchen or doing fund-raising for a charitable organization.

The LHL profile type with the Managing People business core function elevated is likely to be somewhat different. These individuals enjoy the day-to-day aspects of people management, assigning and supervising work, managing work flow in a department, motivating the people who report to them, and providing evaluative feedback. They enjoy getting involved in the nitty-gritty aspects of the operation, not to control it, nor to bring their particular expertise to bear on it, but simply to get the job done. They want to use their people's talents to maximum effect and derive satisfaction from that process. In a sense this type is what many of us think of as the old-fashioned line manager.

Jane McHale headed the finance and control area in a small company. She enjoyed the daily work of her department and managing the people within it. She was not, however, seen as overconcerned about people's feelings or their personal development. If anything, she was too task oriented, and had to overcome other people's perception that she didn't care about her employees.

Managers like Jane who have a strong interest in the Managing People business core function but a low interest in the Counseling and Mentoring function want to get the most from their subordinates but are less interested in the opportunity to develop people. Their interest is in managing people, not in counseling them. Elevation in *both* of these functions means something different from elevation in either one alone. The LHL profile type with both business core functions high is the person who wants to manage the front-line operation *and* who derives considerable satisfaction from the counselor or coach role that managers sometimes take on.

A strong interest in the Managing People business core function, *regardless of other profile features,* is one of our indicators for what we sometimes refer to as a "pure management" career model. If your score on this business core function scale is high, you should refer back to the Managing People section of Chapter 5 for a discussion of the implications of this finding.

THE LLH BUSINESS CAREER PROFILE TYPE

- ♦ *Application of Expertise:* Low
- ♦ *Working with People:* Low
- ♦ *Control and Influence:* High

We don't often see the LLH business career profile type with only the Influence Through Language and Ideas business core function elevated. When we do, the individual is typically engaged in an activity in which interpersonal communication plays the overwhelmingly predominant role, such as pure sales, arbitration and mediation, media training, speech writing, public and investor relations, and some areas of law.

> *Ken Hicks loved nothing more than to exert influence, whether operating behind the scenes on a committee of a charitable organization or getting a reporter from the* New York Times *to interview and run a story about one of his clients. Ken was not interested in personal power per se, preferring to influence events through other people.*

Much more common is the LLH profile type with the Enterprise Control business core function elevated or both functions elevated. With these profile elevations, the LLH profile type is the person we frequently see at the very top of businesses, whether large or small.

These people are, or want to be, CEOs, deal makers, top executives, managing directors or partners of management consulting firms and investment banks, and entrepreneurs.

> *Frank Hollis was described by one of his employees as "unbelievably aggressive." He was a financier and entrepreneur, someone who had to be in control of everything in his life, and had spent his life amassing the wealth and power to do so.*

If both the Enterprise Control and the Influence Through Language and Ideas business core function scale scores are elevated (as they often are), the Enterprise Control function dominates and the Influence Through Language and Ideas function is the means by which the individual gains and asserts control. As the Influence Through Language and Ideas function scale score rises, there may be more of an emphasis on business development, especially in professional services firms (such as in banking, consulting, law and accounting). However, even presidents and CEOs have to sell their ideas within their organizations. In fact, one common cause for career derailment is the mistaken belief that good ideas automatically rise to the top, so that there is no need for the individual to carefully plan an internal marketing and sales campaign for an idea.

LLH profile types are not content to work in the engine room of the ship, or even in the communications center. They want to be on the bridge, in command, setting the course and ensuring that it is followed. They want to be where the action is, engaging with customers or clients, performing transactions, doing deals, making sales. This is equally true for the person who owns a small printing company, the director of a top consulting firm or investment bank, and the CEO of a *Fortune 50* corporation.

LLH profile types tend to be highly dominant, aggressive individuals who want to have an impact. They can be impatient with people who are not as results driven (and personally driven) as they are. In fact, LLH profile types for whom the Enterprise Control business core function is very high often have trouble, especially in the early stages of their careers, when they are not running the show. We often tell such MBA students that they would make wonderful partners in management consulting firms and in Wall Street banks, if only they could get themselves hired right out of business school into those jobs!

> *Joe Cruise was fortunate to find the perfect position for himself. One of the regular recruiters at his business school was a large holding company that had some forty companies in its portfolio. Each year the firm hired a new graduate student to be the assistant to the CEO for a year. After that year the assistant would be installed as president of one of the portfolio companies, with immediate and full responsibility for the management of the company.*

Failing that, unfortunately, they may be in for some rough sledding along the way. Strong LLH profile types may need to remind themselves that it's a long game, and that keeping their eye on the prize, restraining themselves from "swinging for the fence" too early may be wise.

> *Chung Park graduated from business school and, against all advice and conventional wisdom, went into business for himself. The enterprise failed, and he then attempted to start another business, which also failed. (Chung had no experience managing a business of any size or at any level of maturity prior to getting his MBA.) He was in the process of going down this same road yet a third time when we met with him and were able to help him rein in his desires for immediate CEO status.*

At any stage of career, the strong LLH profile type may have to be able to restrain his or her drive and ambition, to modulate the expression of that need for dominance—to "control the need for control." Otherwise, too much of a good thing can cross over the line into being, or at least being perceived as, ruthlessness.

> *David Mann was a manager in a manufacturing company who ran into trouble because he was unable, or unwilling, to control his dominance and aggressiveness. He was relentless in pushing his own agenda forward, was a poor listener, and was unwilling to compromise. These qualities had carried him forward to a point, but*

ultimately impaired his effectiveness to such a degree that he was terminated.

Another note about the LLH profile type has to do with delegating, giving up control. Whether you are an entrepreneur or a manager or executive at Exxon, delegating responsibility and authority is a necessity if you and/or your business are to grow. The annals of business are filled with stories of bright, aggressive entrepreneurs who took a good idea, made it into a business, grew that business, and then killed it because of their unwillingness or inability to give up control. The occupational hazard for the careers of LLH profile types, then, is failing to modulate their need for control and being over-aggressive or not appropriately delegating control to others.

Andy Coulter and his father started a company literally in their garage, having bought patent rights to a new device and then radically changing how it was used and to what purpose. Over the years the company grew to about $30 million in annual sales. Andy's father had retired from the business and urged him to bring in professional management (neither Andy nor his father had any formal business training). Andy had great difficulty giving up any significant measure of control, and did so only when the business was in such trouble that he felt that he had no choice.

THE HHL BUSINESS CAREER PROFILE TYPE

+ *Application of Expertise:* High
+ *Working with People:* High
+ *Control and Influence:* Low

Depending on the area of expertise and whether the emphasis is on counseling and mentoring or on managing people, the HHL business career profile type can be either quite common or rather unusual. If your profile type is HHL, you should refer to the paragraphs in the HHH and HLL sections in which we discuss your particular Application of Expertise elevation(s). Bear in mind that the HHH profile type with your Application of Expertise elevation(s) may be more interested than you are in becoming a CEO, while the HLL profile type may be more interested than you are in remaining in an individual contributor role. Nonetheless, those sections combine to provide a detailed description of the implications of various Application of Expertise business core function elevations.

HHL profile types are generally experts who become managers and love it, or who want to become managers and, when they do, will love it. Engineers who move into project management are often HHL profile types with elevations in the Application of Technology and the Managing People business core functions. Without more elevation in the Enterprise Control function, they will probably be less attracted to general management, in that at a certain point they will be too far away from the engineering work that they enjoy. But project leadership will appeal.

Similarly, financial analysts, portfolio managers, traders, and the like who become satisfied and successful group managers are likely to be HHL profile types with elevations in the Quantitative Analysis and the Managing People business core functions.

Paul Buller had worked in financial services as an equities analyst and portfolio manager before moving into a management role. As a manager he enjoyed being able to leverage his knowledge of the financial markets by working through other portfolio managers. He also enjoyed, somewhat to his initial surprise, the everyday aspects of managing, such as running effective meetings, making policy decisions, and working with his subordinates to improve their investment skills.

The career life cycle of the management consultant follows a predictable course, although the titles at each stage may vary from firm to firm. Cynics (and people who unsuccessfully sought careers in this highly competitive field) put it this way: First you do the work, then you tell other people how to do the work, then you just sell the work. The fact is, of course, that people in management consulting careers work extraordinarily hard during all three stages, from consultant to project manager to partner level. The substance of the work, however, does change at each stage, and the individual who makes a wonderful consultant may make a terrible project manager or partner.

Consultants who are HHL profile types will probably find the transition to manager easier and more rewarding than consultants who do not have an inherent interest in the day-to-day aspects of managing people. As project managers they now have several jobs: still doing a good deal of the intellectual heavy lifting and analysis while attempting to make life as enjoyable as possible for the consultants working on the team and helping them to learn and develop their consulting skills.

> *Todd Rohrer was a mechanical engineer before earning an MBA and going into management consulting. His excellent analytical skills carried him forward to the project manager level, where he was very successful by virtue of his skills in working with people, leading teams, and acting as a mentor to more junior consultants. He developed a following in the firm of other consultants who wanted to work with him on projects and of partners in the firm who wanted him to manage work with their client companies, and was eventually promoted to partner level himself.*

People working in the creative side of advertising who go on to manage those departments are likely to be HHL profile types with elevation in the Creative Production business core function and in the Working with People dimension business core functions. For many creatives, the idea of moving into management seems like a gigantic headache, with all the meetings and budgets and just plain people to manage (people like themselves!); but the HHL profile type finds those aspects of the management job challenging, interesting, and appealing. Without elevation of the Enterprise Control business core function, the creative manager is less likely to strike out and set up his or her own advertising agency, but will enjoy managing a department within an agency.

> *Fran Ellis, whose career we will explore more deeply in Chapter 8, is an example of someone high in both the Creative Production and the Managing People business core functions. Fran had a somewhat unusual pattern of career development. Rather than having an opportunity in management grow out of her success in a creative individual contributor role, she focused on the creative side after proving*

herself in management. After years as a successful marketing manager, Fran realized that her enthusiasm was always higher when working with the marketing aspects of new product ideas. She realized that new product development was closer to her core interest and, over a period of time, was able to move her career in that direction.

Academicians who become deans, and scientists who move into management of research and development, are other examples of HHL profile types. Again, at top levels (president of a major university, vice president for research and development at a large corporation) we would expect to see the Enterprise Control business core function elevated, but at a level of management closer to the actual teaching or research, the HHL profile type would be a good match.

Gail Sunwood was a scientist with a Ph.D. in molecular biology working for a small biotechnology firm. Unlike most of her fellow scientists and technicians, she had good interpersonal skills and a genuine interest in managing and developing the people who worked in her laboratory. These qualities were recognized by the CEO of the company and she was promoted to chief scientist, heading up the firm's research and development efforts.

Stan McCoy was a highly regarded professor of economics in a small college. What he enjoyed most in his work was the counseling and mentoring aspect of dealing with students, more so than the scholarly research and writing required for tenure. He chose to move into administration, becoming dean of students at the college. This allowed him to keep what he enjoyed most about his professorial position while learning to manage the student services departments that fell under his control (which he enjoyed doing). As an added bonus, Stan was able to continue to teach in the economics department as an adjunct faculty member.

In general, then, if you are an individual contributor of some sort but with an HHL business career profile type (with the Managing People business core function wholly or partially responsible for the Working with People dimension being high), you should consider management as a career goal. You might talk with your manager or with someone else in management with whom you have a close relationship—perhaps with a human resource department professional—about this career path. You may decide that you prefer the individual contributor role, but if you are an HHL profile type do your "due diligence" and at least explore the option of management.

A strong interest in the Managing People business core function, *regardless of other profile features,* is one of our indicators for what we sometimes refer to as a "pure management" career model. If your score on this business core function scale is high, you should refer back to the Managing People section of Chapter 5 for a discussion of the implications of this finding.

The HHL profile type with *only* the Counseling and Mentoring business core function elevated is much less common in business. This may be the person who has no interest in managing but for whom relationships within the company, developed and maintained over time, are very important. If this sounds like you, it may be difficult for you to consider leaving a company, even if you think it makes sense to do so, because of the relationships you would be leaving behind. If you are the manager of someone like this, you should take care not to disrupt the individual's personal work relationships (if possible).

> *Nancy Elliot was an expert in the field of precious metals trading. She had no interest in managing other people, but was a wonderful teacher and mentor to people new to the trading desk. She was fiercely loyal to her colleagues and customers, and developed close personal relationships with many of them over the years. When she retired she received calls, letters, and gifts from all over the world— from her customers, the people she had trained, coworkers, and even competitors.*

Another possibility for the HHL profile type with the Counseling and Mentoring business core function as the sole elevation is for an avocational expression of that interest in helping people (like the LHL profile type)—working on a hotline, coaching a soccer team, working with disadvantaged children, or the like. (We might add to this list, "parenting your own children"!)

Many people talk to us about their wish for a mentor—someone who will show them the ropes and help them think through knotty problems, make tough career choices, and understand the politics of an organization. Unfortunately, mentors are in short supply relative to the demand for them. The HHL profile type with the Counseling and Mentoring business core function elevated may be that mentor, the guide to whom more junior members of the department turn for wise counsel. This would not be a formal role; formalizing something like a mentor relationship is like planning to be spontaneous. But experts who want to advise and coach without the headaches they see as being part of formally managing are often HHL profile types with an elevation on the Counseling and Mentoring function.

Tom Wandell was a young investment analyst, very bright but quite unsophisticated in the ways of the world of business. He was, however, a keen observer, eager to learn, and an appealing fellow. Over the years he formed a succession of mentor relationships with elders in his business, learning from them both technically and politically. Eventually, he evolved into serving as a mentor himself to newcomers to the business who needed a helping hand. He was never interested in managing per se but very much enjoyed the role of counselor.

We also find HHL profile types with the Counseling and Mentoring business core function elevated in the role of corporate trainer (assuming that the Influence Through Language and Ideas function is not extremely low). These people can be either internal to the company or external consultants, but with an area of expertise (such as managing change, diversity, sexual harassment) that they teach.

Jerry Walsch had worked as a psychotherapist for many years before moving into corporate training. As a gay man he had special credibility (and personal knowledge) in the area of managing diversity, and he developed a successful program for training managers on this topic.

Theresa Aboud, by contrast, had gone into an analyst program with an investment bank after college, where she had done very well. She was admitted to a top-tier business school and was pursued by Wall Street banks and management consulting firms. She made the difficult decision to turn down those offers, with their prestige and compensation, in favor of work with a consulting firm that specialized in training and development.

We do not want to leave the impression that HHL profile types with the Counseling and Mentoring business core function high who are interested in training are limited to human resource development. Other people with this type find satisfaction teaching marketing, finance, operations management, computer programming, using program applications—whatever their expertise happens to be, as long as there are people interested in learning it.

Alexis Conroy had worked as a middle school teacher before the boom in the use of personal computers. She was an early "techie" and began teaching friends how to use their programs. From that point she moved into doing training on evenings and weekends for a PC retailer. Finally she gave up her day job as a teacher and went to work for a firm that specialized in training other companies' employees in the use of various software programs.

THE LHH BUSINESS CAREER PROFILE TYPE

- *Application of Expertise:* Low
- *Working with People:* High
- *Control and Influence:* High

We think of the LHH business career profile type as the classic general manager, someone who probably does not have a strongly developed identity as an expert in a particular area but who finds the general manager role immensely satisfying because of the very nature of the work, which is *general.* Some salespeople can very successfully sell certain products or services and are disasters at selling others, while other salespeople can sell just about anything with equal enthusiasm and success. Similarly, some general managers can manage successfully only in certain business functions or industries, while others could be just about as happy and successful anywhere they go. This latter characterization fits the LHH profile type. LHH profile types enjoy the *process* of managing, with less concern for what the company does. John Sculley, for example, was the CEO of both Pepsi and Apple Computer, two rather different products.

LHH profile types want to be CEOs, and want to get there through working with people (rather than through having a brilliant idea and the sheer drive to advance it). LHH profile types enjoy managing and leading groups, are comfortable handling conflict and competition, and recognize that their success ultimately depends on their ability to help others succeed.

> *Kenneth Welding was the head of a major division in an investment management firm, with several department heads reporting to him. Kenneth freely admitted that most of the people working for him, including his indirect reports, knew more about the investment process than he did. His strength was in hiring the best people and then in getting those people to perform to their full potential.*

In the early stages of their careers, LHH profile types are attracted to and excel at project management and product management, or, if they are consumer goods oriented, brand management. Unlike individual contributors, however, as they move up and control larger shares of the pyramid—more or larger projects, groups of related products, whole categories of brands—they become increasingly satisfied. They do not feel as if they are getting too far away from the work they enjoy. Running a larger operation is just as satisfying as running a smaller one, only more challenging and more rewarding.

The LHH profile type wants to run things, but is relatively unconcerned with how he or she reaches that position of responsibility. LHH profile types often say to us quite directly that they don't care whether they go up the marketing elevator, the finance elevator, the information systems elevator, or any other. They simply want to move up to a general management level as quickly as possible. If you are an LHH profile type, this has several implications.

First, select an organization that is driven by your chosen function (Procter & Gamble, for example, is known as a marketing driven company). Go where your function is the head of the dog, not the tail. This can be a relatively easy issue to research. Look at the backgrounds of top management over the history of the organization and note the functions that they represented before joining the ranks of general management. Second, if possible choose a company and industry where you have a competitive advantage, or at least no disadvantage. Don't go to work for a firm that manufactures supercomputers or high-tech medical equipment if you are not an engineer, for example. (Some technology firms, however, are very much marketing driven. Do your homework; don't rely on stereotypes.) Third, choose a function where you have a competitive advantage. This may or may not be a traditional function where you have a skill or experience advantage, by the way; it will certainly be a function where your core interests are congruent with the work.

A strong interest in the Managing People business core function, *regardless of other profile features,* is one of our indicators for what we sometimes refer to as a "pure management" career model. If your score on this business core function scale is high, you should refer back to the Managing People section of Chapter 5 for a discussion of the implications of this finding.

Thus far we have been talking about LHH profile types for whom an elevation in the Managing People business core function was at least partially responsible for the Working with People dimension's being high and for whom an elevation in the Enterprise Control function was at least partially responsible for the Control and Influence dimension's being high. This is by far the most common combination in LHH profile types. Occasionally, however, we see people whose sole Working with People dimension elevation is in the Counseling and Mentoring function and whose sole Control and Influence dimension elevation is in the Influence Through Language and Ideas function.

This LHH profile type may find a home in marketing communication or pure sales, depending on what is being sold. Remember that the Counseling and Mentoring business core function is associated with some element of altruism, so these individuals are unlikely to be interested in or successful at selling anything they do not believe in and do not feel is ultimately of value to people and the world. Advertising is usually not a good match over the long term because the nature of the business is to promote whatever accounts are landed, whether the client company sells a cure for cancer or something that causes it.

Kit Neary had worked with emotionally disturbed children before moving into a career in the sales of medical equipment. In talking about her career shift, she made it clear that she would not have made the change if it had been to selling office furniture or fax machines, regardless of the commissions involved.

Elevation in the Counseling and Mentoring and the Enterprise Control business core functions is another uncommon pattern, one we have seen primarily among people who run some sort of human service agency or business. Exactly what the organization does seems less important to these individuals than that it does some kind of good for people, for the environment, etc. They may go in a particular direction because of a personal reason (concern for the elderly, for example) or just because their previous training and experience made it a natural fit for them.

Brian Kelly had a background in management, including human resource management, before he started an outplacement service firm. He was motivated to "do well by doing good," and built a large and very successful business.

Another relatively unusual group is that of people whose sole Working with People dimension elevation is in the Managing People business core function and whose sole Control and Influence dimension elevation is in the Influence Through Language and Ideas function. One example of this profile would be people who are interested in moving into sales *management* from an initial role in direct sales.

Many salespeople would never be interested in sales management, for several reasons. The first is that they prize the autonomy of their positions, having a very loose reporting relationship and the freedom to organize their work schedules as they see fit. No one cares how they do what they do as long as they bring in the numbers. The second is that selling is an endeavor in which you can keep score. If you brought in the sales, it is clear and indisputable. There is no need to self-promote or politick; you can point to the numbers. Like portfolio management, it is a wholly meritocratic function. Also, you don't have to depend on anyone else for your success. As long as you have a good product (or service) to sell and timely delivery, you are on your own. Contrast this with being a middle manager working to implement a new inventory control system that may be opposed by another faction in the company and that depends on the hard work, competence, and cooperation of a whole team of people. Finally, successful salespeople often make substantially more money than their managers, and are typically strongly motivated by earning potential.

There are people, however, who despite all of the above reasons are interested in sales management. These people are likely to be the LHH profile types with elevations in the Managing People and the Influence Through Language and Ideas functions.

> *Brett LaPlante was a very successful salesman in the software industry. He enjoyed his independence, his compensation, and his clear "star" status. After a time, however, he determined to try his hand at management. Despite a lower level of compensation and the fact that he found managing considerably more difficult than selling, he stayed with it until he developed his skills sufficiently for him to succeed in management.*

THE HLH BUSINESS CAREER PROFILE TYPE

- *Application of Expertise:* High
- *Working with People:* Low
- *Control and Influence:* High

Like the LLH and LHH profile types, most HLH business career profile types want to be captains of whatever ships they may be on (assuming that they have some elevation on the Enterprise Control business core function rather than on the Influence Through Language and Ideas function alone). But unlike the LLH and LHH profile types, their route to the top is likely to involve using some sort of expert knowledge, at least in their early career stages. Also unlike LHH and LLH profile types, it usually *does* matter to HLH profile types what business they are in. The LHH and LLH profile types are the "universal donors" of general managers and CEOs. The HLH profile type is probably more interested in industries or businesses that in some way involve his or her area of expertise, whatever that is.

Unlike the HLL profile type, for whom the expert/individual contributor role is the driving career interest, the HLH profile type (who is elevated on the Enterprise Control business core function rather than on the Influence Through Language and Ideas function alone) wants to *run* something. Thus, the person with the Application of Technology and the Enterprise Control functions elevated may be the engineer who dreams of owning his or her own company, or of moving up to the top of the organization in which he or she currently works. The HLH profile type with the Quantitative Analysis function (and, possibly, either the Application of Technology or the Theory Development and Conceptual Thinking function) elevated may be one of the few who become directors in management consulting firms.

HLH profile types become CEOs and general managers in companies in which their expertise and, more important, their *interest* in an area of expertise meld with their interest in Control and Influence to create a formidable combination.

Paul Caswell had received a degree in industrial engineering and had worked in production facilities before studying business in an MBA program. After graduating, he founded a consulting firm that specialized in helping client companies with problems in the areas of production and distribution. Most of the people he hired into the firm also had engineering and business degrees, combining their areas of expertise and interest in Control and Influence.

Unlike LHH profile types (or HHH profile types), the HLH profile type is not oriented toward working with people in a direct line management fashion. HLH profile types are often more interested in the *strategy* of the business than in the day-to-day operations. They are unlikely to be found "managing by wandering around," being more interested in plotting the course of the business. This character-istic has implications for the kind of organizational structure that will provide the best fit for the HLH profile type, namely, one in which there is a president or chief operating officer under the HLH profile type who is the CEO. That structure will provide the HLH profile type with a layer of insulation from the daily operational affairs and allow him or her to concentrate on the bigger picture and on business strategy. This is also true at the level of divisional vice president. A COO analog will make the vice president position a much better fit for the HLH profile type who occupies it.

There is one problem here for HLH profile types who have not yet reached a level where they can have that operations manager working under them. They may still be rising through the ranks themselves, or they may be working in a startup in which (as is the case in most startups) everyone does a little bit of everything. The only solutions are for the HLH profile type either to have as a partner someone whose interest in the Managing People business core function is strong or to tough out those early years.

Like the LLH and HHH profile types, HLH profile types may have difficulty controlling their desire for control until they are in a position to attain it, making the early stage of their careers difficult. Moreover, it may be difficult for them later on in their careers if they have not reached the level of power and control to which they aspire.

If the Influence Through Language and Ideas business core func-tion is elevated *without* the Enterprise Control function, the picture is, again, somewhat different. Here the HLH profile type does not want to run the show but to influence it, often by making the deals. This type of HLH profile type is more transaction oriented, inter-ested more in business development and selling than in being the CEO. Because of the high Application of Expertise dimension, the transactions are likely to involve the person's particular expertise (compare the LLH profile type with the Influence Through Language and Ideas function alone elevated). This is a combination found at the higher levels of many professional service firms such as invest-ment banks, management consulting firms, and public accounting firms (although senior professionals in these settings often have En-terprise Control elevated as well).

Stuart Hamel was a partner in the mergers and acquisitions group of a Wall Street investment bank. A consummate deal maker, he had risen to this level after working in the trenches doing financial analysis on other people's deals. He had no real interest in a senior management role, preferring to move on to the next deal as soon as whatever was currently on the front burner neared completion. He was very interested in the field of finance (his area of expertise and study both as an undergraduate and in business school), but had turned down several offers to work in the finance area within client firms.

Peter Heinz was a definite "techie," who made his living as a computer consultant and trainer. He had passed by opportunities to join the staff of several organizations he consulted to, preferring to maintain his status as an influential outsider. Peter's view on management was "Why would anyone want to do something like that?"

Other careers that lend themselves to the HLH profile type when the Influence Through Language and Ideas business core function is elevated without the Enterprise Control function include business journalism or publishing, marketing communication, and technical writing.

THE LLL BUSINESS CAREER PROFILE TYPE

♦ *Application of Expertise:* Low

♦ *Working with People:* Low

♦ *Control and Influence:* Low

When someone is low on all eight business core functions as measured by the *BCII*, an important question is posed: Is this assessment true and accurate, or is it a false negative, meaning that the person is in fact more interested in one or more of the business core functions than the test has measured? If you took the *Business Career Interest Inventory* and were low on all eight functions, look immediately at the validity statement to see if there is reason to doubt whether the instrument's assessment of your interests was valid. The Response

Range Validity Statement will tell you whether you responded to the inventory with an unusual number of low-range responses (that is, if you responded with 0's and 1's rather than with 2's and 3's much more often than the average inventory-taker).

Of the number of possible reasons for having an unusual number of low-range responses, two are most common. The first involves your mood when you took the test. If you were feeling negative about the world, about life, and especially about work, nothing looked good to you and you were likely to respond accordingly. Think about what kind of mood you were in when you went through the instrument, and if you were feeling especially down at that time, take it again in a few days or weeks when your mood is back to normal.

The second reason you might have a negative response set is that you are just not very interested in a career in business. In this case the assessment of your interest in the eight business core functions as being low is accurate (a "true negative"), and you should consider careers outside business. Also ask yourself if there is some influence operating on you that is making you believe you *should* go into business ("My parents were both in business, and my older brothers and sisters are too. I really want to be an actor, but I really should be a businessman, so I'll take this test and see what is the best fit for me.")

Adam Coltrane came from a family of well-known business people, and had gone to business school simply because it was the "thing to do," socially acceptable, and pleasing to his parents. When he graduated from college, he had no clear calling, so getting an MBA seemed an easy default option. The results were disastrous. He hated business school, felt like a fish out of water, and later described the experience as "the worst two years of my life."

One clue to whether your LLL profile type is an accurate assessment of your interest in business can be found in the General Business Interest Index (GBII) score statement that is reported on the Score Summary screen. This is an index composed of a large number of business-specific items (activities that occur in traditional business settings). Your adjusted standard score on the GBII is compared with the general business sample and is reported on a scale from very low to very high.

If your score is in the high or very high range, your interest in this broad range of business roles and activities is at a level comparable to the general business sample. If your score is in the average range, your interest in the full range of business pursuits is less than that of the general business sample, but not markedly so. If your score is in the low range, your interest in the types of activities and roles typically found in business settings is significantly lower than that of people who actually work in business settings. If your score is in the very low range, your interest in the full spectrum of business activities is markedly lower than that of the general business sample. If you feel that your *BCII* item responses were authentic (not affected by a transitory mood) and your GBII standard score is low or very low, you should pursue approaches to career self-assessment that include a wider range of career options than those found within the traditional business domain. These other approaches might include working with a career counselor and using an interest inventory designed to measure a broad range of career options.

Even if this is the case, you may still be able to learn something from your *BCII* results that will prove useful to you as you consider nonbusiness careers. If, for example, your *relatively* highest score is on the Counseling and Mentoring business core function scale, (even if it was not high in an absolute sense), you might want to consider becoming a counselor of some sort, and perhaps getting a Ph.D. in counseling or clinical psychology, or a master's degree in clinical social work. If your relatively highest score is on the Creative Production function scale, you might want to consider a career in a field such as fine arts, architecture, or fashion design. Remember, however, that the *Business Career Interest Inventory* was not designed to measure career interests in nonbusiness settings. Thus, your absolute score on the Counseling and Mentoring or the Creative Production function, for example, is not an accurate measure of your interests in that area outside the arena of business careers. You should consider only its *relative* (to you) elevation when thinking about it in terms of a nonbusiness career.

If you initially took the test and used an unusual number of lower-range responses, then took it again, this time with more evenly distributed responses, you still have a question to consider: Does this change accurately reflect your more positive feelings (a "true positive") or have you tricked yourself into a more positive stance because, like Adam Coltrane, you believe you should want a career in business (producing a "false positive")?

Obviously, the LLL profile type produces a number of questions that you can answer only after some reflection. Take it as a strong warning that there may be a Sirens' song at work, and heed that warning. Remember that in sound career planning, *should* is always subordinate to *want*. If you follow a path that you "should want," you will either fail along the way or, if you are less fortunate, succeed in getting to a place where you do not wish to be.

Your business career profile type and your specific business core function profile provide a means for understanding the pattern of the deep structure of your life interests and how they may be realized in business work roles. To limit your thinking about your profile to our observations about settings that have attracted individuals with specific profile types would be a mistake, however. The self seeks its fullest, most *differentiated* expression. Interest patterns can be studied to learn about *what* is seeking expression, but they cannot detail a specific path to that expression. Individual career decisions, no matter how closely studied, cannot be predicted solely on the basis of interests. Personal factors such as other personality characteristics, skills, and values play important roles (as we will discuss in Chapter 10). Likewise, important life circumstances, experiences, and events can move two people's very similar patterns of deep structure interests toward different manifestations in the world. In the next chapter, we will focus on the process of career decision making itself and share with you what we have learned about the psychology of career decision conflict, doubt, and choice.

EIGHT

The Alchemical Heat:
Conflict, Doubt, and Choice

CHOOSING MEANS leaving something behind; choosing means loss. The "something" that is left behind may be a particular image of what our life might be. As we grow older, images of this loss return, particularly at midlife, as we imagine what our life might have been: "If only I had. . . ." In our mid-twenties and early thirties, we experience a heightened awareness of choices being made in work, relationships, and other aspects of life. These choices, perhaps for the first time, make us conscious that we are walking down one path and may never again return to the crossroads.

For many of the MBA students we see in our career counseling work, the world has, for virtually all of their lives, opened before them. Choices have been opportunities to gain more alternatives in life, not fewer. In their late twenties, however, these students begin to recognize that meaning and a sense of direction call for a narrowing, rather than a continually widening, focus and involvement. It is at this time in life in particular (and then again, in an often intense and painful reprise, in their forties or early fifties) that different aspects of the self, different voices of the psyche, begin to lay claim to the fate of the whole person. Fundamental questions begin to form. Am I truly dedicated to helping others and laying my hand to the healing of the social ills I see about me? Do I have enough drive and intelligence to become recognized as "successful," as that term is commonly defined by the cultural mainstream? Do I want the recognition of being associated with big-name players of a given industry, or is my best opportunity for personal fulfillment really in an entrepreneurial situation? Will a big risk lead to exhilaration or humiliation? Does taking a highly prized but demanding position mean that I will become a stranger to my spouse and children? What counts, what *satisfies,* what feeds the soul?

Deepening the Conflict

At developmental crossroads such as these, we may become aware, in a gut-wrenching way, that each of us, to paraphrase Truman Capote, has many voices and many rooms. To which voice will I listen? Which room will I occupy? And what about those that I do not heed and do not enter—will they cease to exist altogether?

Alex Kozinski was the oldest son of his East European immigrant parents. With a gift for math and a sense of ambition fostered by his extended family, he was accepted at Columbia University as an undergraduate. He excelled there as an economics major and was courted by several leading investment banks. After two years in a leading bank's analyst program, he applied to several business schools and chose to attend Harvard. He elected to leave the bank early to join a close undergraduate friend in a pregraduate school "fling," working for a struggling startup company in the educational software industry. He found himself working with people he really liked who were caught up in the energy and enthusiasm of their business idea coming to life. By the end of the summer, it was not clear if the company would make it through the next nine months; but Alex, reflecting on his experience as he prepared to enter business school, realized that he had never before known work could be as exciting and engaging as what he had been doing during the previous half year.

As his first semester at Harvard unfolded, Alex became increasingly restless and began to experience periods of down moods. During his undergraduate years and at the bank he had learned to push through low points such as these in order to complete a paper, cram for an exam, or meet a work deadline. For a while, this act of will worked well enough for him to remain active in class discussions and keep up with his business cases. As his restlessness contin-

ued, however, he realized that this struggle required a strategy other than pure willpower and the suppression of uncomfortable feelings that were becoming more and more difficult to ignore.

By the time Alex attended our career assessment workshop and career discussion group at Harvard, he had become more able to articulate his dilemma. He seemed to have two visions for meaningful work. On one hand, he was in a position that many of his colleagues would envy. With impressive academic credentials and work experience with an industry-leading company, he was on the verge of launching a successful investment banking career. In fact, he had been told by the managing director of his area that there would be a place for him after business school. Moreover, he truly liked the work in corporate finance that he had done at the bank. The recognition he received for his natural analytical ability had shown him that this was a place where he could not only do well but feel a growing sense of self-confidence and accomplishment. It would have been hard to imagine a more perfect fulfillment of the dream career that had dominated his thinking and feeling during his junior and senior years at college.

On the other hand, Alex's experience at the software startup had touched something in him that was also familiar, if less accessible. It was a sense of adventure that was a bit scary, a sense of not really knowing what the day would bring, but that there would be companionship and excitement in meeting whatever came up. As we listened to Alex talk in the career discussion group, we caught a glimpse of a part of him that seemed a source of energy that had been partly walled off, but was still alive. Was this a sense of adventure and fun that had been suppressed during childhood or adolescence? Was this part of his psyche a threat to the strongly focused achiever that graduated first in his high school class? Was it a threat to the worldview of his family?

We recognized in Alex's experience something that we had worked with many times before. His situation serves as a good illustration of the way in which a career dilemma can constellate a polarized field of energy. The charge passing across this energy field, like an electric shock, is always upsetting to the psychological status quo. It also sets up a vital opportunity for a true deepening of the self, and the capacity for greater satisfaction that can be had if we are able to understand and work with the nature of psychological polarity and conflict.

When we have two opposing and compelling options or points of view, our first instinct is to achieve a compromise, because the tension involved in choice and the uncertainty entailed in change are unsettling. Unfortunately, compromise when considering career options often does not work; it does not lead us into a deeper understanding of who we are and what work will hold meaning for us. On the contrary, if we are to gain this knowledge, we must paradoxically first *deepen* the conflict. We sensed that Alex was resisting this deepening.

Conflict and indecision are basically the psyche's message that our present way of understanding and approaching the world is no longer working. The current solutions, compromises, and allocations of our personal energies are no longer in line with an emerging need to be more engaged, to get more from life. We begin to sense that something larger out there is not being grasped or even fully perceived. This sense of dissatisfaction and uncertainty is painful, and we want to move away from it. We want to reinstall the old compromises between the warring voices of the self and return to the familiar. But if we are honest, we come to the point where we have to admit that the old compromises are no longer working: Something is missing.

The experience would be easy if what is new is immediately both clear and clearly better than what we have known; but it is neither. If we have been on a path of growth, intermittent as it might have been, we have achieved some hard-won victories. We have staked out a psychological homestead, realized in the realms of love and work, that has nurtured us and given us a sense of place. The demand to pull up stakes and move into new territory is naturally resisted, but the energy of the emerging self gathers with a growing intensity. What happens next follows a pattern that is easier to describe than it is to live. It is a progression, not automatic but requiring conscious effort, from vague, unacknowledged emotions, to deeply experienced new feeling, to an imagination that allows us to connect our feelings with a course of action in the world. And conflict itself provides the fuel for making the journey.

Unarticulated emotions are the vanguard of new consciousness, and they break the barrier into awareness by causing some sort of unrest. Something is "opposed" to an established position, to a previous image of who we are and how the world works. At first this contrast is experienced emotionally, rather than as fully articulated images and thoughts. We have yet to become aware that we are in the midst of a psychological shift of perspective. Episodes of anxiety and excitement may cycle with feelings of boredom and apathy. Dreams of being chased or of wild animals or burglars entering the house are common during these times. If we are able to bring patience and attention to these emotional states, they may deepen into more recognizable feelings connected with specific people and events. Eventually, paying attention to our emotional experience yields images that better communicate the nature of what is happening. This last step in the process is the most crucial and the most difficult. To stay with feelings of conflict for long is hard, but we have to if we are going to let them speak their message fully.

Alex spoke about the opposing career settings of investment bank and small startup company in a way that seemed generally accurate, but not very personal. He was not yet able to *imagine* himself in either life, although he had experienced something of both. He would talk briefly about one option and then switch quickly to another focus. That he was both excited and somehow disturbed about the possibility of the small-company direction was clear, but *what* disturbed him was not clear. It may have been that it was not the new career possibility itself that was disturbing, but rather the experience of being "lost," uncertain, and without a plan for resolving his uncertainty. He was avoiding staying with the conflict and discovering what it might yield. We observed that he was trying to make a career decision from a level that was too abstract and intellectual. We encouraged him to return to the uncomfortable, unsettled feelings of conflict and wait for them to speak in the language of more specific images. His career dilemma needed more *heat*.

Psychological Alchemy

Carl Jung spent many years studying the symbolism of medieval and Renaissance alchemy. He saw the alchemists not as deluded, primitive chemists in search of material riches, but as the first depth psychologists, trying to understand the processes of the self. He found in their work rich language to describe the very sequence of transformation that changed not lead into gold but vague emotion into deep feeling, and this new feeling into a rich imagination that could open up the scope of a person's life. An idea fundamental to the alchemical process is that of heat.

The alchemical process of self-development is fundamentally a process of heating or "cooking." Psychological heat is the friction of things that are "going wrong," from the perspective of the established, comfort-seeking ego. This heat, which sooner or later requires conscious attention, provides the energy source for the transformation of feelings, memories, sense impressions, ideas, and enthusiasms into the gold of a newly imagined life. In various alchemical descriptions this heat is used to cook, or incubate, raw life experience until it yields true imagination (rather than abstract fantasy). Psychologically, no real change happens without the psychological heat of conflict, doubt, and uncertainty.

Alex needed to return to the uneasy feelings of indecision, to the feelings of being lost, and wait there with an active, open attention. What might he see and feel on such a psychological "vision quest"? Memories, perhaps, of what it felt like in the past when he was truly excited about work, and life generally; recognition, perhaps, that he really does not like a certain activity, although he has always assumed that he does; fear, perhaps, that may portend real danger, or be merely a phantom of his ego's resistance to change; anger, perhaps, that he has often based his decisions on the unexamined opinions of others; surprise, perhaps, that his established direction is, in fact, more likely to satisfy him than a recent enthusiasm. These insights will emerge only from deliberately allowing images to come to him spontaneously as he imagines himself being in either work situation. Some of the images may be ineffable, leaving an enduring feeling that never develops into insight, or does so only after years pass. Other images will evoke memory, thought, and more images. If Alex can stay with the images and allow them to speak, without an attempt to repress, intellectualize, analyze, simplify, or alter them, and without artificially bringing them to a conclusion, he will learn the difficult craft of psychological alchemy.

The more time Alex can spend at *both* poles of the opposition, gathering images there, the deeper the ultimate resolution. He needs to return in his mind's eye to the investment bank and wait there to see what will happen. He needs to go back in his mind to the bench in the park across the street from the small startup and wait to see who from that group shows up, and how he feels talking with them. He may be surprised when his father shows up instead, and has a long talk with him about how he feels about him, about work, or about his own choices in life. This process of active imagination more often than not has surprises in store for the ego, that part of ourselves that seemed to have things all figured out. The conflict must be felt deeply; it will respond with the messengers of imagination that beg to be heard.

This is the work we do with our career counseling clients. We urge them deeper into their sense of unease, fear, and uncertainty. We ask them to go back into that place of sitting by the alchemical fire. We want specific images, and we want to see how those images affect their feeling, their bodies, their posture, their tone of voice, their rate of speech, their associations, their memories. This work of active imagination needs to be done in small doses. Five minutes of concentrated, undistracted focus can be psychologically wearing. One clear image can reveal a great deal as it is turned over, in the counseling session and in the days that follow. What are we looking at? What are we learning about how the deeper self feels and thinks? Sometimes we will give our clients specific prompts: to talk about a previous work situation and return there in the imagination. Sometimes we will pick up on a sense of excitement our client has about some recent work experience or work-related reading, perhaps in the business press. We will go back to the experience or to the magazine article. What really grabbed the person—what passage or image was most striking? What happens as our client recalls that image, and lets it live on in his or her present mind?

There is a fear inherent in emotionally returning to a conflict to do the work of image-gathering, fear of becoming stuck there and having our "deepening" turn into the "depths" of depression and inertia. Maybe, fear says, the conflict will last forever. Maybe there is no answer and work will always be work: Something that by its very nature is hard and lacking in pleasure. Sometimes depression *is* a part of career decision making. It results, however, not from too much conflict or doubt, but from the attempts to avoid conflict and doubt, with their concealed energy for transformation. If we can help our clients find the fear or anger behind the depression and stay with those feelings, the images that emerge become a source for movement. Sometimes we have to sit with the slow, smoldering ember heat of the depression itself and allow the psyche to speak in its own time. At other times things get too hot and there is too much change and intensity for a single life: job loss, divorce, death of those who are close. At these times we need to avoid, on one hand, becoming numb and distanced from our feelings and, on the other, trying to deal with and resolve everything at once. When there is too little heat, nothing changes; when there is too much, we can be burned.

The Nigredo

Some alchemical texts talk about the process of transformation as occurring in three eternally repeating self-making phases represented by the three colors black, white, and red. The black, or *nigredo,* phase is where any true transformation begins. The nigredo represents the experience of being in conflict, stuck or depressed without a course of action—a difficult, black time. The advice of the alchemical adepts at this point is always the same and is represented by an ancient alchemical motto: "Make the black blacker than black." In other words, stay with the conflict, go into it, imagine each of the conflicting poles as deeply as possible, let the distance between them increase.

This, needless to say, is counterintuitive and the very last thing that the ego wants to do. Better to find a compromise—surely there is a job that has all the qualities we want. Better to seek *the answer* from a career counselor, or trust that some psychological test will, in itself, produce the answer. Better to wait another year until our résumés are more impressive. The ego is never without its apparently rational arguments for not moving closer to the heat. "Making the black blacker than black," however, means *increasing* the sense of conflict by amplifying the images associated with opposing choices. It means feeling and accepting the sense of loss entailed in leaving one path for another. It means acknowledging death and the brevity of life: We cannot do everything; we must choose! We must not become embittered by missed opportunity or defeat; we must turn our attention to what actually is, to "that which is given." We must feel this deeply; we must find the courage to stay with conflict, even as it gets deeper and blacker. We must be partners in the blackening.

When Alex, or any of us, spends time paying attetion to the feelings and images associated with a polarized career choice situation, we begin to engage psychological material from other realms of our lives as well. Different paths in work will allow different aspects of ourselves to emerge and live more fully. During a career choice crisis, parts of the self that have been repressed or buried for years have an opportunity to call to us, one more time, asking to be allowed to emerge from the shadows and be lived. During times of difficult career choices, we can find ourselves reliving old conflicts, doubts, and injuries and find ourselves dealing with surprisingly intense feelings of hurt, guilt, shame, regret, and anger. We are reminded of old paths-not-taken; we find ourselves replaying arguments that we had with our parents years ago about values; we begin to second-guess earlier work and relationship decisions; we recall memories of personal defeats and painful mistakes. The energy generated by the heat of the career dilemma becomes a catalyst, setting off unanticipated reactions in our alchemical laboratory of self.

This return of emotion from the past adds an unsettling intensity to what the ego represents as a straightforward decision amenable to some sort of cost benefit analysis. The intensity is itself a warning that deeper issues are at stake, and that we should not slide by or take the easy default option, but instead to redouble our efforts to pay attention, feel and think things that we have been putting off. The poet Robert Bly uses a wonderful image to describe just such disturbing opportunities for enlarging the self. Bly employs the metaphor of all human beings coming into the world psychologically as radiant spheres of light. This radiant sphere represents full, unbroken access to all the energies of the self. When we watch an infant, it is easy to see that nothing is held back. As very young children we repress nothing and experience the full spectrum of our emotional, sensual, and cognitive range.

It does not take us long, however, to learn that certain parts of our experience are not acceptable to important others that we rely on for love and survival. Perhaps our mother doesn't like our rage, or our reckless abandon creates anxiety and brings admonitions from our father. Perhaps one of our parents has not really come to terms with a loss in his or her own life, and thus finds it difficult to tolerate our sadness. As we grow older, we become proficient at unconsciously figuring out what these important people in our lives want from us, and what parts of our being need to be repressed in order to give them what they want.

Bly continues his metaphor to say that we begin to store away unacceptable parts of our full, radiant self into a "long black bag" that we trail behind us through life. The problem with this process is that we need the full range of our personal energies in order to be fully engaged in our world of relationships and work. This does not mean that emotions should be impulsively or gratuitously expressed. It does mean that we need access to the deep reservoir of our emotional experience, so that our energy is available to take us in the right direction.

In business we need to be in touch with our anger if it is going to be transformed into power for constructive action. We need to know when we feel hurt so that we do not retaliate unconsciously, perhaps targeting someone who was not responsible for a previous emotional injury. The parts of our being that have been relegated to the long black bag do not die or disappear; they wait in the shadows for an opportunity to emerge and be reintegrated into our lives. When they return, they are often disturbing because they have become strangers to us. Where, at age forty, is all of this rage coming from, when I am known as such a rational and easygoing senior manager? I never liked this company anyway, so why does the prospect of leaving now bring such feelings of grief? Career crossroads, because they force us into a deeper connection with our feeling world, often create an opportunity for an opening of the black bag, and a chance to reconsider the value of enlarging our lives with its contents.

This disturbing intensity of feeling, fed by unintegrated feelings, is part of the nigredo world. It appears that we are not the mature, settled person we had always thought we were! Is there no end to uncertainty? Is happiness inevitably a mirage? Why are the rational aspects of this career decision so much more complicated than they should be? An important psychological life skill is that of acquiring an awareness of the *feel* of the nigredo experience. When we *know* that we are in a nigredo period, as difficult as it may be, we can work with it. When we do not recognize it for what it is, we too easily feel that this dark, disturbing vista on life is who we really are and who we will always be. The alchemists tell us that we will cycle through nigredo periods many times during the psyche-making voyage of our lives. We must become adepts who, like wily Odysseus, learn through experience how to navigate storm-tossed waters.

Working with nigredo requires patience. We must remind ourselves that this *experience* is not us and is not permanent. We are being worked on, and our job is to stay awake, to feel deeply, and to be ready to follow the images for a new direction or attitude that inevitably will emerge from the dark. It is critically important not to hasten to premature action in order to avoid the discomfort brought on by the emotional intensity of this time.

As we move deeper into the nigredo, change does not come from clever analysis or force of will. We do not work out the solutions to our career and other life choices with our discursive intellect. As the sense of conflict deepens, the distance between alternatives seems to grow, and we begin to feel more lost or confused than ever.

At times such as these we should remember the counsel of the alchemists who assure us that the dedicated adept, who has done the work of deepening in the nigredo, will find a change in the work of transformation coming not from the ego but from the deeper layers of the psyche. The change will be heralded by a *whitening,* or a movement into the next phase of the change process, the *albedo.*

The Albedo

This "white" phase should not be confused with a sudden breaking into the sunlight, with a clear sense of direction. It is not an "Ah ha" experience of definitive enlightenment. It is, rather, more like the light of the moon, a light that allows us not to banish the darkness of ambivalence and uncertainty, but to begin to see our situation in a *new* light. At this point we may see that our conflict is not between different jobs but between different ways of working. Or we may realize that change is needed not at our workplace but in an importat relationship or in our family life. We may see that our search for an ideal job is an illusory Sirens' song. We may recognize that we carry old conflicts with parental figures with us to new jobs, and that it is these conflicts that need attention. We may come to recognize the voice of a harsh internal judge who has not allowed us to take pleasure in our accomplishments. Working on changing our relationship with this judge, rather than changing jobs, then becomes our task. Sometimes a very different light is cast: We realize that our job unhappiness is not of our own making but, in fact, has much to do with a subtly shaming and demeaning supervisor. We may see that a certain strongly held belief or assumption about ourselves has been self-defeating. We may recognize that a deep passion, previously exercised only avocationally, needs to be primary. By working with the images produced by conflict, our experience of our situation changes, and we may begin to have a new way of seeing life and our path through it. The notion of career itself may change.

Fran Ellis was thirty-four years old and a well-paid marketing manager in a relatively small electronic game manufacturing company in New York. At least that was what her job description said; when she consulted us she wasn't doing much marketing or managing. Her company was undercapitalized, and top management was striving to contain operating expenses in order to shore up the company balance sheet while they sought new investors. Many projects were on hold or woefully underfunded. Fran was working on a marketing project that, due to lack of support from her top management and an unrealistic business plan, was going nowhere. From week to week she would get mixed signals as to the project's fate. Fran was frustrated and angry. More difficult, however, was the realization that her situation felt all too familiar.

Unlike many of the more senior managers at her company, Fran did not have an MBA. Nor did she have an engineering degree like many of the team leaders in product development. Fran had gained her position through native intelligence and intuition for marketing issues. She was self-conscious about her lack of academic credentials and from time to time thought about returning to school for an MBA. At this stage of her career, however, the opportunity cost for that path would be exceptionally high. In the past four years Fran had held positions with two other toy companies prior to working for her current employer. She had been unhappy about the circumstances of her leaving in both cases. Fran was beginning to wonder if she needed to look at some aspect of her own psychological makeup.

In our initial meeting Fran cast her career dilemma as a choice among the three alternatives of staying with her company, joining a competitor, or following the longtime dream of starting her own company. The idea of having her own company was emotionally charged for Fran. Ten years earlier she and several friends had started a magazine subscription business that had failed after three difficult years. She could see that that failure was limiting her ability to evaluate the advisability of launching a new entrepreneurial venture. At the same time we saw that her resentment of her distant, critical, and uncommunicative boss was activating feelings she had about her own family, preventing her from accurately assessing her value to her current employer and to others.

Fran feared that if she took a position with a competitor she would soon find herself in a similar position: locked in conflict with a father-figure boss and feeling that she had missed her chance to follow her heart by starting her own business. There were painful feelings evoked by focusing at either pole of her go-or-stay dilemma. We discussed the personalities and organizational dynamics of her current position and how they mirrored her family. As Fran explored her situation more deeply she began to feel worse. Fran's career dilemma had clearly led her into a difficult nigredo period that was opening up old wounds.

During the course of Fran's self-assessment work we discovered that her interest profile was dominated by the Creative Production business core function. Fran knew that creativity had always been important to her, but she was surprised at the extreme elevation of her score in this area, and by the fact that her Creative Production interest was far higher than interest in any other core function. We talked at length about the opportunities for the creative in Fran's life. She shared a lifelong vision of renting a studio and taking up painting again.

As we discussed creativity in the workplace as such, Fran recognized that she had always been most satisfied with her work at the beginnings of a new product campaign. She realized that she often felt her job as marketing manager did not have enough of the true beginnings: She envied her colleagues in product design, and felt locked out of what she saw as the most creative aspect of the work by her lack of an engineering degree.

After a hiatus of several months we heard from Fran again. During that time, she had marshaled the resources to move her product idea closer to reality. She was full of enthusiasm when she talked about her new computer game. Some things, however, had not changed. The company was still struggling and costs were being scrutinized ever more closely. Fran still wondered if she should get out altogether and had given her résumé to some executive search firms so that she could consider alternatives.

Fran's work with us certainly could not be characterized as a Pollyanna tale of sudden insight leading to a major decision and a totally new direction. But in another sense, she had a much firmer grasp of what she really wanted to do. She realized now that she needed to create and be involved in the imaginative beginnings of business projects, whether she was working for others or for herself. Certainly issues from her past and current life situations continued to be active and affect the way she felt about herself and her work, but she knew more now about what was important, even if significant obstacles lay in the way of its realization.

Career counseling had not turned out as Fran expected. There was not a complete release from the tensions of old conflicts; rather, a subtle shift in perspective had allowed her to experience those conflicts in a new light. The whitening of the albedo had not banished the darkness, but had brought better night vision. Old conflicts, in the light of the rising moon, seemed less dense and impenetrable.

The Rubedo

The final phase in the process of alchemical change is called the *rubedo*, or red, phase. We do not have a rubedo ending to supply for

Fran's story. The rubedo phase of the alchemical process of self-making represents the final stage of a hard-won extension of self: the realization in the world of newly available personal energies. It often manifests as a clearer sense of direction and more power to pursue that direction: A promotion brings new authority, a book is published, a product comes to market, ideas for a paper start to flow, the conclusion of a major deal strengthens our position, our vision for a project is adopted by the organization, a decision about a new career direction leads to definitive action, a relationship shifts into a period of mutual respect and enjoyment.

In the rubedo phase some inner workings of the psyche break through into daily reality. What was previously a vaguely perceived inner sense of shift in perspective now is seen as real and solid. The rubedo is not necessarily represented by the common currencies of success such as promotions, raises, and new titles, although these are often rubedo artifacts or outcomes. The rubedo does not entail freedom from the sense of loss that comes with a difficult choice, but its hallmark is an increased ability to move in a chosen direction with a sense of commitment.

This metaphor of the rubedo must be understood in terms of its position within the alchemical sequence. It comes out of the nigredo conflict and the new perspective of the albedo. It does not appear spontaneously or randomly, nor is it purely the consequence of an act of will. True rubedo has its roots in the darkness of the nigredo. Many contemporary cultures focus excessively on the rubedo aspects of life. The visible indications of energy, success, and a new direction are often taken as the totality of career development. This does a grave disservice to the understanding of the actual process of personal development through work.

In our career consultations we commonly see business professionals whose focus on the results of the rubedo world have led them away from the process of self-discovery. By emphasizing the rubedo, we risk drawing attention away from the vital struggles of nigredo and albedo periods, which require great personal courage, stamina, and commitment. However, a reluctance to leave the sunshine of the rubedo world for the darkness of the creative depths will ultimately lead to stagnation and a sense of emptiness. As Goethe observed:

And so long as you haven't experienced
This: to die and so to grow,
You are only a troubled guest
On the dark earth.

Some alchemical texts talk about a premature appearance of a red coloring in the alchemical vessel not as an indication that a shortcut has been found but, rather, as a sign that the work has been spoiled and must be begun anew, with a return to some earlier place of authenticity. A new job or title does not in itself imply true rebedo—a greater sense of energy or authority. Setting our sights on higher rungs of the ladder, without paying attention to what being there actually means, can lead to our being stuck, even if our altitude has increased. We must learn to distinguish between the rubedo-like *appearances* of career success and the actual activities that feed the self.

The alchemical metaphor of the nigredo, albedo, and rubedo phases may be seen as a model of the creative process, which involves a period of disturbing destruction of old patterns and viewpoints before a new vista can be achieved. The artistic medium in this case is the self, created through a series of hard-won insights, choices, and commitments. D. H. Lawrence believed that none of his literary achievements was as important as what he created by his choices in daily life. He referred to the work of day-to-day self-making as "that supreme work of art," and he chose as his personal emblem the alchemical image of the phoenix, the bird that emerges only from ashes.

We will cycle through this process of career decision as self-making many times in the course of our lives. It provides the opportunity to become more conscious participants in the work of attending to and working with the energies of the emerging self. We do so as we participate more fully in the act of transforming the experience of discontent and conflict into a new imagination and reality of meaningful work. There is no end to this cycle, but if we may speak of a goal it would be a sense that we have opened up a new room in the house of psyche and that our life has become not easier but more spacious. Thus, we can speak about working with the heat of career indecision as the work of making a self that is bigger, with more room for contradiction and paradox, more tolerance for the voices of different parts of the self, and more depth of feeling. This increased depth includes the recognition that our path is ours precisely because we have taken it and left other paths behind.

NINE

The Business Career Profile: Case Examples

THIS CHAPTER will present in greater depth several examples of people we have worked with who represent various business career profile types. As with other case examples, we have changed people's names and enough of the specifics to protect the identities of the individuals, while still providing the essence of their stories. Our goal in this chapter is to help you gain a greater understanding of how these complex interest patterns play out in actual career decision situations. We believe that this will enable you to better apply what you have learned about your personal business career profile type to your own career planning.

We will describe in some detail the career paths, choice points, and motivations for one or more individuals who fall into each of the seven possibilities for a designation of high in one or more of the three fundamental dimensions that underlie the eight business core functions. As with the information contained in Chapter 6, these profiles are not intended to be used as a cookbook. Even if two people had identical profile types, differences in their aptitudes, personality traits, life stage, and values could result in dramatically different manifestations of their interests. The profiles, then, should be used to stimulate your thinking about your own unique set of life circumstances. We will begin by revisiting the three people we described briefly in this book's introduction: Mark Young, Caroline Greeley, and Elaine Littleton. We will then discuss in somewhat greater depth several other individuals we have worked with in recent years. In each case we will begin by showing you a copy of the individual's actual *Business Career Interest Inventory* Score Summary screen.

Mark Young (HHH, QHH)

Score Summary

Application of Technology	36	
Quantitative Analysis	56	
Theory Development and Conceptual Thinking	42	
Creative Production	51	
Counseling and Mentoring	57	
Managing People	63	Personal High
Enterprise Control	56	
Influence Through Language and Ideas	63	Personal High

Business Career Profile Type: HHH

General Business Interest Index: Very High

To recap, Mark had held several management positions, principally in marketing, within a manufacturing company. A relatively young senior executive team and low turnover led to his career progression stalling, with no promise of advancement in the near future. When Mark came to us he was considering several alternatives. He could purchase a share of a small business in an area related to his current employment, take over as vice president of marketing in the business of a college friend, or move to a marketing position with a company that was a direct competitor of his current employer. He had worked for only one company thus far in his career, so his frame of reference in assessing his opportunities was quite limited.

Mark's business career profile type was HHH, but by far his dominant individual business core function elevations were on the Managing People and the Influence Through Language and Ideas scales. Mark's father was a successful entrepreneur, as were two of his older brothers, and Mark's unspoken definition of success was to have his own business.

What he enjoyed most, however, was working with people, networking, and influencing—not being alone at the top. People loved Mark, and he loved the fact that they loved him. He enjoyed getting to know people, playing tennis with them, remembering their birthdays, and so forth. If he were the president/CEO, he would not be able to have his coworkers as his friends. In addition, if it were his money in the business, he knew that he would spend his time worrying about it. However, he also wanted very much to please his father and make his own fortune.

After a rather agonizing decision-making process, feeling pushed and pulled by what he was really best suited for and what he felt he should do, Mark chose to accept the marketing director position for the larger consumer goods company that had been pursuing him through an executive recruiter. Because the organization was somewhat larger, this position held more opportunity for growth than his previous position and did not put Mark at the helm, either as captain or first mate. The position gave him ample opportunity to be a day-to-day manager.

Caroline Greeley (LLH)

Score Summary

Application of Technology	43	
Quantitative Analysis	44	
Theory Development and Conceptual Thinking	44	
Creative Production	47	
Counseling and Mentoring	38	
Managing People	51	
Enterprise Control	56	Personal High
Influence Through Language and Ideas	62	Personal High

Business Career Profile Type: LMH

General Business Interest Index: Very High

Note: Based on full assessment data, Caroline's medium designation was assessed to be low range for purposes of profile classification. In considering her case, however, you should keep in mind her actual elevations on all business core function scales.

Caroline Greeley was a highly intelligent and extremely creative woman in her early twenties. She was a strikingly beautiful woman and had always received a great deal of attention for her looks. As a result, her appearance became a large part of Caroline's self-identity. Despite her intelligence and creativity, Caroline lacked self-confidence, and this was her primary career limitation. At the time she consulted us she was working in what in many ways was a good position for her in the movie business. As we talked, Caroline posed the question: "I basically like the work I'm doing, so why do I feel so uncomfortable in this job?"

Caroline's parents had divorced when she was a young girl, and her father, a very successful businessman, had subsequently been married twice, each time to a much younger, highly attractive woman. Not surprisingly, Caroline had internalized the message that what is of greatest value, at least for a young woman, is physical appearance. Caroline's *BCII* business career profile type was LLH, with elevation primarily in the Influence Through Language and Ideas business core function. Thus, it seemed that her current work was, in terms of interests, a good fit for her.

Unfortunately, in the entertainment industry appearance, if not all that matters, is very highly valued. Further, because it is such a difficult industry to get into (great demand, small supply of openings), employers can get exactly what they want in the people they hire. Caroline was never sure whether she was getting ahead because of her competence or her beauty; and she was surrounded by people who made no bones about the overriding importance of physical appearance.

Caroline, then, was in a good position in a good industry *in terms of her interests* but not in terms of her feelings about herself. After consultation she determined to remain in the marketing area, but to move to another industry (direct-mail marketing) that did not have the cultural elements of the entertainment industry that troubled her. Her new setting placed a premium on her interest in the area of Influence Through Language and Ideas.

Elaine Littleton (HLL; A,Q,TLL)

Score Summary

Application of Technology	68	Personal High
Quantitative Analysis	66	Personal High
Theory Development and Conceptual Thinking	55	
Creative Production	42	
Counseling and Mentoring	40	
Managing People	45	
Enterprise Control	52	
Influence Through Language and Ideas	39	

Business Career Profile Type: HMM

General Business Interest Index: Very High

Note: Based on full assessment data, Elaine's profile was assessed as HLL for purposes of profile classification. In considering her case, however, you should keep in mind her actual scores on all of the business core function scales.

Elaine Littleton left a successful career in management consulting out of her unhappiness with the lifestyle her work demanded (seventy- to ninety-hour workweeks with extensive out of town travel). Elaine was an exceptionally intelligent individual who loved solving problems and learning about new businesses, so in many ways a consulting career was ideal for her. Her career dilemma was how to satisfy her desire for a continual flow of new problems to solve without spending three or four days on the road and working the hours she had been.

In addition, Elaine had an exceptionally difficult time tolerating the incompetence or ineffectiveness of colleagues. As a consultant she had no problem with her observation that she and her fellow consultants were generally brighter and harder working than their clients. After all, she reasoned, that was why they had been hired in the first place. When someone from her own firm was not as bright, highly motivated, or dedicated as she was, however, she had trouble containing her displeasure. She worried that if she went to work in industry (for a former client company or the equivalent thereof) she wouldn't be able to stand it.

Elaine's *BCII* business career profile type was HLL. Her results were somewhat unusual for a management consultant, in that her score on the Influence Through Language and Ideas business core function scale was low. Her interests in the Application of Technology and the Quantitative Analysis business core functions were very high, however, and she secured a position with an investment management firm in which she could put her interests both in financial analysis and in technology to work with colleagues who were generally very bright. She was also now able to control her own travel schedule.

Pat Heller (LLH)

Score Summary

Application of Technology	35	
Quantitative Analysis	38	
Theory Development and Conceptual Thinking	41	
Creative Production	45	
Counseling and Mentoring	46	
Managing People	51	
Enterprise Control	65	Personal High
Influence Through Language and Ideas	63	Personal High

Business Career Profile Type: LMH

General Business Interest Index: Average

Note: Based on full assessment data, Pat's profile was assessed as LLH for purposes of profile classification. In considering his case, however, you should keep in mind his actual scores on all of the business core function scales.

Pat was a true survivor. He had led a marginal life as a young boy, moving from apartment to apartment (sometimes sleeping in the car) as he and his mother and half-brother were evicted for not paying the rent. Pat's mother was an alcoholic and put her own needs before anyone else's, including those of her children. As young children Pat and his brother were frequently left alone nights while their mother went out drinking. Pat's father had abandoned the family when Pat was an infant, never to be heard from again. His mother was involved with a succession of men, one of whom was the father of his half-brother, many of whom were also alcoholics and were verbally and physically abusive. In addition, the frequent moves meant that Pat never stayed in the same school for more than a few months, and so was never able to develop a network of social support that might have helped to stabilize his otherwise chaotic life. All in all, it would be hard to imagine a more unstable environment in which to grow up.

Pat later described his life as that of an "army brat" but without all the other army brats for company. He meant that he learned to make friends quickly and to end those relationships just as quickly, never becoming too deeply involved ("Velcro relationships," we called them). Pat became adept at fitting in and getting along. He was attractive and athletic and had a smile that rarely left his face, making him someone to whom other children were drawn.

Pat was natively intelligent but had been quite poorly educated. The constant start-stop nature of his early education had laid a poor groundwork for future higher education, and he completed only slightly less than a year of college before dropping out to go to work. His lack of a college education embarrassed him, even though no one would ever surmise from his self-presentation that he was not well educated. He was articulate, had an extensive vocabulary, and had educated himself sufficiently to be able to hold his own in most social conversations about politics, world affairs, music, and art. Nonetheless, this sense of having a "secret" persisted. In fact, over time it increased as he became more successful and traveled in higher social and economic circles.

After a few years of floundering, Pat found his career niche. He talked his way into a position selling office supplies to retailers and large end users (such as banks, law firms, and hospitals), and within just a few months was exceeding his manager's expectations, despite having been given a very difficult territory to work. After several years of consistently "making his numbers" in this area, Pat successfully crossed over into the high-tech field, working for a firm that produced software applications for use by a wide variety of businesses. Pat had no technical training or knowledge, but he learned what he needed to know in order to sell the products, relying on technical sales support people to handle the detailed technical issues. Again, he was quite successful, and with the higher profit margins in this industry Pat's income skyrocketed into the $200,000-plus range.

It was at this point that Pat first considered moving into management, when he was asked if he wanted to apply for a regional sales manager position that was vacant. With this company, if he had succeeded in management, the potential financial upside would be great, with stock options and bonuses. Pat wisely decided not to pursue the move into management. He correctly recognized that his only real interest was in actually selling. He enjoyed the entire process: learning about the products, learning about the customers' needs, anticipating their objections and questions, listening carefully to their questions and comments, negotiating selling prices, and, finally, closing the deal. He also enjoyed the product: the tangible, unarguable numbers, the "keeping score" aspect of the work. He did not want the headaches of managing other people's performance, he did not want to be responsible for them, and he did not want his bonus to be dependent on their sales.

Pat's business career profile was LLH, with low- or average-range scores on all the business core function scales except Enterprise Control and Influence Through Language and Ideas, on which he was very high. It seems likely that his early life of having to learn to make relationships quickly had helped cement a skill that reinforced his interest in interpersonal influence. It is Pat's interest in working collaboratively with people that places his Managing People score in the average range. When we discussed this it became clear that monitoring the work of others and motivating them is not attractive to him. Pat's interest in Enterprise Control illustrates an important point regarding that business core function, which is that Enterprise Control can indicate wanting to run business *or* "do the deals," make the sales, handle the transaction (or both). In Pat's case the latter was definitely the source of his interest. The idea of being in charge per se did not have significant appeal for him.

Jerry Gilchrist (HHH, THH)

Score Summary

Application of Technology	39	
Quantitative Analysis	53	
Theory Development and Conceptual Thinking	64	Personal High
Creative Production	48	
Counseling and Mentoring	64	Personal High
Managing People	42	
Enterprise Control	43	
Influence Through Language and Ideas	52	

Business Career Profile Type: HHM

General Business Interest Index: High

Note: Based on full assessment data, Jerry's profile was assessed as HHH for purposes of profile classification. In considering his case, however, you should keep in mind his actual scores on all of the business core function scales.

Jerry, famous for his passion for the stock market, was the only son of immigrant parents who had never completed high school. They saw the value of education, however, and encouraged Jerry to work to his highest potential in school. He attended an exam school in New York City that was oriented to the sciences, where he devoted himself single-mindedly to his studies.

Jerry went on to attend the City University of New York as an engineering student, where he was first exposed to the world of finance. He took an elective economics course, enjoyed it, and followed that with a business finance course, which he loved. He also excelled in it and caught the eye of the instructor, who, a graduate of the school, worked on Wall Street and taught one course pro bono as a way of giving something back to the institution that had given him his start.

His teacher arranged for Jerry to have an interview with a colleague in the trading area of the brokerage firm for which he worked, and Jerry landed a summer job doing clerical work for the traders. Grunt work it may have been, but Jerry loved the excitement of "the Street." He met other bright, ambitious people and saw an opportunity for someone with street smarts who wanted to work hard. All the people he met seemed to live and breathe their work, and before long Jerry did too.

He changed his major from engineering to business, with a concentration in finance, and continued to work summers for the investment bank. By the time he graduated he was working part-time during the school year as well, and on graduating he walked into a full-time job as an assistant trader. Jerry was in heaven. He was doing something he loved, working with other people who loved their work as well, and was making more money than he had ever dreamed he could. He was as single-minded in his devotion to his work as he had been to his studies, and he excelled in it. The trading group was small, and Jerry was able to get the help he needed to become a more seasoned professional.

For the next several years Jerry devoted himself to two things only: his work and his family. He continued to live with his parents, who were aging, in poor health, and no longer working (Jerry had been born relatively late in their lives), and he assumed financial responsibility for them. As a trader he worked very hard while the market was open but was then free to head home to spend the evening with his parents. As the years went on Jerry was promoted from assistant trader to trader, where he took positions on the bank's account. Although not a big personal risk taker, he was generally successful in his reading of the market and netted profits for the bank ranging from very good to exceptional. He also grew into the role of "big brother" to the younger, less experienced traders who were coming onto the floor.

When the head trader left for another firm, Jerry was asked to assume this responsibility. In addition, the decision was made to dramatically grow the trading group and expand its capabilities. This meant building a new trading room and, more important, bringing in more people. Jerry both loved and hated this new role. As head trader he was now part of management, which meant meetings that he saw as a waste of time. It also meant working more directly and frequently with people whose ambition, it seemed to Jerry, was to rule the world. He personally would have been happy to live out his days trading equities and had no desire to become managing director of the bank (let alone of the known universe). He was a doer, and anything that took him away from the trading floor, where the action was, was interference.

But he found that he loved building the business from a small franchise to a major profit center and a player. The part he loved most was hiring and training new talent. His "kids" were, as he had been, mostly bright, hungry, aggressive recent college graduates (not MBAs, as most of the people on the investment banking side were). If they were eager to learn, he was eager to teach, and Jerry's reputation grew on the Street as one of the best people to train you early in your career.

When someone was not so hardworking or eager to learn, however, Jerry learned that he disliked something else about managing: motivating people who were not like him (in his view, lazy). Motivating them aside, he had a hard time even tolerating their presence, and on a number of occasions really lit into people who, in his estimation, were not pulling their own weight. This impatience with incompetence was not limited to the traders who reported to him. If there were a problem with the information systems, for example, and the IS department was slow to fix it, that department head could expect to hear about it.

Jerry was supremely dedicated to the firm, and his dedication only increased after his parents died. He saw his role as partly that of a change agent and partly as the upholder of standards for how the business should be run. As his influence in the firm grew, he used it in service of both roles (needless to say, not always to other people's liking). Tolerating the gap between the ideal and reality was difficult, sitting in the meetings was boring, and managing people who were not as keen as he would have liked was frustrating. Nevertheless, Jerry could not imagine going back to a pure individual contributor role, and not simply because to do so would mean less prestige or less money.

Jerry was in all respects an HHH business career profile type. He was interested in applying his expertise in the financial markets, to be sure, and if that were all he might have never left his role as a trader. But he was also interested in the Working with People dimension (specifically, in Counseling and Mentoring them, not in Managing People per se). Even if these two dimensions stood alone, Jerry might have been satisfied as an individual contributor who, as he had done before becoming head trader, would have mentored people on the side. Jerry was also interested in the Control and Influence dimension, however, which is what led him to a management role. Interestingly, it was the Influence Through Language and Ideas business core function that was elevated, and not the Enterprise Control function. This was congruent with Jerry's desire to use his position as a platform from which to influence the organization, while not wanting to actually run it himself. Similarly, he was high on the Counseling and Mentoring business core function scale but not on Managing People, which was congruent with his liking to teach but not to manage those who really needed managing.

Jerry's career followed an interesting path. It first provided him with an arena (as a trader–individual contributor) in which to express his interest in applying the expertise that he had discovered in college. In working in this position, he discovered another interest—in acting as a mentor and counselor to more junior traders. This in turn led to his discovery of his interest in exerting his influence to help shape the course of events in the organization. We often find that people who have elevated interests in more than one of the three fundamental dimensions may have discovered these interests serially, as one work opportunity allows for the uncovering of another interest dimension (and possibly that other to a third).

Diane Vance (LHL)

Score Summary

Application of Technology	50	
Quantitative Analysis	44	
Theory Development and Conceptual Thinking	38	
Creative Production	46	
Counseling and Mentoring	51	
Managing People	69	Personal High
Enterprise Control	54	
Influence Through Language and Ideas	43	

Business Career Profile Type: MHM

General Business Interest Index: High

Note: Based on full assessment data, Diane's profile was assessed as LHL for purposes of profile classification. In considering her case, however, you should keep in mind her actual scores on all of the business core function scales.

Diane, a brand manager in the consumer packaged goods industry, came to us as a result of having trouble when a new manager took charge of her group. She experienced Jack as aloof, autocratic, and confrontational, and after several months of poor relations Jack suggested that Diane consider other career options. Diane felt devastated. She had never failed at anything, and her confidence was badly shaken. To her credit, she took advantage of the opportunity to take a close look at herself and to consider all options, including radical departures from her current career path.

Diane was one of two children, and she described the messages she and her brother received, in several ways, from her parents as "Play it safe, go by the book, don't stand out." One way this had been communicated was verbally, through suggestions that she stick to activities and school subjects at which she was already good, and that she avoid taking unpopular positions that might lead to confrontation ("If you can't say something nice, don't say anything at all"). The other, equally potent ways she had received this message were by the example of her mother's remaining in a very secure job for many years despite not really enjoying it; and by her observing, during her high school years, her father start a business that ultimately failed.

The resultant psychological stress and financial hardship on the family had produced two powerful reactions in Diane. The first was an intense desire for success and the financial security it would bring. The second was, not surprisingly, an aversion to any form of risk-taking. These two forces had become the key determinants of Diane's career. She worked hard, moved into an area in which she had a natural affinity and talent, worked for brand-name companies, and avoided conflict whenever possible. She also sought to keep all options open, to close no doors. She had seen her father go down a path (which, unfortunately, turned out to be a dead end) from which it was difficult to return, and she was determined not to do the same.

When she graduated from college, Diane was utterly lost. She had gone to an Ivy League college, majored in American studies (not wanting to close any options), and had no idea what she wanted to do after leaving school. She did not go through the college's recruiting process, graduated without a job, and proceeded to begin her career as a temporary secretary (despite having graduated summa cum laude). In retrospect she saw that her risk aversion and fear of failing had extended even into applying for jobs and risking being rejected.

The theme of not trying (or not trying her hardest), so she could not fail, persisted for some time, until someone at a bank where she was working recognized that she was grossly underemployed and virtually took charge of her career. This individual got Diane into the bank's commercial lending officer training program, where she again excelled. With the structure of the bank's lending policies to support her, Diane did well in her new role. After several years her mentor persuaded Diane to apply to business school, and she spent the next two years earning her MBA. This was a learning and growing process for Diane, especially insofar as she wanted to be liked by everyone and not "stand out," but required class discussion of business cases was the program's primary pedagogy. There was simply no way to avoid taking positions and having to argue for her point of view.

Diane went into marketing almost as a default, not finding any other function she was more interested in and deciding that experience in product management would be useful in a number of business settings going forward (again, keeping the options open). She was hired by a large firm, which had quite a structured training program, and received very positive reviews. She enjoyed the teamwork involved in marketing and was good at attending to the details that were essential to top-quality marketing management. Although not the most creative manager, she was reasonably good at the analytic side of the work and a standout on execution.

Jack, the manager who had suggested that Diane consider other careers, was unlike any manager Diane had experienced. He was direct, confrontational, and aggressive, and expected the people who reported to him to be similarly direct. Whereas Diane worked to ensure that everyone liked her, Jack saw making the occasional enemy as part of the cost of doing business. To say the least, this was not a relationship Diane enjoyed.

As she considered her future career path, she wondered whether she should go for top management, feeling that she had the potential to do so but questioning whether she was being swayed by what her MBA classmates would say. Diane's business career profile type, LHL, loaded on the Managing People business core function. From her *Business Career Interest Inventory* we saw that Diane was in the moderate range on the four Application of Expertise business core functions and on both of the Control and Influence business core functions. These results suggest that Diane's questioning whether she would enjoy running the whole show was well founded. In fact, they suggest that she might find more satisfaction not as the CEO but as a general manager within a larger company, or perhaps as head of a smaller, slow- to moderate-growth company (in which the managing of people would be more important than planning strategy).

We have worked with a number of excellent, top-level managers who, like Diane, are primarily interested in managing people (as opposed to managing processes, "doing deals," or controlling the operation). As one such individual said to us, "All of the people who work for me know more about what they do than I do, but I know about hiring the right people, keeping them happy, and getting them to do their best work." This individual was well known as an excellent manager, and would have been successful managing in virtually any setting. In our consultation with Diane, he provided a model for her to grow toward.

Sue Knight (HHL)

Score Summary

Application of Technology	56	Personal High
Quantitative Analysis	64	Personal High
Theory Development and Conceptual Thinking	54	
Creative Production	34	
Counseling and Mentoring	41	
Managing People	56	Personal High
Enterprise Control	46	
Influence Through Language and Ideas	41	

Business Career Profile Type: HHM

General Business Interest Index: Very High

Note: Based on full assessment data, Sue's profile was assessed as HHL for purposes of profile classification. In considering her case, however, you should keep in mind her actual scores on all of the business core function scales.

Sue was one of four children, the daughter of immigrants. Her father worked in a steel mill in Pittsburgh until he was injured in an accident while working. After his accident, which occurred when Sue was in her early teens, the family's standard of living dropped dramatically and remained low during the rest of her youth. In addition, both of her parents, never overly positive in their attitudes toward life, grew depressed. Demonstrations of love, affection, and pride in the children's accomplishments were so rare that Sue was unable to recall a single instance in which she or any of her siblings were praised for any achievement.

What she could recall was a steady diet of criticism—of comparison with others and with an ideal of behavior and achievement. The net effect of her parents' depression and criticism was that Sue grew into adulthood with a terribly distorted sense of herself and of her self-worth, and a great deal of anger. Although the anger may have been a healthy response from a psychological standpoint, Sue had difficulty in the workplace, tending to personalize criticism and see herself as being treated unfairly. No doubt much of the time she was correct in her perceptions, but there were clearly other situations in which she assumed that others were treating her as badly as a part of her believed she should be treated.

Having grown up in a depressive atmosphere, both economically and psychologically, and being innately quite intelligent, Sue had turned to books for solace and stimulation from an early age. She read voraciously, and found herself particularly drawn to materials dealing with science. As a high school student, she had been discouraged from taking science and math courses by her parents in favor of more "practical" courses, but she stuck to her guns and took all the courses available to her.

On graduating, Sue secured a position as a technician, working nights in a medical testing laboratory and taking courses on a part-time basis at a local college during the days. During this period she was introduced to computers and, more specifically, to programming. Sue was entranced with this new world of languages and code writing, and, just as some people find learning French or Portuguese naturally easy, she found programming similarly easy. Sue soon found more highly paid employment doing programming for a large commercial bank in the city, which also paid for her to finish her degree in computer sciences.

Fortunately, in her line of work Sue's talent was indisputable, and combined with her strong work ethic and ambition, she received very positive performance reviews (despite her occasional flare-ups of anger). At first she anticipated every review with dread and anxiety, a holdover from the days when she would take her report cards home to her parents and be subjected to cross-examination, no matter how well she had done. Over time, however, the consistently positive feedback she received for her work began to have a positive impact on Sue's sense of herself. She began to recognize that the "mirroring" she had received from her family was distorted, something like the mirrors in the fun house at a carnival, and that the reflections she was getting from people in her current world were more accurate. Her self-esteem increased so that it was more nearly in line with the actuality of her value, both as a worker and as a person.

After working for several years as a senior programmer and systems analyst, and completing most of her course work for a master's degree in information technology, Sue was recruited for a position in Boston. The move was lateral in terms of title, but it presented new challenges and a much higher compensation level, so she accepted the offer. Again Sue excelled in her new position, and her competence and productivity were quickly recognized and rewarded. Freed from the rather stifling influence of her family, Sue blossomed. She made friends in her new workplace, bought a condominium, took advantage of Boston's cultural opportunities, learned to sail and ski, began dating, and eventually married.

Sue did experience guilt and ambivalence over having achieved a much higher level of success than either her parents or any of her siblings. Only her youngest sister, the youngest of the four, had gone on to college, and was working as a registered nurse back home. Her other sister had married soon after graduating from high school and now worked as a receptionist in a dental office. Her brother, an alcoholic who also suffered from depression, had failed to finish high school and worked as an unskilled laborer.

Sue had spent her early career as an individual contributor, albeit as someone to whom others turned for expert advice with their programming and systems problems. She had also been project leader on a number of initiatives, but had never had management responsibilities as such. After several years in her new position, she was asked to take on such a role. Despite some misgivings, she accepted the position of group manager and found that she very much enjoyed it. She gained a reputation as one of the better managers to work for, someone who both knew her stuff and was a good people manager.

Sue's business career profile type was HHL. She has high interests in the Application of Expertise dimension (with elevation in both the Application of Technology and the Quantitative Analysis business core functions), which are consistent with her interest in the systems analysis side of her work. Interest in the Working with People dimension (the Managing People business core function) accounts for her enjoyment of working in a management role. Thus, Sue fits the pattern of the expert individual contributor who moves successfully into a management role and finds that role satisfying and fulfilling.

Kim Oliver (HLH)

Score Summary

Application of Technology	33	
Quantitative Analysis	48	
Theory Development and Conceptual Thinking	40	
Creative Production	62	Personal High
Counseling and Mentoring	46	
Managing People	43	
Enterprise Control	53	
Influence Through Language and Ideas	63	Personal High

Business Career Profile Type: HMH

General Business Interest Index: High

Note: Based on full assessment data, Kim's profile was assessed as HLH for purposes of profile classification. In considering her case, however, you should keep in mind her actual scores on all of the business core function scales.

Kim had lived a childhood many people would envy. Her family was quite wealthy, with homes in Manhattan, in Florida, and on an island off the coast of Maine. She had two brothers, who were eight and ten years older, and so, as she described it, she grew up mostly as an only child. Her father was an extremely successful investment banker and her mother was active in charitable causes. Kim's parents' marriage was marked by a good deal of strife, with many battles precipitated by her father's affairs with other women. Her mother grew depressed, and ultimately the marriage ended, when Kim was fourteen, in a bitter divorce.

Kim was sent to one of the best prep schools in the city, where she had considerable difficulty with the work, especially in the area of mathematics and the sciences. In addition, she had a difficult time coping with her parents' divorce and with her mother's depression. Kim became depressed and socially withdrawn, and began abusing alcohol and other drugs. Her parents arranged for her to see a psychiatrist, and she spent the next several years in psychoanalysis. Kim found the therapy of little help, and ended the relationship when she went away to college.

Due to her poor grades, Kim was not admitted to a top-tier college, which was a great disappointment to her family, all of whom had gone to Ivy League schools. She did attend a respectable college, where she made reasonably good grades as an English major. She was interested in theater set design, and worked during the school year in the college theater productions and during summers for a theater company in upstate New York. Her depression persisted, however, and by the time she graduated she was still something of a lost soul. Over the next several years she had several jobs of varying duration, in the retail industry, financial services, working for an interior design firm, and in advertising (all secured through family connections). None of these positions lasted for more than a year or so, and in none was she particularly satisfied or successful. She had difficulty taking criticism and was generally unprepared for the rough-and-tumble, competitive aspects of the business world.

She did find a psychotherapist who was of help to her, and on her recommendation Kim began to take an antidepressant medication. The combination of therapy and medication made an enormous difference in her mood. Her depression lifted, and she was able to begin to think more clearly about her career. Then her therapist recommended that she go to Boston for a career consultation.

In our work we developed several career possibilities that appeared to have promise for Kim, including event planning, public relations, publishing, advertising, arts management, and fashion design. Kim began sampling these fields. She took a couple of courses at the Fashion Institute of Technology and in public communications, and used her family network to gain access to people in all the fields she was considering, talking to them about careers in the various areas.

Kim had enjoyed the creative elements of working in the advertising industry but had difficulty with the highly political nature of the field. She was drawn to the product of the publishing industry but did not want to work on the editorial side of that business. She ultimately found her niche, in essence, by combining the two: working as a publicist and then as a marketing manager for a large publishing house in New York. The work was not highly remunerative, but it allowed her to work with other bright, creative people in a less cutthroat environment than she had found in advertising.

Kim's *BCII* business career profile type was HLH (converted from HMH), with elevations in the Creative Production and Influence Through Language and Ideas business core functions. This profile type is characterized by a strong need for creative variety and a wish to be a player, someone of influence, but not to be the person at the top of the organization. Kim had no desire to have her own publishing imprint or to head an advertising agency or public relations firm, as we might have expected given her average Enterprise Control function scale score. Nor did she want to manage other people, as an elevation in Working with People would have indicated.

Mark Twomey (LHH)

Score Summary

Application of Technology	38	
Quantitative Analysis	41	
Theory Development and Conceptual Thinking	46	
Creative Production	46	
Counseling and Mentoring	51	Personal High
Managing People	39	
Enterprise Control	50	
Influence Through Language and Ideas	52	Personal High

Business Career Profile Type: MMM

General Business Interest Index: Average

Note: Based on full assessment data, Mark's profile was assessed as LHH for purposes of profile classification. In considering his case, however, you should keep in mind his actual scores on all of the business core function scales.

Mark Twomey grew up in a lower-middle-class family in northern New Jersey. He was the oldest of four sons in an Irish American family that respected hard work, humility, and family loyalty. Mark was never an exceptional student in high school, but he was well liked by both friends and teachers and worked hard enough to earn respectable grades. Mark went to a local college that was a popular choice of graduates from his school.

In college, social life continued to be important for Mark, but he worked harder than he had in high school and maintained a B average. He initially considered an economics major but in his junior year switched to business administration, preferring the more practical emphasis. When Mark graduated in 1990, the job market was difficult. He lived at home during what turned out to be an extended job search. Mark became depressed during this period and in retrospect realized that he had no role models or other resources for helping him determine a career direction. He was the first person in his family to go to college, and there seemed to be no path that naturally opened before him.

Mark eventually went to work for a temporary help agency and continued to live at home. After a year of uninteresting assignments, he accepted a position with a pharmaceutical manufacturing company in the human resources department. After two years, Mark was promoted. Most of the time he enjoyed meeting with employees individually and helping them with their concerns. He did not, however, like doing all the paperwork that was required. After two years Mark was becoming clear about one thing: he genuinely enjoyed some aspects of his work, and others made him want to call in sick. He liked the individual counseling; he disliked the extensive record keeping. He became interested in the legal aspects of the work and made friends with two of the attorneys who represented the department in disputed unemployment and workers' compensation cases.

Unfortunately for Mark, there was little opportunity for expanding his role. More and more he felt as if the senior managers and attorneys were doing the "real" work, and he was keeping the records for them. Four years after joining the company, Mark's interest in and sense of commitment to his work had begun to suffer to the point that he was beginning to be seen as a problem employee. He was told that he was moody, and he fell behind in some of the more tedious record-keeping aspects of his work. When a new manager became head of Mark's area, he recognized Mark as a capable worker who was, for unknown reasons, in danger of losing his job. He recommended that Mark see someone outside the company concerning his difficulties at work.

In our interviews Mark talked about his ambivalence toward his work. From our discussion and from psychological testing and letters from people who knew Mark well, it became clear that the Counseling and Mentoring business core function was indeed an important aspect of work satisfaction for him. It also became clear, however, that his interests associated with the Influence Through Language and Ideas business core function were just as important, if not more so. Mark's counseling and mentoring interests were being only intermittently met in his current position, and his influence-based interests, given his status within the department, were barely realized at all. In terms of the business core function model, Mark had a statistically unusual LHH profile characterized by elevations in Counseling and Mentoring (but not Managing People) and in Influence Through Language and Ideas (but not Enterprise Control).

Mark's conversations with us made it clear that the strongest image he had of exciting work was that of the lawyers he had encountered at the company. He saw them as respected authorities who influenced policy at the highest levels. He was relatively well informed about the realities of their work activities, and the more he considered their work, the more attracted he became to pursuing an occupation in labor relations law. This was not the first time that Mark had considered going to law school. He had considered it briefly on other occasions but had been unable to imagine a work role in the law that was compelling enough to overcome his lack of self-confidence in being accepted to and completing law school.

Mark's contact with the lawyers at work, combined with his career consultation, helped him develop his imagination of satisfying work enough that he was able to overcome the psychological obstacles to applying to law school. Mark enrolled in an LSAT preparation course and was eventually admitted to a local law school.

Emmanuelle Lenoir (HLL; A,Q,T,CLL)

Score Summary

Application of Technology	71	Personal High
Quantitative Analysis	64	Personal High
Theory Development and Conceptual Thinking	55	
Creative Production	57	
Counseling and Mentoring	38	
Managing People	49	
Enterprise Control	46	
Influence Through Language and Ideas	50	

Business Career Profile Type: HMM

General Business Interest Index: Very High

Note: Based on full assessment data, Emmanuelle's profile was assessed as HLL for purposes of profile classification. In considering her case, however, you should keep in mind her actual scores on all of the business core function scales.

Emmanuelle grew up in a middle-class family in a Paris suburb, the elder of two children. She described her father as a very reserved, intelligent, introverted person who "should have done more" with his life. Emmanuelle always felt that he would have made a good engineer, but he had not had the opportunity to attend college and instead made his career working in the government. She had always identified with her father and recalled fondly spending time as a girl playing chess with him, and later solving mathematical puzzles together. Meanwhile, her younger sister was closer to their mother, who was a homemaker. She married and began a family quite young, following in her mother's footsteps.

It was clear early in her life that Emmanuelle was bright and talented. She learned languages easily, becoming fluent in English and German and proficient in Spanish and Italian. She had an ear for music, and played piano and sang well. Most significantly in terms of her career, Emmanuelle was an outstanding student in mathematics and the sciences. She earned admission to the École Polytechnique, a top science and engineering school (the French equivalent of Massachusetts Institute of Technology), where she excelled and earned her bachelor's degree in physics.

Rather than go directly into the workforce, Emmanuelle decided to pursue an advanced degree in industrial engineering, and came to the United States to study for her master's degree. Again, she was an excellent student, and on graduating she received offers from a number of American manufacturing companies and consulting firms. Recognizing that the opportunities available to her in the United States were greater than those in France, Emmanuelle made sponsorship for permanent resident visa status her top priority in evaluating her offers, and as a result took a position with a large international management consulting firm that promised to sponsor her for a green card. Emmanuelle proved herself to be an outstanding analyst of business problems, showed a strong work ethic, and was a good team player.

As a result she received strong performance reviews. We noted that she did not, however, get rave reviews from clients, as some of her peers did. This is not to say that clients found fault with her work, simply that she was perceived more positively within the firm than outside.

After three years as a consultant, Emmanuelle was promoted to the role of project manager, which included many of the responsibilities present in the consultant role. Added to those were the duties of conceptualizing the business situation being studied, breaking the study into components and determining a time sequence for addressing those components, distributing the work among the team members, motivating them and monitoring their progress, building and maintaining a positive working relationship with the client company's primary contact person, taking the lead on presentations of progress reports and the final outcome to the client company, and working with the partner for whom she was managing the case. As when she was a consultant, Emmanuelle was more successful at aspects of her work that were internal to the firm than external. She found herself wanting to defer one-on-one meetings with the client, and she didn't like doing presentations to the client's executive team any more than she had as a consultant. In fact, now that she was the person responsible for the success of those presentations, she disliked them even more than she had in the past. She gave over much of the airtime during client presentations to members of her team, which at first was perceived as generous but later came to be seen as avoidance. In addition, Emmanuelle found the team management aspects of her new role somewhat difficult. Like many managers, she had no problem if a person reporting to her was hardworking, competent, and willing to function as part of the team (that is, if the person didn't need real management). When she had to push, exert her authority, energize someone who was feeling discouraged, or deliver negative performance reviews, however, Emmanuelle had real trouble. In other words, she continued to excel at the more analytical and technical side of the work, but did not fare so well in the managerial work. This discrepancy between her interest in, success in, and comfort with the internal technical work and the external or managerial activities continued, and after some time Emmanuelle realized that she would not be promoted to partner. She also realized that she would not *want* to be in that role, in which business development and management constitute the great majority of the work.

In the meantime, Emmanuelle had met and married an American, and considered herself to be in fact as well as in visa status a permanent resident of the United States. Her husband was a partner in a Wall Street investment bank, so Emmanuelle was, moreover, a permanent resident of New York City. She considered several career options. She could remain in consulting but in more of a "knowledge base" consulting role, doing research and writing, almost as she would do in a public policy think tank. She could move into a strategic planning role for a telecommunications company for which she had managed several projects. She could try to get into the venture capital industry, where her analytical skills would be of great value. Or she could use her connections in the financial services field to facilitate a move to a position as an equities analyst for either a "buy side" investment management firm or for a "sell side" investment bank. She wisely agreed that an individual contributor role was a better match for her than a management position.

Emmanuelle had a rather difficult time making a decision among her options, and a look at her *BCII* score summary gives us a strong clue as to why. We see that she is not elevated on either of the Working with People business core functions—Counseling and Mentoring, and Managing People. Nor is she elevated on either of the Control and Influence business core functions—Enterprise Control, and Influence Through Language and Ideas. But she is elevated on *all four* of the Application of Expertise business core functions. While it is true that her interests in the Application of Technology and Quantitative Analysis functions are surpassingly high, she has definite interests in Theory Development and Conceptual Thinking and in Creative Production as well. Essentially, when she began planning her next career move, Emmanuelle was trying to find a career position and path that would allow for expression of all four of those areas of expertise. Not surprisingly, such an opportunity proved to be elusive.

At one point Emmanuelle was leaning toward venture capital, figuring that it would provide the best overall mix of activities to suit her. On further reflection and networking, she learned that, at least at that time, there was so much capital in venture capital firms that a large part of the job had become selling the capital to the entrepreneurs, much as a commercial lender sells loans to businesses. Emmanuelle fortunately recognized that this would again eventually put her in a position in which she would not be comfortable. She eventually chose to pursue a career in investment management with a firm that highly valued its analysts (and compensated them accordingly). She would cover the telecommunications industry sector for them. This allowed her to express her very strong interests in the Application of Technology and the Quantitative Analysis functions, with some possibility for Theory Development and Conceptual Thinking. Creative Production was left for avocational expression.

At this point we want to turn our attention from looking within and assessing our patterns of deep structure interests to looking outside ourselves, at the world of work. Clearly, it is crucial to have an accurate picture of who you are. It is equally crucial to have a means of assessing work opportunities. Unlike shopping for a new suit, where if you know your size you can easily identify those suits that will fit, work opportunities come without labels attached. Chapter 10 will give you the tools you need to measure work opportunities you may consider.

TEN

Evaluating Work Opportunities

LEARNING ENOUGH about what a work opportunity will be like to evaluate it fairly can require a great deal of detective work, so you need to consider how to gather information about an industry, a specific company, and a particular position within it. The first step in the evaluation of a work opportunity is to read whatever you can about the industry and company in the business and general press. Call the company's investor relations department (if its stock is publicly traded) and ask that information be sent to you. Ask the reference librarian at your public or university library for help in locating information. If your city or university has a library dedicated to business research, that is even better. Also, the Internet has a growing number of services dedicated to providing career resource information. This trend is likely to continue and to become an important source for information.

Ask questions in interviews, especially as the balance of power shifts from them (with you acting as the salesperson for yourself) to you (with the firm's representatives trying to sell you the job), and after you have an offer. If you are being recruited by an executive recruiting firm ("headhunter"), ask the recruiter for detailed information about the job, the person you would report to, the office, the firm. Make use of your network of friends, fellow college and/or graduate school alumni, and business associates to obtain other points of view on the company and position. When visiting a company, pay attention not just to how *you* are treated but also to how people seem to treat each other; be an anthropologist, examining the habits of a new tribe. Take notes on all of your observations, so you don't lose any important data.

It is important to look at the macro level (industry and company) as well as at the micro level (the particular office, the group with which you would be working most closely, and the specific job you would have), since they will all account for some of the variance in your experience. At the most macro level of industry, different industries can have radically different cultures. High-tech companies tend to be less formal than trust companies, for example. At the level of company, different organizations have different cultures. Procter & Gamble, for example, promotes primarily from within, resulting in an extremely strong culture and sense of loyalty among middle and upper management. Finally, at the level of specific settings, different offices within the same company can have very different microcultures.

Most important, be ruthlessly honest and objective as you go about it. A person-position match is always either a win/win or a lose/lose situation. Don't deceive yourself into taking the wrong job just because you want or need a change, or you are likely to find yourself in a lose/lose scenario. When that happens, the individual almost always loses more than the company.

Think in terms of a one- to two-year time frame in considering the fit between yourself and a specific work opportunity. You should also consider an *opportunity* as part of a longer career *path,* with a five- to seven-year time frame.

When evaluating a given work opportunity, you'll find many factors to take into account, such as location, compensation, benefits, and the opportunities that this position may open up for you. While making a good match between your core interests and the opportunity a particular position will provide for the expression of those interests is of great importance, this is clearly not the only thing that matters. The impact of a career change or physical move on your spouse or partner's career, on your children's educational and social lives, and on your relationships with other family members and friends may be of critical importance in your consideration of a work opportunity, perhaps overriding the goodness of fit between the opportunity and your interests. We are not able to address those issues in this book. Many articles and books have been written about how to negotiate compensation packages, how to weigh different variables such as location and dual career issues, and so on.

In our career assessment work we focus on three general aspects of an individual in terms of a match with a specific work opportunity: aptitudes, personality traits, and reward values. Although we focus on a number of personality traits, for all of the reasons discussed in earlier chapters we consider the deep structure of interest patterns to be most important. We will discuss briefly aptitudes and reward values, and then discuss at some length how you can evaluate a work opportunity in terms of its match with the deep structure of your interest patterns.

Aptitudes

It is important to keep in mind that skills and aptitudes are what we call *threshold variables.* In other words, to be successful in a particular work role you need *at least* the threshold amount of any specified ability. Greatly exceeding that threshold may or may not be to your advantage, but not breaking the threshold will lead to failure in the position.

Consider, as a concrete and very measurable example, the work of a refuse collector—picking up garbage cans and dumping their contents into the back of the collection truck. For this position the aptitude in question is ability to lift weight, and the threshold is, let us say, one hundred pounds. Someone who is unable to lift one hundred pounds will not be able to do this work successfully; someone who can lift that amount will. Will greatly exceeding the threshold make someone better at the work? Perhaps, but not necessarily. Being able to lift five hundred pounds may be entirely superfluous in terms of success. Once a particular aptitude threshold is broken, other variables may become more important to success, such as dependability, strength of the body's autoimmune system, and so forth.

When you consider a work opportunity in the world of business, ask what aptitudes and skills the work requires, *at a minimum,* for success; and then think about whether you meet that threshold. Bear in mind that people tend to overestimate what will be required, to mentally set the bar higher than it really is. For example, we have heard several excellent salespeople say that they wouldn't consider high-tech sales because they know nothing about computers or software. In fact, for many products all the salesperson has to know is what the program can and can't do, and enough about competing products to champion his or her own. The salesperson has the backup of technical support people to answer highly technical customer questions. Ability to write code is not even on the list of requirements; even a priori knowledge of how to use the product is far less important than skill at selling.

As another example, consider a more abstract aptitude—the capacity for critical thinking. Critical thinking is the hard work of intellectual functioning: correctly defining problems, determining what information is needed to solve those problems, recognizing unstated assumptions in arguments, formulating hypotheses on the basis of available data, and assessing the validity of inferences being drawn on data. Assume that for a particular job you need to be at least at the 50th percentile in your capacity for critical thinking. Will being at the 99th percentile be to your advantage, making you more successful? Perhaps so, at least over the short term. But being that bright may lead to your feeling bored a great deal of the time, so in fact it might *not* make for greater success in that particular work opportunity.

Another consideration when we think about aptitudes is that of development. Some aptitudes can, with effort, be developed. A particular job may be a stretch for you, but something that you can grow into. The key here is in distinguishing between being stretched and broken. Someone who can currently lift only eighty pounds is likely to be able to gain strength quickly enough to be able to survive the first few weeks on the job and then be at or above the threshold of one hundred. But someone with a bad back who can barely carry a twenty-pound bag of groceries may wind up with a herniated disk.

Lack of an engineering background may be an initial disadvantage, but not a fatal one, if the company you work for makes a technical product whose end user is a nonengineer consumer (personal computers sold to individuals for home and business use, for example). In this case you might have to stretch to gain the requisite technical expertise, but it is likely that you will succeed. If, however, your product is a sophisticated supercomputer whose end user is a team of aeronautical engineers, your lack of a very high level of engineering knowledge and aptitude is likely to be too much of a stretch.

In summary, to evaluate a work opportunity you need to look carefully and objectively at the aptitudes the work will require you to have, and at what levels. Then look equally carefully and objectively at yourself to see which of those aptitudes you possess, and at what level; and to see which of those aptitudes you will likely be able to raise to the required level in a reasonably short amount of time.

Values

People mean many different things when they speak of values; there are family values, national values, and spiritual values, among others. Our focus here is on work reward values. Many different rewards are available to people for their work. The term *work reward values* refers to the degree to which you value those different rewards.

In our consulting practice we regularly use an instrument, the *Management and Professional Reward Profile*, which we developed to help people prioritize their valuing of thirteen different work rewards. The list is not meant to be exhaustive (no list could be), but these are the rewards we most commonly find to be most salient for people in business:

- *Intellectual Challenge:* The position offers consistent intellectual challenge.

- *Financial Gain:* The position provides excellent opportunity for exceptional financial reward.

- *Security:* The position offers a great deal of security in terms of predictable salary, benefits, and future employment.

- *Power and Influence:* The position offers the opportunity to exercise power and influence (to be an influential decision maker).

- *Affiliation:* The position offers a setting with enjoyable colleagues with whom I feel a sense of belonging.

- *Recognition:* The position is in an environment where individual accomplishments are recognized with praise from peers and superiors.

- *Managing People:* The position offers the opportunity to manage and direct other people.

- *Positioning:* The position offers experience and access to people and opportunities that will position me well for my next career move.

- *Lifestyle:* The position allows ample time to pursue other important aspects of my lifestyle (family, leisure activities, etc.).

- *Prestige:* The position is with an organization that commands a great deal of prestige in its field.

- *Altruism:* The position offers the satisfaction of regularly helping others with their individual or business concerns.

- *Autonomy:* The position offers considerable autonomy and independence.

- *Variety:* The position provides a great deal of variety in the nature of the work performed.

Although we are not able to include the *Management and Professional Reward Profile* in this book, you can produce your own personal work reward value hierarchy in an informal way. First copy each reward title and its description on a blank note card. Then lay them all out on a table and arrange them so that they are assembled in order of importance. If two or more are tied, place them side by side. If any are of no importance to you whatsoever, set them aside.

Keep in mind that each reward is self-defined: What constitutes exceptional financial gain for one person may be an austerity budget for another. One person's good lifestyle may be traveling abroad extensively, while another would want to be home most every evening and on the weekends. As you look over the cards and sort them out, think about what each reward means *to you.* Make a note of the order in which you placed the cards, and then set them aside for a week or two. Revisit this exercise, and see if there are any shifts you feel should be made. If there are any changes, repeat this step until you feel confident that your hierarchy accurately reflects your values.

Three cautionary notes are necessary. First, this exercise is completely transparent and easy prey for your valuing highly what you "should" value and not valuing what you "shouldn't." Be as honest as you possibly can. If prestige is important to you, for example, you won't do yourself a favor by pretending it isn't because you think it shouldn't be. Second, values change. They don't change overnight, or even in a matter of weeks or months, but over the course of several years they may change substantially. If you highly value financial gain and then make $10 million in the stock market, your valuing of that reward may diminish. If you are just beginning your career, you probably place a much higher value on positioning for the future than if you were near to retirement. If you are "footloose and fancy free," with no debt, mortgage, or family responsibilities, and then you marry, buy a house, and have triplets, your valuing of security is likely to increase. Third, the disadvantage of this exercise is that it does not tell you if the distance between your most highly valued reward and the second most highly valued reward is the same as the distance between the second and the third. In psychometric terms, this exercise provides you with ordinal data (the order of the reward values). We developed the *Management and Professional Reward Profile* in order to provide interval data (so that one reward could have a value of 12, the next a value of 9, the next an 8, and so forth, giving us information about the *relative distance* between the different values). Thus, you need to ask yourself whether the distances are equal, and if not, how much difference really exists.

Think of the three or four rewards you valued most highly as a shopping list in considering work opportunities. These data are important: If you do not receive the rewards in some abundance, you are unlikely to be happy in that position for long. In addition, being clear about what you are looking for as rewards for your work helps you to shop more efficiently. Just as you can evaluate a potential computer purchase much more quickly if you have in mind a handful of "must have" features you can't live without, you can evaluate a work opportunity more easily if you have in mind those rewards you can't live without.

Use the same techniques described at the beginning of the chapter in evaluating the rewards that specific work opportunities offer. Then compare what they offer with what you want. Consider carefully whether you can live with any great differences between the two. Again, be honest and you won't get the wrong job.

Interests: Evaluating the Core Function Profile of a Work Opportunity

At the heart of your evaluation of any work opportunity should be an evaluation of the extent to which it provides a good match with your business core function profile. You have already analyzed your interest profile. In this section you will learn how to do a core function profile analysis of specific work opportunities. You will do this by comparing the information you have gathered about a work opportunity with the statements listed below for each of the eight business core functions; think in terms of a time frame of one to two years in evaluating what the opportunity offers in each of the function areas. Your goal in this analysis will be to arrive at a rating on a scale from very low to very high for each function. If you are already working in business, evaluate your current or most previous position using this schema. This will accomplish two things: It may help you to clarify what you do and do not enjoy about this work; and it will provide you with a baseline against which to compare future work opportunities.

As you read the five statements for each of the eight business core functions, make a careful determination of *between which two statements* the position in question best fits. Do this for all eight categories. Then revisit each of the eight and refine your evaluation. If, for example, you decided that a work opportunity you are considering falls somewhere between a 2 and a 3 on the Quantitative Analysis business core function, ask yourself whether the position is really closer to a 2 or to a 3—or is squarely in the middle between the two—and give it a rating of 2, 2.5, or 3. Any work opportunity or position will be described for *each business core function*, then, as a 0, 0.5, 1, 1.5, 2, 2.5, 3, 3.5, or 4. Following are a series of statements to use as anchors for the integer points on the scales.

Application of Technology

  0: No use of technology is involved in the work opportunity and no technological skill or knowledge is required.

  1: Minimal application of technological skill and knowledge is required. For example: positions requiring use of standard business software applications such as word processing and scheduling programs, and use of office equipment and systems such as fax machines, voice mail, and electronic mail.

2: Application of technological skill and knowledge is a regular part of the work, but not a central determinant of success. For example: marketing or selling medium- or high-tech products; positions involving some use of spreadsheet, database, and desktop publishing software.

3: Application of technological skill and knowledge is a central determinant of success. For example: product management of high-tech products; positions requiring daily and frequent use of sophisticated technologies such as spreadsheet, database, desktop publishing, and financial modeling software in the service of a nontechnical goal (such as financial analysis or marketing analysis).

4: Application of technological skill and knowledge is the major component of the work and the central determinant of success (and is in the service of a technical goal). For example: management of research and development, engineering-oriented consulting, manufacturing process engineering, electrical engineering, information systems analysis and management or consulting, computer-assisted design of machinery.

Quantitative Analysis

0: No use of quantitative analysis is involved in the work opportunity.

1: Minimal use of quantitative analysis is required. For example: sales or other customer service roles where records must be kept and reported, but where only basic mathematical computations of the records are required; creation of annual budgets for a small department.

2: Quantitative analysis is a regular part of the work, but not a central determinant of success. For example: sales roles where sales analyses and forecasting are expected; supervisory and management roles that require the creation and use of complex budget systems.

3: Quantitative analysis is a central determinant of success. For example: positions where business analysis such as cash-flow analysis, analysis of sales or market trends, or general analysis of corporate financial reports is required on a regular basis.

4: Quantitative analysis is the major component of the work and the central determinant of success. For example: equity analysis, public accounting, actuarial analysis, credit analysis, market research analysis, designing and building financial and economic models.

Theory Development and Conceptual Thinking

0: No theory development or conceptual thinking is involved in the work opportunity.

1: Minimal theory development and conceptual thinking are required. For example: sales positions that require characterization of the needs or buying patterns of potential customers in new markets.

2: Theory development and conceptual thinking are a regular part of the work, but are not a central determinant of success. For example: management positions that require program or organizational design; operations- or production-oriented management consulting ("process reengineering").

3: Theory development and conceptual thinking are central determinants of success. For example: developing marketing strategies, new business development, merger and acquisition strategy planning or consulting, design of compensation systems.

4: Theory development and conceptual thinking are the major components of the work, and the central determinants of success. For example: professor of business in a research-oriented university, research scientist in a consulting firm, business policy analyst in a government agency, designing and building financial and economic models.

Creative Production

0: No creative production is involved in the work opportunity.

1: Minimal creative production is required. For example: positions that require the production of slides for internal business presentations or the creation of customized versions of standard products such as spreadsheet or word processing templates.

2: Creative production is a regular part of the work, but is not a central determinant of success. For example: positions that require desktop publishing layout, writing copy for or designing internal publications, designing slides and graphics for sales presentations, writing extensive correspondence.

3: Creative production is a central determinant of success. For example: public relations, meeting or event planning, advertising account manager, director of communications or publications, designing corporate training and development programs.

4: Creative production is the major component of the work and the central determinant of success. For example: graphic designer, advertising copy writer, new product designer, architect, author of business books, business journalist, publisher or editor of a business press.

Counseling and Mentoring

0: No counseling or mentoring is involved in the work opportunity.

1: Minimal counseling and mentoring are required. For example: many expert individual contributor roles.

2: Counseling and mentoring are a regular part of the work, but not a central determinant of success. For example: most middle management or first-line supervisory positions.

3: Counseling and mentoring are a central determinant of success. For example: managing a group in which developing new employees is a major part of the management role; managing the relationships among and the efforts of a team working closely together in a high-stress environment; work in which maintaining close personal relationships with clients is important.

4: Counseling and mentoring are the major component of the work and the central determinant of success. For example: human resource development, outplacement counseling, executive coaching; work in which maintaining close personal relationships with clients is essential, such as private banking or private client services for high net worth individuals.

Managing People

0: No management of people is involved in the work opportunity.

1: Minimal management of people is required. For example: a professional role (such as consultant, portfolio manager, banker) that includes managing an administrative assistant; supervising occasional temporary workers.

2: Managing people is a regular part of the work, but not a central determinant of success. For example: a project management role in which other members of the team operate with moderate autonomy, requiring coordination of efforts and management of group resources.

3: Managing people is a central determinant of success. For example: a general management position (such as division head, president, CEO); managing the work of a group of employees on permanent assignment while being involved in broader issues within the organization such as business strategy, internal policies, organizational structure, or hiring decisions in addition to direct reports.

4: Managing people is the major component of the work and the central determinant of success. For example: supervising the day-to-day work of a large group of permanent blue- or white-collar employees (without having substantial involvement in broader organizational issues).

Enterprise Control

0: No enterprise control is involved in the work opportunity.

1: Minimal enterprise control is required. For example: first-line manager in an operating company; shift supervisor of a franchised business.

2: Enterprise control is a regular part of the work, but not a central determinant of success. For example: head of a trading or sales desk in an investment bank or investment management firm; managing other salespeople while maintaining personal responsibility for sales within a territory; a player-coach role.

3: Enterprise control is a central determinant of success. For example: plant manager, regional sales manager, manager of a large office of business professionals (such as consultants, accountants) with responsibility for the profitability of the group as well as maintaining personal client relationships

4: Enterprise control is the major component of the work and the central determinant of success. For example: president, chief executive officer, chief operating officer, chief financial officer, vice president (general manager) of a division or subsidiary, vice president of sales, managing director in an investment bank or consulting firm, managing partner of a law firm; principal in a transaction-intensive work role. Profit and loss responsibility is implied.

Influence Through Language and Ideas

0: No influence through language and ideas is involved in the work opportunity.

1: Minimal influence through language and ideas is required. For example: handling in-bound calls from mail-order purchasers.

2: Influence through language and ideas is a regular part of the work, but not a central determinant of success. For example: managing an organization consisting largely of volunteers, inspiring their efforts in service of the mission of the organization; manager of a customer service function.

3: Influence through language and ideas is a central determinant of success. For example: management positions in an organization in which informal networks of influence are important in accomplishing goals; working as a member of the board of directors of a charitable organization where fund-raising is one responsibility.

4: Influence through language and ideas is the major component of the work and the central determinant of success. For example: sales, director of public relations and communications, speech writer, labor negotiations, writing press releases, writing advertising copy, holding public office, arguing a case in court, writing for the business press.

Once you have determined a rating on each of the business core functions for a work opportunity, use the chart below to assign a description of the extent to which the work opportunity offers activities associated with each of the business core functions:

Rating	Range
0	Very Low
.5 or 1	Low
1.5, 2, or 2.5	Average
3 or 3.5	High
4	Very High

Compare these ratings with the ranges of the eight business core functions on your own profile. At the heart of your analysis, of course, should be the match between your profile and the work opportunity on those business core functions that are most important for you. You should also beware, however, of a work opportunity that demands a significant amount of time devoted to activities associated with business core functions that are significantly *low* for you. A work opportunity where a highly important core function will be realized, but where much time will be required in core function activities that hold little interest for you, may be problematic.

Ultimately, you will have assessed a work opportunity's business core function profile, the aptitudes it will require, and the work rewards it will provide, and then compared these features of the opportunity with your own profile of aptitudes, reward values, and deep structure interests. If there are significant mismatches between you and the opportunity on any of these three factors, you may well be unhappy in the position and/or fail in it.

It is in the final stage of assessing a work opportunity that the Sirens' songs can be most compelling. "What if I don't get another offer?" "What if I don't get a better offer?" "All my friends think I should take it." "I know I'll be miserable for a while, but I can stand it." "Things are looking pretty dicey in my current company/industry—I don't want to wait around and be reengineered out of a job." These kinds of statements can lead people to abandon their planning and impulsively take a bad job. The usual process is first to lie to ourselves, convincing ourselves that this really is a good job for us, then to tell the "truth" (which we have made up) to the prospective employer, convincing the company to hire us. (Meanwhile, employers may be doing the same thing, misrepresenting to some degree what the job will be like. Both parties get what they want, but neither gets what they need.)

Over the past fifteen years we have worked with many hundreds of MBA students, as well as business professionals at advanced stages in their careers, and the overwhelming concern expressed is "Will I get a job?" Rarely do we hear "I don't want to get the *wrong* job." Many people consider a job search essentially completed when they receive an offer. In truth, that moment calls for a renewed effort at paying attention to the voice of the emerging self.

OUR WORK IN career research and counseling is a lifetime endeavor. We will be sharing that work in several ways, including via a "site" on the World-Wide Web where we will publish further research and information about career self-assessment, planning, and management. We offer intensive training workshops for career development professionals interested in becoming certified users of the *BCII*. In these workshops we teach participants how to interpret *BCII* results and how to integrate them with other career assessment instruments such as the *Management and Professional Reward Profile* and the *Myers-Briggs Type Indicator*®, both with individuals and in a workshop or class format. Information about these workshops is available on our web site or by calling 617-739-1976.

We want to hear your comments about this book and the *BCII*: what you found most helpful and least helpful, what you think we should include in our next edition, and any questions you would like us to address. Although we are not able to respond individually, if we hear similar concerns or questions from a number of readers, we will respond through the Web page. We also want to use this as a way of learning what you, our readers, are thinking about, how you are managing your careers, what your choices and dilemmas are—what is going on out there in the world of business work that we may be able to address through our writing and seminars. Finally, if you would like to add your *BCII* results to our database of business professionals, that would be very helpful to us as we go forward in our work. The *BCII* disk automatically creates a file that is easy to attach to an e-mail message. The file will be sent without your name attached; your privacy is assured. Full directions for sending us your comments and your file are available on our Web home page. We invite you to visit us there; our address is http://www.careerdiscovery.com.

Percentile Equivalents of Adjusted Standard Scores for the Eight Business Core Function Scales

THE TABLES IN this appendix will allow you to find the general business sample percentile equivalent for your adjusted standard score on each of the eight business core function scales. A percentile equivalent tells you how many individuals in the general business sample had scores higher and lower than you on a given scale. For example, if your score is at the 30th percentile, approximately 30% of the general business sample of your same gender had scores that were lower than yours and approximately 70% had scores that were higher. If your score is at the 75th percentile, approximately 75% of the sample of your gender had scores that were lower and approximately 25% had scores that were higher.

To find a percentile equivalent, first find the table for the appropriate scale; make sure that you are looking at the column **for your own gender** when finding your percentile equivalent. Find your adjusted standard score on the scale (as provided by the *Business Career Interest Inventory* score summary screen) in the left hand column of the table and then read the corresponding approximate percentile equivalent for your adjusted standard score. For those who are curious about how their interests in the core functions compare with the interests of our combined sample of business men and women, we have provided that information on our web site (http://www.careerdiscovery.com). Each adjusted standard score actually corresponds to a percentile range that extends from the percentile representing the previous standard score through the percentile corresponding to the percentile equivalent for your standard score. For example, let us say that your percentile equivalent on a given scale is the 50th percentile and that the percentile equivalent for the next lower standard score is the 46th percentile. The actual percentile range represented by your adjusted standard score is from the 46th to the 50th percentile.

Application of Technology

Men		*Women*	
Adjusted T Score	Approximate Percentile	Adjusted T Score	Approximate Percentile
26 or lower	1	26 or lower	1
27	1	27	1
28	1	28	1
29	1	29	1
30	1	30	1
31	1	31	1
32	1	32	1
33	1	33	1
34	1	34	1
35	2	35	1
36	3	36	2
37	4	37	3
38	9	38	5
39	12	39	6
40	15	40	8
41	19	41	14
42	23	42	17
43	30	43	25
44	31	44	26
45	34	45	29
46	38	46	35

Application of Technology (*continued*)

Men		Women	
Adjusted T Score	Approximate Percentile	Adjusted T Score	Approximate Percentile
47	41	47	40
48	45	48	44
49	49	49	49
50	54	50	55
51	57	51	59
52	60	52	60
53	65	53	63
54	69	54	66
55	72	55	70
56	75	56	75
57	77	57	77
58	81	58	78
59	83	59	81
60	86	60	84
61	87	61	85
62	88	62	86
63	89	63	88
64	91	64	91
65	92	65	91
66	95	66	92
67	96	67	93
68	96	68	94
69	97	69	96
70	98	70	97
71	98	71	97
72	99	72	98
73	99	73	98
74	99	74	98
75 or higher	99	75 or higher	99

Quantitative Analysis

Men		Women	
Adjusted T Score	Approximate Percentile	Adjusted T Score	Approximate Percentile
26 or lower	1	26 or lower	1
27	1	27	1
28	1	28	1
29	1	29	1
30	1	30	1
31	2	31	1
32	2	32	1
33	3	33	1
34	4	34	1
35	6	35	1
36	8	36	2
37	10	37	2
38	13	38	4
39	14	39	5
40	21	40	10
41	23	41	11
42	27	42	14
43	30	43	17
44	34	44	23
45	36	45	27
46	39	46	35
47	42	47	37
48	44	48	42
49	49	49	45
50	52	50	48
51	54	51	54
52	56	52	57
53	58	53	65
54	63	54	69
55	66	55	71
56	71	56	78

Quantitative Analysis (*continued*)

Men		Women	
Adjusted T Score	Approximate Percentile	Adjusted T Score	Approximate Percentile
57	72	57	79
58	74	58	80
59	78	59	81
60	83	60	84
61	85	61	85
62	86	62	86
63	89	63	88
64	92	64	88
65	94	65	90
66	95	66	92
67	96	67	94
68	96	68	95
69	97	69	97
70	97	70	97
71	98	71	98
72	99	72	98
73	99	73	99
74	99	74	99
75 or higher	99	75 or higher	99

Theory Development and Conceptual Thinking

Men		Women	
Adjusted T Score	Approximate Percentile	Adjusted T Score	Approximate Percentile
26 or lower	1	26 or lower	1
27	1	27	1
28	1	28	1
29	1	29	1
30	1	30	1
31	1	31	1
32	1	32	1
33	1	33	1
34	1	34	2
35	1	35	2
36	3	36	3
37	4	37	4
38	6	38	5
39	9	39	7
40	12	40	9
41	16	41	11
42	18	42	12
43	23	43	17
44	25	44	21
45	30	45	25
46	34	46	29
47	38	47	29
48	42	48	36
49	46	49	40
50	50	50	48
51	54	51	49
52	60	52	54
53	63	53	55
54	68	54	59
55	71	55	65
56	76	56	69

Theory Development and Conceptual Thinking (*continued*)

Men		*Women*	
Adjusted T Score	Approximate Percentile	Adjusted T Score	Approximate Percentile
57	78	57	71
58	81	58	75
59	84	59	80
60	86	60	82
61	89	61	87
62	91	62	90
63	92	63	92
64	94	64	93
65	96	65	94
66	98	66	96
67	98	67	97
68	99	68	99
69	99	69	99
70	99	70	99
71	99	71	99
72	99	72	99
73	99	73	99
74	99	74	99
75 or higher	99	75 or higher	99

Creative Production

Men		*Women*	
Adjusted T Score	Approximate Percentile	Adjusted T Score	Approximate Percentile
26 or lower	1	26 or lower	1
27	1	27	2
28	1	28	2
29	1	29	3
30	1	30	3
31	2	31	4
32	3	32	4
33	4	33	6
34	6	34	8
35	8	35	10
36	9	36	11
37	11	37	14
38	13	38	14
39	14	39	15
40	16	40	16
41	18	41	20
42	21	42	20
43	25	43	21
44	29	44	29
45	32	45	31
46	37	46	34
47	44	47	37
48	45	48	40
49	46	49	44
50	48	50	46
51	54	51	50
52	59	52	52
53	63	53	56
54	68	54	57
55	70	55	63
56	74	56	66

Creative Production (*continued*)

Men		Women	
Adjusted T Score	Approximate Percentile	Adjusted T Score	Approximate Percentile
57	75	57	69
58	78	58	74
59	80	59	78
60	83	60	80
61	86	61	86
62	88	62	92
63	90	63	95
64	92	64	99
65	94	65	99
66	95	66	99
67	96	67	99
68	98	68	99
69	99	69	99
70	99	70	99
71	99	71	99
72	99	72	99
73	99	73	99
74	99	74	99
75 or higher	99	75 or higher	99

Counseling and Mentoring

Men		Women	
Adjusted T Score	Approximate Percentile	Adjusted T Score	Approximate Percentile
26 or lower	1	26 or lower	1
27	1	27	1
28	1	28	1
29	1	29	1
30	1	30	2
31	1	31	2
32	1	32	3
33	1	33	3
34	2	34	4
35	4	35	5
36	8	36	6
37	8	37	10
38	11	38	11
39	13	39	14
40	16	40	15
41	19	41	16
42	22	42	20
43	24	43	20
44	29	44	25
45	33	45	29
46	36	46	34
47	39	47	37
48	44	48	42
49	49	49	50
50	55	50	52
51	57	51	55
52	64	52	59
53	66	53	59
54	68	54	63
55	71	55	68
56	75	56	70

Counseling and Mentoring (*continued*)

Men		Women	
Adjusted T Score	Approximate Percentile	Adjusted T Score	Approximate Percentile
57	77	57	75
58	81	58	78
59	82	59	79
60	84	60	79
61	87	61	83
62	88	62	86
63	89	63	90
64	91	64	93
65	94	65	94
66	96	66	95
67	96	67	98
68	97	68	99
69	97	69	99
70	99	70	99
71	99	71	99
72	99	72	99
73	99	73	99
74	99	74	99
75 or higher	99	75 or higher	99

Managing People

Men		Women	
Adjusted T Score	Approximate Percentile	Adjusted T Score	Approximate Percentile
26 or lower	1	26 or lower	1
27	1	27	1
28	1	28	1
29	1	29	1
30	1	30	1
31	1	31	1
32	1	32	2
33	1	33	2
34	2	34	3
35	3	35	3
36	4	36	4
37	4	37	5
38	8	38	6
39	10	39	8
40	12	40	10
41	16	41	13
42	19	42	16
43	22	43	20
44	25	44	24
45	32	45	28
46	34	46	31
47	40	47	33
48	43	48	35
49	47	49	43
50	50	50	46
51	56	51	49
52	60	52	53
53	63	53	57
54	69	54	59
55	72	55	66
56	74	56	67

Managing People (*continued*)

Men		Women	
Adjusted T Score	Approximate Percentile	Adjusted T Score	Approximate Percentile
57	77	57	73
58	81	58	76
59	82	59	78
60	87	60	82
61	89	61	84
62	90	62	88
63	93	63	90
64	94	64	93
65	96	65	94
66	97	66	95
67	97	67	97
68	98	68	97
69	99	69	98
70	99	70	99
71	99	71	99
72	99	72	99
73	99	73	99
74	99	74	99
75 or higher	99	75 or higher	99

Enterprise Control

Men		Women	
Adjusted T Score	Approximate Percentile	Adjusted T Score	Approximate Percentile
26 or lower	1	26 or lower	1
27	1	27	1
28	2	28	1
29	2	29	1
30	2	30	1
31	2	31	1
32	3	32	3
33	3	33	3
34	4	34	4
35	4	35	5
36	5	36	5
37	7	37	6
38	8	38	6
39	11	39	7
40	13	40	10
41	16	41	12
42	18	42	16
43	20	43	16
44	23	44	17
45	27	45	20
46	31	46	25
47	33	47	30
48	37	48	31
49	42	49	35
50	45	50	38
51	47	51	44
52	51	52	47
53	59	53	53
54	64	54	59
55	69	55	63
56	74	56	70

Enterprise Control (*continued*)

Men		Women	
Adjusted T Score	Approximate Percentile	Adjusted T Score	Approximate Percentile
57	77	57	74
58	82	58	77
59	84	59	82
60	87	60	86
61	91	61	88
62	93	62	89
63	97	63	93
64	99	64	93
65	99	65	95
66	99	66	97
67	99	67	98
68	99	68	99
69	99	69	99
70	99	70	99
71	99	71	99
72	99	72	99
73	99	73	99
74	99	74	99
75 or higher	99	75 or higher	99

Influence Through Language and Ideas

Men		Women	
Adjusted T Score	Approximate Percentile	Adjusted T Score	Approximate Percentile
26 or lower	1	26 or lower	1
27	1	27	1
28	1	28	1
29	1	29	1
30	1	30	1
31	1	31	1
32	2	32	1
33	4	33	2
34	4	34	3
35	5	35	4
36	7	36	5
37	8	37	5
38	9	38	7
39	12	39	8
40	14	40	11
41	15	41	13
42	17	42	16
43	19	43	18
44	23	44	20
45	28	45	22
46	32	46	25
47	35	47	27
48	40	48	32
49	44	49	38
50	47	50	44
51	52	51	48
52	57	52	53
53	61	53	57
54	67	54	64
55	71	55	65
56	76	56	69

Influence Through Language and Ideas (*continued*)

Men		Women	
Adjusted T Score	Approximate Percentile	Adjusted T Score	Approximate Percentile
57	78	57	74
58	80	58	78
59	85	59	80
60	88	60	84
61	88	61	85
62	90	62	87
63	94	63	89
64	94	64	92
65	96	65	95
66	98	66	97
67	99	67	98
68	99	68	99
69	99	69	99
70	99	70	99
71	99	71	99
72	99	72	99
73	99	73	99
74	99	74	99
75 or higher	99	75 or higher	99

━ CHAPTER NOTES

Epigraph

LaVelle, Louis, *The Dilemma of Narcissus* (translated by William Gairdner) (Burdett, NY: Larson Publications, 1993).

Chapter Two

Thomas R. Piper, Mary C. Gentile, and Sharon Daloz Parks, *Can Ethics Be Taught?: Perspective, Challenges, and Approaches at the Harvard Business School* (Boston: Harvard Business School Press, 1993).

Chapter Three

Mihaly Csikszentmihalyi, *Flow: The Psychology of Optimal Experience* (Harper Perennial, 1991), p. 71.

The authoritative work on memory and imagination in Renaissance thinking is Frances Yates, *The Art of Memory* (London: Routledge and Kegan Paul, 1966).

Robert Bosnak uses a similar approach to memory training for active imagination in his excellent work on the psychology of dreams, *A Little Course in Dreams* (Boston: Shambhala, 1988).

Chapter Five

Correlations cited are with scale scores from the Strong Interest Inventory and the Campbell Interest and Skill Survey.

Chapter Eight

"The Holy Longing," by Goethe (translated by Robert Bly) from *News of the Universe,* edited by Robert Bly. Copyright 1980 by Robert Bly.

Reprinted with permission of Sierra Club Books (San Fancisco: Sierra Book Club, 1980).

For an extended discussion of the "long black bag" image see Robert Bly's *A Little Book on the Human Shadow,* edited by William Booth (San Fancisco: Harper and Row, 1988).

Chapter Ten

The definition of critical thinking is based on the work of P. Dressel and L. Mayhew, published in *General Education: Exploration in Evaluation* (Final Report of the Cooperative Study of Evaluation in General Education) (Washington, D.C.: American Council on Education, 1954).

— INDEX

Accountant, 81
Active imagination, 44, 47
  distasteful jobs, 55
  feelings of accomplishment,
    55–56
  flow, 50–52
  images, 45–48
  job envy, 53–55
  letters about you, 57–58
  reading patterns, 56–57
  self observation and daydreaming,
    57
  training the mind's eye, 48–50
  work history interview, 52–53
Active imagination exercises, scoring
  and analyzing, 92
  combining ratings, 100–03
  integrating with *BCII* scores,
    103–04
  sample ratings, 94–100
  scorable activities, examples, 93–94
Activity-based business core functions,
  78–90
Adjusted standard score, 63, 224
Adult development, 85
Advertising, 83, 90, 136
Affiliation, 212
Age, 65–67
Aggressiveness, 35–36
AHH, 119–21
Albedo (white phase), 173–76
ALL, 130–33
Altruism, 213
Ambition, 23, 26

Anger, 171–72
Anxiety, 167
Apathy, 167
Application of Expertise, 125, 137
  Application of Technology, 79–81,
    119, 130
  Creative Production, 83–85, 106,
    124, 135
  high, 114, 128, 146, 156
  low, 140, 143, 152, 159
  profile type, 106
  Quantitative Analysis, 81–82, 121,
    133
  Theory Development and
    Conceptual Thinking, 82–83,
    106, 123, 134
Application of Technology, 78,
  130–33
  business core function model,
    79–81
  core function profile analysis,
    215–16
  interests, 79, 110
  percentile equivalents, 225–26
  profile type, 106
  scorable activities, 93
  score interpretation, 80
  skills, 79
Aptitude, 14, 210–12
Architecture, 84
Art, 83–84, 135
Authentic writing, 49–50
Autonomy, 213
Average standard score, 68

Bank manager, 86
BCII. See *Business Career Interest Inventory*
Black phase, 170–73
"Blank page" job description, 84
Bly, Robert, 171–72
Bookkeeper, 81
Boredom, 167
Business Career Interest Inventory (BCII), 59, 108–13
   database, adding your results, 223
   on disk, 60–61
   interpreting your scores, 74
   scale scores, 61–63
   scoring questions and answers, 63–71
   and skills, 81
   understanding your profile type, 74–75
   validity statements, 71–74
Business career profiles, case examples, 180–81
   Gilchrist, Jerry (HHH, THH), 188–91
   Greeley, Caroline (LLH), 182–83
   Heller, Pat (LLH), 185–88
   Knight, Sue (HHL), 195–98
   Lenoir, Emmanuelle (HLL; A,Q,T,CLL), 203–07
   Littleton, Elaine (HLL; A,Q,TLL), 184–85
   Oliver, Kim (HLH), 198–200
   Twomey, Mark (LHH), 201–03
   Vance, Diane (LHL), 192–95
   Young, Mark (HHH, QHH), 181–82
Business career profile type, 74, 114
   analyzing, 105
   determining, 106–08
   HHH, 114
      AHH, 119–21
         Application of Expertise functions, 125–28
      CHH, 124–25

Control and Influence functions, 116–17
      QHH, 121–23
      THH, 123–24
   HHL, 146–52
   HLH, 156–59
   HLL, 128
      ALL, 130–33
      Application of Expertise functions, 137–40
      CLL, 135–37
      QLL, 133–34
      TLL, 134–35
   how to use your scores, 108–13
   LHH, 152–56
   LHL, 140–43
   LLH, 143–46
   LLL, 159–62
Business core function model, 78–79
   Application of Technology, 79–81
   business core function profile, 91
   Counseling and Mentoring, 85–86
   Creative Production, 83–85
   Enterprise Control, 89–90
   Influence Through Language and Ideas, 90
   Managing People, 86–89
   Quantitative Analysis, 81–82
   Theory Development and Conceptual Thinking, 82–83
Business core functions, 11, 76
   activity-based, 78–90
   evolution of, 76–78
   explanation of term, 77
   scorable activities, examples, 93–94
   understanding your profile, 91
Business teaching, 83, 86

Calling, work as a, 17–18
   distinguished from Sirens' song, 30–31
Capote, Truman, 164
Career course distractions
   fears and discomforts, 31–38

lack of knowledge about self, 40–43
lack of knowledge about the world, 38–40
sirens' songs, 18–31
Career decisions and development, 12
Career interest inventories, 17
Career psychology research, 12
Career, word origin, 17
CEO, 89, 157
CFO, 89
Chamber of Commerce executive, 89–90
CHH, 124–25
Choices, and loss, 163, 171
CLL, 135–37
Coaching, 85
"Cognitive dissonance," 40
College professor, 82
Colors, in transformation process, 170
Commercial artist, 83, 135
Communications skills, 90
Competitive strivings, 23–25
Compromise, in career choices, 166
Computer programmer, 79, 81
Concentration, 50
Consistency Validity Statement, 71–72
Control and Influence, 106
    Enterprise Control, 89–90, 106
    high, 114, 143, 152
    Influence Through Language and Ideas, 90, 106
    low, 128, 140, 146, 159
Core functions. *See* Business core functions
Corporate trainer, 90
Counseling, 85
Counseling and Mentoring, 78
    business core function model, 85–86
    core function profile analysis, 218–19
    interests, 111
    percentile equivalents, 233–34
    profile type, 106

scorable activities, 94
skills, 85
Creative Production, 78, 135–37
    "blank page" job description, 84
    business core function model, 83–85
    core function profile analysis, 218
    employment pattern, 84–85
    interests, 111
    percentile equivalents, 231–32
    profile type, 106
    scorable activities, 94
    skills, 83
Credit manager, 81, 86
Critical thinking, 211
Csikszentmihalyi, Mihaly, 50–51
    "flow," characteristics of, 50

Database (*BCII*), adding your results, 223
Deep structure interests, 13–16
Depression, 169–70
Descriptive writing, 49–52
Design, 83
Development of, 81
Disk contents, 60–61
Dream analysis, 47
Drifting, 14–16

E-mail, sending to authors, 223
Economic analysis, 83
Editor, 90
Ego, 45–46, 170
    comfort-seeking, 168, 170
    and imagery, 45
    narrative of, 46
Elected public official, 89–90
Emotional content of images, 47
Emotions, 171–72
    unarticulated, 166–67
Engineer, 79–80
Engineering degree, as "membership card," 80
Engineering profession, and "nonengineers," 80

Enterprise Control, 78, 116
  business core function model, 89–90
  core function profile analysis, 220
  interests, 112
  percentile equivalents, 237–38
  profile type, 106
  scorable activities, 94
  skills, developing with experience,
    89
Entrepreneur, 31, 35, 89, 124
Envy, 20–21, 53–55, 96–97
Event planning, 83
Expectations, 21–23, 25–27

Failing, fear of, 32–34
"False negative," 68
Family expectations, 22–23
Family influence, 23–27, 41
Fantasies, 46
Fashion, 84
Fears, 31–38
  of being aggressive, 35–36
  of being disliked, 36–37
  and courage, 31
  of failing, 32–34
  of losing success, 34–35
  of success, 37–38
Finance, 81
Financial gain, 212
Financial planner, 81
"Flow," 50–52
  exercise, sample rating, 95
"Flow of success," 34
Food service manager, 86
Future employers, 12

GBII. *See* General Business Interest
    Index
Gender, 26, 37, 63, 224–25
General Business Interest Index,
    69–71
General managers, 157
Goethe, 177–78
"Golden handcuffs," 14

Guidance counselor, 85–86
Guilt, 171

Harvard Business School, 2, 79–80
HHH business career profile type,
    114
  AHH, 119–21
  Application of Expertise functions,
    125–28
  CHH, 124–25
  Control and Influence functions,
    116–17
  QHH, 121–23
  THH, 123–24
HHL, 146–52
High scale scores, 63–67
Hillman, James, 52
HLH, 156–59
HLL business career profile type,
    128
  ALL, 130–33
  Application of Expertise functions,
    137–40
  CLL, 135–37
  QLL, 133–34
  TLL, 134–35
Holland, John, 78
Homer, 19
Hospital administrator, 86, 89
Hotel manager, 86
Human resources director, 86
Humiliation, 32
Hurt, 171–72

Imagery, 45
Images, 45–48
  autonomous, 46
  differentiating from fantasies, 46
  emotional content of, 47
  persistence of, 45
  writing and recording, 49–51
Imagination. *See* Active imagination
Inconsistency, 72
Indecision, 166–69

Influence Through Language and
  Ideas, 78
  business core function model, 90
  core function profile analysis,
    220–21
  interests, 112
  percentile equivalents, 239–40
  profile type, 106
  scorable activities, 94
  skills, 90
Influences, from family and friends,
  18–19, 21, 23–27, 41
Information systems consulting, 81
Insurance agent, 90
Intellectual challenge, 212
Interest patterns, 14
  underlying, 87
Interests, 12–16, 215–22
Interpersonal functioning, 87
Investment banking, 88
Investment management, 88
Investor relations, 208

Job envy, 53–55
  exercise, sample rating, 96–97
Journal, recording in, 49–51, 54–57,
  100
Journalism, 84
Jung, Carl, 41, 47, 167–68

Knowledge, lack of, 38
  about ourselves, 40–43
  about the world, 38–40

Law, 80, 89–90
Lawrence, D. H., 178
Lawyer, 90
Leadership, 86–90, 117
Learning by doing, 10–12
Letters about you, 57–58
  exercise, sample rating, 98–99
LHH, 152–56
LHL, 140–43
Lifestyle, 213

LLH, 143–46
LLL, 159–62
"Long black bag," 172
Low-range responses, 159–60
Low scores, 68–71

Management, 86, 129–30, 213
Management consulting, 82, 88
Management development programs,
  89
*Management and Professional Reward
  Profile*, 212–14, 223
Managing People, 78
  business core function model, 86–89
  core function profile analysis, 219
  interests, 111–12
  interpersonal functioning, 87
  percentile equivalents, 235–36
  profile type, 106
  "pure management" career model,
    88
  scorable activities, 94
  score comparison, 87
  score in early stage of career, 87
  skills, 86
  value, 213
Manufacturer's representative, 90
Marketing, 83, 90
Marketing director, 89–90
Mathematical analysis, 81
Mathematics skills, 80–81
Mathematics teacher, 81
Mechanical crafts skills, 79
Media executive, 89–90
Medical illustrator, 83
Memories, 168
Memory exercise, and active
  imagination, 48–49
Mentoring, 151
Merchandising, 86
Military officer, 89
Mind's eye, 48–50
Money, 15
  and status, 19–21

Mood, effect on test results, 69
Music, 83
Myers-Briggs Type Indicator®, 223

Negotiations, 90
Nigredo (black phase), 170–73
Non-profit organizations, 86
Nursing home administrator, 85–86

Odyssey, The, 19
Office management, 86
Omitted Items Validity Statement, 68, 71
Opportunity, as part of a career path, 209

Paradox, of discovery, 10
Parks, Sharon D., 34
Partners in professional services firms, 89
Pattern of interests, 12–16, 78
    aptitude and, 14
    drifting, 14–16
    stability over time, 65
Percentile equivalents, 224
    Application of Technology, 225–26
    Counseling and Mentoring, 233–34
    Creative Production, 231–32
    Enterprise Control, 237–38
    Influence Through Language and Ideas, 239–40
    Managing People, 235–36
    Quantitative Analysis, 227–28
    Theory Development and Conceptual Thinking, 229–30
Percentile scoring, 63
Persistence of images, 45
Personal high scores, 63–67
Personnel director, 85
Photography, 83
Politics, 89–90
Positioning (for next career move), 213

"Potential self," 12
Power and influence, 212
President, 89
Prestige, 213
Product design, 79, 82–83
Production and operations management, 81
Production and operations process analysis, 79
Production and systems planning, 79
Professor, 82
Profile type, 74–75
Psychological alchemy, 163–70
Psychological heat, 168
Psychologist, 86
Public accounting, 81
Public administrator, 90
Public relations, 90
Public speaking, 90
Publishing, 84
"Pure management" career model, 88, 118

QHH, 121–23
QLL, 133–34
Quantitative Analysis, 11, 78, 133–34
    business core function model, 81–82
    core function profile analysis, 216–17
    interests, 110
    percentile equivalents, 227–28
    profile type, 106
    scorable activities, 93–94
    skills, 81

Reading, 47
    as part of imaginative process, 47
    patterns, 56–57
Realtor, 89–90
Rebellion, 25–26
Recognition, 212
Recruiters, 208
Red phase, 176–79

Regret, 171
Repression, 171–72
Research and development manager, 79, 82
Researching companies, 208
Response Range Validity Statement, 69, 72–74
Retail manager, 86
Rubedo (red phase), 176–79

Sales, 90, 210–11
Scale scores, 61–63
School administrator, 85, 90
School superintendent, 86
Science, 82
Scientists, 131
Scorable activities, examples, 93–94
Scores, 61, 69
    adjusted standard, 63
    and age, 65–67, 87
    average standard score, 68
    consistency over time, 65
    high and low, 63–71, 127
    how to use your *BCII,* 108–13
    integrating active imagination and *BCII,* 103–04
    interpreting, 74
    page for, 75
    percentile, 63
    questions and answers, 63–71
    standard, 62
    three-letter designations, 106–08
    and underlying interest patterns, 87
Scoring and analyzing, active imagination exercises, 92
    combining ratings, 100–03
    integrating with *BCII* scores, 103–04
    sample ratings, 94–100
    scorable activities, examples, 93–94
Security, 212

Self, 10, 12, 46–47
    assessment, 44, 48, 59
    consciousness, 50
    development process, 168
    knowledge, 40–44
    observation, 57
Self-understanding
    descriptive writing and, 49–52
    effect of time on, 53
    images and, 47–48
"Shadows," 41
Shame, 171
Sibling rivalry, 24–25
Sirens' songs, 18–31
    common scenarios, 27–31
    competitive strivings, 23–25
    expecting too much, 21–22
    family expectations, 22–23, 25–27
    money and status, 19–21
Skills, 14,
    Application of Technology, 79
    Counseling and Mentoring, 85
    Creative Production, 83
    Enterprise Control, 89
    Influence Through Language and Ideas, 90
    lack of, 79
    Managing People, 86
    Quantitative Analysis, 81
    Theory Development and Conceptual Thinking, 82
Social services, 85
Social worker, 85
Societal influence, 18
Sociologist, 82
Software, 60
Specific interests, 13–16
Standard score, 62
Statistician, 81
Strategic finance, 83
Strategic planning, 81–82
Strategy consulting, 81–82
Success, 37–38

Supervisory skills, 86
Systems analyst, 79, 81

Teacher, 119
Team leader, 89
Theory Development and Conceptual
    Thinking, 78, 134–35
  business core function model,
      82–83
  core function profile analysis, 217
  interests, 110–11
  percentile equivalents, 229–30
  profile type, 106
  scorable activities, 94
  skills, 82
THH, 123–24
Threshold variables, 210
TLL, 134–35
Training workshops for career
    development professionals,
    223
Transformation process, phases, 170,
    178
True calling, 17–18, 30
"True negative," 69

Underlying dimension, 106
Underlying patterns of work interest,
    12
Undifferentiated, 68

Validity Statements, 68–74
Values, 212–14
Variety, 213
Venture capital, 88
Vocational interest tests, 17
Vocations, 17
Volunteer work, 142, 151

Wealth, lure of, 19–21
Weighted average, 101–02
White phase, 173–76
Work history interview, 52–53
  exercise, sample rating, 97–98
Working with People, 106
  Counseling and Mentoring, 85–86,
      106
  high, 114, 140, 146, 152
  low, 128, 143, 159
  Managing People, 86–89, 106
Work opportunities, evaluating,
    208–10
  aptitudes, 210–12
  interest patterns, 215–22
  work reward values, 212–14
Work reward values, 212–14
  informal hierarchy, 213
  list of, 212–13
World-Wide Web, 223
  authors' home page, 223
Writer, 90
Writing, 49–51, 82–84, 90